"In exploring the international development community's expanded the focus from MDGs to SDGs, this timely and well-written book offers a refreshing look at the synergies between the SDGs and Africa's own development agenda and stresses the critical role that African leaders can play in achieving the SDGs."

Francis Owusu, Professor and Chair of the Department of Community & Regional Planning, Iowa State University

"As an African researcher and educationist who lives on the continent, I believe *From Millennium Development Goals to Sustainable Development Goals* will be a point of reference for many years to come. The book is a brilliant piece of work in which the informed contributors give great thoughts for Africa's positive way forward. It suggests practices that will shape the attainment of Sustainable Development Goals in Africa and brings unimaginable prospects in Africa closer in time and space. I highly recommend this comprehensive and well-reasoned contribution to the world."

Professor Hany Besada, Deputy Executive Director, Diamond Development Initiative

From Millennium Development Goals to Sustainable Development Goals

Millennium development goals (MDGs) and sustainable development goals (SDGs) have significant implications for global development, in particular for African countries. This book seeks to assist Africa's policy-makers and political leaders, multinational corporations and non-governmental organizations, plus its increasingly heterogeneous media landscape, to understand and better respond or negotiate the evolving development environment of the twenty-first century.

In this collection of nuanced essays, the contributors interrogate the relationship between the MDGs and SDGs in key areas of African development to enhance our understanding and knowledge of the evolving nature of development. They address issues of governance, agriculture, South–South cooperation in a context of foreign aid, natural resource governance and sustainable development, export diversification and economic growth as well as emerging topics such as the Internet of Things or the sharing economy, climate change, conflict and non-traditional security. The varied, yet interlinked foci present a holistic overview of Africa's development aspirations, and ability to transform the SDGs' universal aspirations into local realities.

This book will be of use to academics and students in Development Studies, Contemporary African Studies, Political Science, Policy Studies and Geography, and should also appeal to policy-makers and development practitioners.

Kobena T. Hanson is CEO of Strategic Outlooks, a research consultancy and advisory firm in Ghana, and a Knowledge Management Consultant to the African Development Bank (AfDB).

Korbla P. Puplampu is in the Department of Sociology at Grant MacEwan University, Edmonton, Canada.

Timothy M. Shaw is Faculty Fellow, Department of Conflict Resolution, Human Security and Global Governance; McCormack Graduate School, University of Massachusetts Boston (UMB).

The International Political Economy of New Regionalisms

Series Editor: Timothy M. Shaw

The International Political Economy of New Regionalisms Series presents innovative analyses of a range of novel regional relations and institutions. Going beyond established, formal, interstate economic organizations, this essential series provides informed interdisciplinary and international research and debate about myriad heterogeneous intermediate-level interactions. Reflective of its cosmopolitan and creative orientation, this series is developed by an international editorial team of established and emerging scholars in both the South and North. It reinforces ongoing networks of analysts in both academia and think-tanks as well as international agencies concerned with micro-, meso- and macro-level regionalisms.

For a full list of titles in this series, please visit www.routledge.com/The-International-Political-Economy-of-New-Regionalisms-Series/book-series/ASHSER-1146

Post-Colonial Trajectories in the Caribbean: The Three Guianas
Edited by Rosemarijn Hoefte, Matthew L. Bishop and Peter Clegg

Post-Hegemonic Regionalism in the Americas
Toward a Pacific-Atlantic Divide?
Edited by José Briceño-Ruiz and Isidro Morales

From Millennium Development Goals to Sustainable Development Goals
Rethinking African Development
Edited by Kobena T. Hanson, Korbla P. Puplampu and Timothy M. Shaw

Understanding Mega-Free Trade Agreements
The Political and Economic Governance of New Cross-Regionalism
Edited by Jean-Baptiste Velut, Louise Dalingwater, Vanessa Boullet and Valérie Peyronel

From Millennium Development Goals to Sustainable Development Goals

Rethinking African Development

Edited by Kobena T. Hanson, Korbla P. Puplampu and Timothy M. Shaw

First published 2018
by Routledge
2 Park Square, Milton Park, Abingdon, Oxon OX14 4RN

and by Routledge
605 Third Avenue, New York, NY 10017

First issued in paperback 2021

Routledge is an imprint of the Taylor & Francis Group, an informa business

Publisher's Note
The publisher has gone to great lengths to ensure the quality of this reprint but points out that some imperfections in the original copies may be apparent.

British Library Cataloguing in Publication Data
A catalogue record for this book is available from the British Library

Library of Congress Cataloging-in-Publication Data
Names: Hanson, Kobena, editor, author. | Puplampu, Korbla P., editor, author. | Shaw, Timothy M., editor, author.
Title: From millennium development goals to sustainable development goals : rethinking African development / edited by Kobena T. Hanson, Korbla P. Puplampu and Timothy M. Shaw.
Other titles: International political economy of new regionalisms series.
Description: New York : Routledge, 2017. |
Series: The international political economy of new regionalisms series | Includes bibliographical references and index.
Identifiers: LCCN 2017011198| ISBN 9780415785938 (hardback) | ISBN 9781315228068 (e-book)
Subjects: LCSH: Sustainable development–Africa. | Economic development–Africa. | Africa–Economic policy. | Africa–Economic conditions.
Classification: LCC HC800.Z9 .E5444 2017 | DDC 338.927096–dc23
LC record available at https://lccn.loc.gov/2017011198

Typeset in Times New Roman
by Out of House Publishing

ISBN 13: 978-1-03-209656-8 (pbk)
ISBN 13: 978-0-415-78593-8 (hbk)

Contents

Figures and tables

Figures

Tables

Contributors

Peter K. Arthur is Associate Professor of Political Science and International Development Studies at Dalhousie University, Canada. Dr Arthur's research focuses on sub-Saharan Africa, with emphasis on the contribution of small-scale enterprises, new regionalism, capacity development and post-conflict reconstruction, and the governance of natural resources. His works have been published in a number of edited volumes and journals, including *Africa Today*, *African Studies Review*, *Commonwealth and Comparative Politics*, and *Journal of Contemporary African Studies*.

Damilohun D. Ayoyo is a PhD student in the Department of Sociology, University of Alberta, Canada. He teaches Criminology in the undergraduate program at King's University, Edmonton. His research interests encompass the differential impact of policing, human rights, crime and criminality, and human security.

George O. Essegbey is Director of the Science and Technology Policy Research Institute (STEPRI) of the Council of Science and Industrial Research (CSIR) of Ghana, a member of the Nairobi-based Scientific Board of AfricaLICs and the ten-member group supporting the United Nations Technology Facilitation Mechanism with the UN Inter-agency Task Team on Science, Technology and Innovation for the SDGs. Dr Essegbey was a former member of the Ghana National Development Planning Commission and has also served on several international bodies such as the FAO, UNESCO, UNCTAD, UNEP, WIPO and the World Bank. His research areas range from science and technology policy research, innovation studies, to new technologies and climate change. He has published in several academic journals including *Technology and Investment*, *Tailoring Biotechnologies*, *Perspectives on Global Development and Technology* and also contributed chapter essays in edited volumes such as *Agribusiness and Innovation Systems in Africa*.

Kobena T. Hanson is CEO of Strategic Outlooks, a research consultancy and advisory firm in Ghana, and a Knowledge Management Consultant to African Development Bank (AfDB). Dr Hanson's areas of expertise cover knowledge management, natural resource governance, regional development, and public policy. He has published in numerous journals, including *Africa Today*, *African Geographical Review*, *Environment and Planning*, *GeoJournal*, *Journal of African Development*, and *Review of Applied Socio-Economic Research*. He has edited and co-edited several books including *Contemporary Regional Development in Africa* and *Managing Africa's Natural Resources: Capacities for Development*.

Abbi M. Kedir is with the Centre for Regional Economic and Enterprise Development, the University of Sheffield, United Kingdom. He has also worked in many regions of the world and served as government civil servant and economic affairs officer at the United Nations Economic Commission for Africa. His research areas are in applied quantitative development economics, specifically analysing and modelling issues of employment, entrepreneurship, climate change, tax compliance and evasion, debt, firm performance and agricultural productivity. His current research is focused on undeclared work in the European Union and informal economy in developing countries, emerging economies and other global sub-regions such as Africa. His publications can be found, among others, in *Oxford Bulletin of Economics and Statistics*, *Journal of African Economies*, *European Journal of Industrial Relations*, and *Entrepreneurship Theory and Practice*.

Isaac Odoom is in the Department of Politics and International Relations at Lancaster University, Ghana. His research interests include Africa's international relations, Africa–China relations, the politics of emerging powers and South-South cooperation, critical international relations theory, and the political economy of development. His research publications have appeared in the *Third World Quarterly*, *Journal of Asian and African Studies* and the *African Review of Economics and Finance* as well as edited volumes such as *Africa Yesterday, Today and Tomorrow: Exploring the Multi-dimensional Discourses on 'Development'*.

Temitope B. Oriola is an Assistant Professor of Sociology in the Department of Sociology at the University of Alberta, Canada. His research interests include resource conflicts and 'state-organized' crime, use of force and weaponization policy in North America; and terrorism studies. Dr Oriola's publications can be found in leading scholarly journals, such as *Studies in Conflict and Terrorism*, *Review of African Political Economy*, the *British Journal of Criminology, Critical Studies on Terrorism, and African Security*. He is also the author of *Criminal Resistance? The Politics of Kidnapping Oil Workers*.

Korbla P. Puplampu is in the Department of Sociology at Grant MacEwan University, Edmonton, Canada. His research interests are in state and non-state actors in the African political economy, the global restructuring of agriculture and higher education and the politics of knowledge production and propagation; transnational and global citizenship, diaspora and identity politics in multicultural societies. Dr Puplampu has publications in academic journals such as *Canadian Journal of Learning and Technology* and *Alberta Journal of Educational Research*. He has co-edited and contributed to several books including *The Public Sphere and the Politics of Survival: Voice, Sustainability and Public Policy in Ghana* (with Wisdom Tettey) and *African Education and Globalization* (with Ali Abdi and George Dei).

Timothy M. Shaw is Faculty Fellow, Department of Conflict Resolution, Human Security, and Global Governance; McCormack Graduate School, UMB. Previously he directed the Institute of Commonwealth Studies at the University of London where he remains professor emeritus. Prof. Shaw also is a visiting professor at Mbarara and Stellenbosch Universities. His most recent co-edited works include *Development in Africa: Refocusing the Lens after the MDGs*, *Africa and IR in the 21st Century*, *Africa's Challenge to International Relations Theory* and *Comparative Regionalism for Development in the 21st Century: Insights from the Global South*.

Vanessa T. Tang is a lecturer in International Economics in the School of Accounting, Economics and Finance, University of KwaZulu-Natal (UKZN), Durban, South Africa. She has consulted for various organizations, including the African Capacity Building Foundation, National Research Foundation, Midlands Meander Tourism Association, the Institute of Natural Resources, and the KwaZulu-Natal Provincial Treasury. She is the principal UKZN investigator for the Network for Regional Integration Studies (NETRIS) and a co-editor for the *International Journal of African Integration*. Her research interests are economics of education, time-series analysis, international trade, comparative regional integration, special economic zones and the open-economy policy-making in the global south. She has published in journals such as *South African Journal of International Affairs* and *Investment Management and Financial Innovations* and also contributed to several edited books.

Acknowledgements

This volume reflects the dedication and commitment of many people who, individually and collectively, supported the process in diverse invaluable ways. It started out with brief observations and conversations on Africa's future which is also our shared and collective future. Those informal interventions developed a desire to publish a book on the continent's journey of transformation. We are grateful to all who provided instrumental guidance, engaged us in discussions, as well as reviewed and or commented on our initial thoughts, draft chapters and ultimately the compiled manuscript. Your insights, encouragement, constructive criticisms and thought-provoking questions helped us to rethink issues, refocus arguments and crystallize viewpoints. For that and more others, we are most grateful.

To the contributing authors, our sincere appreciation for the very nuanced and informative submissions without which this volume would not have materialized. We also appreciate your dedication to the project as demonstrated by your often timely response to our many email and phone requests and follow-ups. Our shared commitment to the contribution to knowledge and to Africa's quest to seize the second half of the twenty-first century brought us together. It has been a pleasure working with each and every one of you. As the African proverb goes: 'Knowledge is like a baobab tree, no one can embrace it all.' We could not have managed to wrap our minds around the many issues ourselves. But together, the task has been more expressive and definitely rewarding.

Appreciation also goes to the anonymous reviewers at Routledge for your insightful critiques that helped us to sharpen our arguments, interrogate issues in more detail, and articulate ideas more clearly. By your actions, you have demonstrated once again that scholarship is a cooperative enterprise. We are privileged to receive your help in the review of this manuscript.

To Rob Sorsby, Claire Maloney and the entire production team at Routledge, we say a big thank you for your priceless support, critical yet valued comments, encouragement and continuous patience with us even when we missed deadlines, and requested extensions. The production of this volume could not have been possible without your commitment to knowledge generation and scholarship.

Finally, we couldn't have done it without the support of our loved one and families. So, this is to you all – you have been, and continue to be, the wind beneath our wings. Thanks for your love, support and encouragement.

Acronyms

ACBF	African Capacity Building Foundation
AfDB	African Development Bank
APRM	African Peer Review Mechanism
AU	African Union
BRICS	Brazil, Russia, India, China and South Africa
CAADP	Comprehensive Africa Agriculture Development Program
CCDA	Climate Change and Development in Africa
CoP21	Conference of the Parties on Climate Change in Paris
CRGE	Climate-Resilient Green Economy
CSOs	Civil Society Organizations
EAC	East African Community
ECOWAS	Economic Community of West African States
EU	European Union
FARA	Forum for Agricultural Research in Africa
FOCAC	Forum on China-Africa Cooperation
GASFP	Global Agriculture and Food Security Program
HHR	Hausmann, Hwang and Rodrik measure of sophistication
IAR4D	Integrated Agricultural Research for Development
IDPs	Internally Displaced Persons
IoT	Internet of Things
IPOB	Indigenous People of Biafra
IR	Industrial Research
ISIL	Islamic State of Iraq and the Levant
MASSOB	Movement for the Actualization of the Sovereign State of Biafra
MDG	Millennium Development Goal
MMR	Maternal Mortality Rate
NBA	Niger River Basin Authority
NEPAD	New Partnership for Africa's Development
OECD	Organization for Economic Co-operation and Development
ORB	Okavango River Basin
RECs	Regional Economic Communities
RFID	Radio-Frequency Identification

SADC	Southern African Development Community
SDG	Sustainable Development Goal
SSA	Sub-Saharan Africa
SSC	South–South Cooperation
UN	United Nations
UNECA	United Nations Economic Commission for Africa
UNFCCC	United Nations Framework Convention on Climate Change
UNIDO	United Nations Industrial Development Organisation
WCED	World Conference on Environment and Development
WFP	World Food Programme

1 From MDGs to SDGs

African development challenges and prospects

Korbla P. Puplampu, Kobena T. Hanson and Timothy M. Shaw

Introduction

There was both a great fanfare and hopeful exuberance when the United Nations endorsed the millennium development goals (MDGs) on the dawn of the third millennium, and also launched the sustainable development goals (SDGs) in the second decade of the current millennium (UNDP 2003, UNDP 2015). Both the MDGs and SDGs – now also 'global goals' – have significant implications for global development, particularly in the case of African countries (Nayyar 2012; Sachs 2012). The SDGs have expanded and specified some of the targets that would shore up African development. In expanding the MDGs, the SDGs incorporate a 'range of key areas that were not fully covered in the MDGs, such as energy and climate change; and reflect equally the economic, social and environmental dimensions of sustainable development and the interconnections between them' (UNECA *et al.* 2015). But the SDGs still tend to overlook varieties of conflict, especially non-traditional security, and the water-energy-food relationship. Unlike the MDGs, the SDGs 'apply to all nations, developed and developing, bridging governments, civil society, and the private sector to create innovative ways to achieve sustainable development while "leaving no-one behind"' (Besada *et al.* 2016: 2) (see figure 1.1).

While some African countries did attain their MDG targets, hence the plausibility of 'Africa Rising', the overall state of African development continues to assume attention in the global development discourse (Ayittey 2015; Taylor 2014; United Nations 2015a, 2015b). As Bianchi (2015) points out, while Africa overall registered positive rates of economic growth over the past 15 years or so, thus the claim to 'African agency', poverty remains widespread and unemployment is reaching alarming levels (see also ACBF 2016; Beegle *et al.* 2016; Kharas and Biau 2015). Making the development process sustainable thus represents a key challenge for the future of the continent, and calls for urgent regional and country-specific actions (Bianchi 2015; Hanson 2015). In terms of the general assessment of MDGs and African development, a recurring theme has been the state of institutions, particularly in terms of the discourse of knowledge, regionalism, policy and capacity imperatives; the

Figure 1.1 The SDGs: 17 goals to transform our world

Source: www.un.org/sustainabledevelopment/blog/2015/12/sustainable-development-goals-kick-off-with-start-of-new-year/#prettyPhoto[gallery13821]/0/

order of factors is in part a function of which state and what analytic perspective (Hanson 2015; Hanson *et al.* 2012; Shizha and Abdi 2014; Shizha and Diallo 2015).

In view of the broader concern about Africa's development agenda, this book addresses two main issues. First, it seeks to interrogate the dynamics between the MDGs and SDGs in key areas of African development; for example, the changing role of the state in sustainable development and democratic governance, agriculture, natural resources management, environmental sustainability and climate change, technology and private sector, and development aid.

Second, it is clear that the extent to which the SDGs will advance the African development agenda will depend on global, continental and regional imperatives. The SDGs have an enhanced and universal aspiration that has to be grounded in global, continental, regional and national realities. The integrated and indivisible nature of the SDGs results from learning from the MDGs. Experience suggests that a solo approach to development yields limited results (Robinson 2017). Consequently, there is an ongoing effort globally, and Africa is no exception, to review development planning visions and strategies, align them with the SDGs, and to carefully set out country priorities. In fact, the SDGs not only 'underline and underpin the African Union's (AU) Agenda 2063, "The Africa we Want", which also calls for a paradigm shift and profound economic and social transformation' (Besada *et al.* 2016: 4–5), but also align with the African Development Bank's (AfDB) High-5s (the Bank's five strategic priority areas) meant to guide its approach to the continent's development over the next ten years (AfDB 2015). The five strategic areas are: light up and power Africa; feed Africa; industrialize Africa; integrate Africa; improve the quality of life for the people of Africa. These areas stem from the AfDB's (2013) Ten-Year Implementation Plan to transform Africa and are also consistent with the AU Agenda 2063.

Indeed, there is synergy between the SDGs and Africa's ambitious Agenda 2063, including AfDB's first Ten-Year Implementation Plan. The SDGs line up almost perfectly with the vast majority of the goals of the Ten-Year Implementation Plan, and a detailed look at their respective targets illustrates the strong commonality between the agendas. The integrative potential of the SDGs and the continental initiatives cannot be underestimated, but as Robinson cautions, only 'through action at the national level, and cooperation internationally, can transformation be achieved' (2017: xiv).

The requisite action and agency needed to ensure transformation across Africa has been documented by a number of studies (Besada *et al.* 2016; Bischoff *et al.* 2016; Brown and Harman 2013) as well as contributors to this volume. Today, African actors can clearly claim a degree of agency rather than endure continuing dependency (Brown and Harman 2013). In areas of transboundary resources management, regionalism (Hanson 2015), security management, and the continent's engagement with global partners (Bischoff *et al.* 2016), Africa's agency is undoubtedly manifest (Besada *et al.* 2016). The establishment of the Africa Progress Panel (www.africaprogresspanel.org); the Africa Mining Vision (www.africaminingvision.org); or the launch of the *Africa Capacity Indicators Report* (now *Africa Capacity Report*) by the African Capacity Building Foundation (www.acbf-pact.org), are all evidence of the growing agency of contemporary Africa (Hanson *et al.* 2012; Shaw 2015a, 2015b). Elsewhere on the continent, other novel forms of African agency are visible in regional conflict zones such as the Great Lakes, the Horn of Africa and the Sahel, and in the energy and minerals sectors (Besada 2010; Ismail 2014; Shaw 2015a).

The dramatic breakthroughs in communication and information technologies on the economy (the sharing economy) and the transformation of markets and financial transactions (M-Pesa) offer both opportunities and challenges in the development process (Oppong 2015; Saeed and Masakure 2015; Wallis 2016). In the case of the environment and climate change, the water-energy-food security link underlays security concerns, typified by such actors as Boko Haram, Al-Shabaab, and the worsening security environment in countries such as Libya, Somalia, Kenya, Nigeria and Chad (Besada 2010; Kedir 2014; Ismail 2014; and see Ayoyo and Oriola this volume). In the unfolding dynamics, while the state continues to occupy a role, even if a minimal one, the activities of civil society groups including faith-based organizations also deserve attention and analysis especially in terms of democratic governance. For example, in the case of natural resource governance, new forms of overseas development aid and foreign direct investment with the emergence and changing fortunes of China, other BRICS partners, and Taiwan, India, China and Korea (TICKs).The aforementioned all go to reinforce the view that 'the key to delivering the vision and transforming people's lives lays in how seriously governments, the United Nations (UN), international organizations, CSOs and business take their roles, together and in partnership, in implementing the SDGs' (Robinson 2017: xv).

African governments must meet their commitments if they are serious about delivering the promise of Article 10 of the UN's *Declaration on the Right to Development* to all their citizens by 2030. To do so, they need to move rapidly beyond rhetoric and political differences to make the right to development a reality for all. The real work to deliver on the right to development is only now starting, thanks to the SDGs, the Paris climate change agreement (CoP 21) and the 2015 Addis Ababa action agenda, which created a global framework for financing development. However, without a renewed commitment and finance, the ground-breaking SDGs will not be met by their target date of 2030, and will remain an empty promise without appropriate political and financial commitment, regulation, management and related safeguards (Dodds *et al.* 2017; South Centre 2016). The role and significance of an appropriate foreign policy and equally relevant international organization cannot be overemphasized (Warner and Shaw 2017).

While issues such as poverty reduction, gender equality, hunger eradication, hunger, health and education are still very much central to the 2030 Agenda for Sustainable Development, there are also some new entries among the SDGs that are particularly salient for Africa (Bianchi 2015). These notables include SDG 16 on peaceful and inclusive societies for sustainable development; SDG 11 on inclusive, safe, resilient and sustainable settlements; and SDG 9 on resilient infrastructure, inclusive and sustainable industrialization, and innovation (see figure 1.1).

In light of this background, this book seeks to assist Africa's policy-makers and political leaders, multinational corporations and non-governmental organizations (NGOs), plus its increasingly heterogeneous media landscape, to understand and better respond to or negotiate the evolving development environment of the twenty-first century. The book, as alluded above, also crystallizes perspectives and discernments on Africa's ongoing transition from MDGs to SDGs, drawing on both the wider extant literature as well as nuanced developments taking place at the global and national levels, to provide useful insights into Africa's agency and drive to attain sustainable development. The next section overviews and justifies our selection of topics and authors which highlight the rationale and sequence of chapters.

Perspectives and discernments

Arthur, in Chapter 2, interrogates the relationship between the African state and development initiatives, arguing that attaining the objectives in development initiatives such as the SDGs in Africa will hinge on good governance. That requires a political environment characterized by transparent, participatory and accountable decision-making processes. The political system should also be grounded in the promotion of the rule of law, anti-corruption mechanisms, participation of civil society in decision-making and effective political leadership.

Next, Ayoyo and Oriola, in Chapter 3, highlight the pertinent issue of conflict and insecurity in Africa, and its implications for continental efforts to transition from MDGs to SDGs. The SDG 11 call for inclusive, safe, resilient communities on sustainable principles means security is integral to the development of any society. The chapter surveys the conflict and insecurity connection on the continent, from Nigeria in West Africa and the consequences for peace in the region, to East African countries such as Kenya, Somalia, South Sudan and Sudan, and North Africa. The chapter contends that the poor performance of many African states during the MDGs era is strongly connected to conflict and insecurity situations on the continent, and cautions that resolving conflicts and security challenges on the African continent would constitute a central issue in achieving the SDGs by 2030.

In Chapter 4, Puplampu and Essegbey examine the policy and institutional aspects of the MDGs situating the performance of African agriculture relative to MDGs 1 and 8. In so doing, they help to contextualize the extent to which the SDGs, as a follow-up program, are able to attain desirable policy and institutional outcomes in the agricultural sector, a vital aspect of Africa's development agenda. Central to the chapter, is the focus on threats and pitfalls in implementing global, continental, regional or national policies as well as the institutional imperatives for desirable outcomes in agriculture. The chapter submits that underpinning agricultural policy and institutional performance are problems linked to the availability and access to resources.

While the previous chapters looked at broader policy and institutional issues, Odoom, in Chapter 5, shifts the attention to the rapidly growing and contentious role of China's development cooperation practices in Africa. The chapter undertakes a comparative analysis of the traditional and contemporary sources of development assistance, placing the analysis in a relevant historical context. Demonstrating Chinese development assistance in several African countries, the chapter closely looks into the case of Ghana. Based on the Ghana case, Odoom reveals key features of China's development practice in Africa and draws attention to the underlying forces likely to shape Africa's post-MDGs political economy and how such practices will shape the attainment of the SDGs.

Chapter 6 by Puplampu and Hanson explores the nexus between natural resource governance and sustainable development in Africa. The chapter examines the extent to which relevant aspects of the MDGs and SDGs support natural resource governance and sustainable development, focusing on the role of oil and water. Furthermore, the chapter demonstrates the tensions in the relationship between natural resource governance and sustainable development. First, natural resources are public goods, but require private capital for their exploration. Second, the infrastructure for a regional approach to water resources, for example, also requires significant financial commitment, mostly from foreign public and private entities. In each case, the role of the state in natural resource governance and sustainable development is key. However, the African state has been the site of significant contestations due to or in response to forces of globalization.

In Chapter 7, Tang addresses the impact of the growth of exports and their effect on middle-income African economies. The chapter notes that the growth of the richer middle-income African nations is somewhat linked to increased sophistication and innovations in trade. Tang also contends that Africa's service industry is not only growing, but more productive and tradable as reflected in the spread and success of Nigerian Nollywood films, Ivorian *Coupé Décalé* music, and call centres in Kenya. Central to the contention is a call for a combined effort (public and private) to invest and create an environment conducive to the promotion of exports, a key requirement as set out under SDG 17 and associated target 12 in the 2030 Agenda for Sustainable Development.

Chapters 8 and 9 examine, albeit in unique ways, the threats and possibilities of emerging issues. In Chapter 8, Hanson and Puplampu focus on what the emerging technologies and a fast evolving landscape by way of the sharing economy and Internet of Things (IoT) mean for African countries as they strive to attain the SDGs. The chapter indicates several promising trends of the sharing economy and the IoT. They argue that these trends have the potential to drive Africa in its quest to meet its SDG targets, particularly in terms of grassroots delivery of health care and education, positively transforming communities; a prospect that would have been unimaginable just a few years ago. In Chapter 9, Kedir draws attention to one of Africa's evolving challenges, the environment and climate change, highlighting the overlap between MDGs and SDGs with regard to goals that address environmental and climate change concerns, while mapping out the progress realized to date. Kedir situates his study relative to continental and global initiatives on the environment and climate change. The chapter calls for further research into ways to *domesticate* the SDGs to local realities, a careful and robust analysis and monitoring of global environment regimes, for example, CoP21, to ascertain the impact on the environmental sustainability of African economies and finally the potential role (positive or negative) of the informal sector in environmental protection and degradation.

The final Chapter 10 by Hanson, Puplampu and Shaw crystallizes the emerging Africa Rising narrative arguing that transformative leadership, capacity development and the prioritization of policy implementation are crucial to achieving the 2030 Agenda for sustainable development – a position which also mirrors Article 10 of the UN's *Declaration on the Right to Development*. The authors also highlight Africa's agency plus creative engagement with disruptive technologies in a new development environment.

MDGs, SDGs and Africa: forging a way forward

Africa's transformation agenda will require both sufficient and necessary conditions for successful outcomes. A key requirement is the multilevel political dimensions of the development agenda. As Africa tries to seize the twenty-first century, and crystallize the Africa Rising narrative (see Chapter 10 at end), it faces a globe confronted with multiple crises, climate change, crime and security (Boko Haram, Al-Shabaab), leadership malaise, natural resource governance (illicit financial flows), youth unemployment. As a result of these and more, the challenges for realizing the social-ecological transformation envisioned by the UN SDGs or global goals are formidable in Africa and its diasporas, as elsewhere.

Across much of sub-Saharan Africa in particular, the youth face particular challenges, from high poverty and unemployment rates and low job security (ACBF 2016; Kharas and Biau 2015), to the looming impact of climate change and environmental degradation (South Centre 2016; also see Kedir this volume). Climate change is directly and indirectly threatening the full and effective gratification of a range of human rights by many across the globe (South Centre 2016). The impact of climate change are borne by people and communities already in disadvantaged situations, including indigenous peoples, who have historically contributed the least to greenhouse gas emissions (see Kedir this volume) and under whose stewardships 80 per cent of the world's remaining biodiversity has been preserved (South Centre 2016).

The aforementioned notwithstanding, contributors to this volume, individually and collectively, speak to initiatives at the local, national, regional, continental and global levels all aimed at ensuring Africa seizes the twenty-first century. Already, the region can point to a series of innovations, from the Maputo Corridor to trans-frontier peace parks or the Tripartite Free Trade Agreement between the Southern African Development Community (SADC), East African Community (EAC) and Common Market for Eastern and Southern Africa (COMESA) (www.tralac.org). Elsewhere the continent is defining its own science and technology policies (Opoku-Mensah 2016; Hanson and Puplampu this volume) including how it embraces and utilizes emerging technologies, while proactively planning for climate change with green growth planning (Kedir, this volume). Similar trends are evident in areas of governance, regional security, natural resource management, agriculture, trade, and international relations.

According to UN experts, central to developing real partnerships to deliver change are transparency, effective participation and accountability at national and international levels (South Centre 2016). As Dodds *et al.* (2017) further demonstrate, unlike the MDGs, at the core of the SDGs is the recognition that these goals and targets are interlinked and need to be addressed as an integrated package. Can the continent negotiate its challenges and seize the opportunities ahead, thus crystallizing the 'Africa Rising' or 'Lions on the Move' narrative? Who should spearhead this drive, developmental states, regional bodies or continental bodies? What should 'success' look like: fragile and post-conflict versus developmental states; leaders for life versus transformative leaders? The chapters in the book address these links in novel and imaginative ways and attempt to beat a path towards the envisioned future.

References

ACBF (2016) The Challenge Of African Youth Unemployment, Occasional Paper No. 26. Harare: African Capacity Building Foundation.

AfDB (2013) *At the Center of Africa's Transformation Strategy for 2013–2022.* Tunis: African Development Bank.

———. (2015) AfDB's High 5s: A Game Changer in Africa's Development Discourse. Available at www.afdb.org/en/the-high-5/ (accessed 5 January 2017).

African Union, Economic Commission for Africa; African Development Bank and United Nations Development Programme (AU/ECA/AfDB and UNDP) (2016) *MDGs to Agenda 2063/SDGs Transition Report 2016: Towards an Integrated and Coherent Approach to Sustainable Development in Africa.* Addis Ababa: AU/ECA/AfDB and UNDP.

Ayittey, G. (2015) Post-MDGs and Africa's development conundrum. *Journal of International Development*, 27 (3): 345–61.

Beegle, K., Christiaensen, L., Dabalen, A. and Gaddis, I. (2016) *Poverty in a Rising Africa.* Washington, DC: World Bank.

Besada, H. (2010) (ed.) *Crafting and African Peace and Security Architecture: Addressing Regional Peace and Conflict in the 21st Century.* London: Routledge.

Besada, H., Xu, J., Mathers, A. and Carey, J. (2016) Advancing African agency with the new 2030 transformative development agenda, *African Geographical Review*, dx.doi.org/10.1080/19376812.2016.1138232.

Bianchi, A. (2015) From MDGs to SDGs – Where Does Africa Stand?, ISPI Commentary (5 October 2015). Istituto per Gli Studi di Politica Internazionale.

Bischoff, P-H., Aning, K. and Acharya, A. (2016) (eds) *African IR Africa in Global International Relations: Emerging Approaches to Theory and Practice.* London: Routledge.

Brown, W. and Harman, S. (2013) (eds) *African Agency in International Politics.* London: Routledge.

Dodds, F., Donoghue, D. and Roesch, J. L. (2017) *Negotiating the Sustainable Development Goals: A Transformational Agenda for an Insecure World.* London and New York: Routledge.

Hanson, K. T. (ed.) (2015) *Contemporary Regional Development in Africa.* Farnham: Ashgate.

Hanson, K. T. and Kararach, G. and Shaw, T. M. (2012) (eds) *Rethinking Development Challenges for Public Policy: Insights from Contemporary Africa.* Basingstoke: Palgrave MacMillan.

Ismail, O. (2014) The Boko Haram insurgency and the changing patterns of regional security arrangements in Africa. In K. T. Hanson (ed.) *Contemporary Regional Development in Africa.* Farnham: Ashgate, pp. 201–24.

Kedir, A. M. (2014) Debating critical issues of green growth and energy in Africa: thinking beyond our lifetimes. In K. T. Hanson, C. D'Alessandro and F. Owusu (eds) *Managing Africa's Natural Resources: Capacities for Development*. New York: Palgrave Macmillan, pp. 185–220.

Kharas, H. and Biau, J. (2015) Africa looks forward to the post-2015 development agenda. Foresight Africa: top priorities for the continent. In The Brookings Institution, *Africa Growth Initiative*. Washington, DC: Brookings.

Nayyar, D. (2012) *The MDGs after 2015: Some Reflections on the Possibilities*. Background paper prepared for the UN System Task Team on the Post-2015 UN Development Agenda. New York: United Nations.

Opoku-Mensah, A. (2016) The Internet of Things in Africa: What Will it Take? 28 April. Available at www.linkedin.com/pulse/internet-things-africa-what-take-aida-opoku-mensah (accessed 11 November 2016).

Oppong, J. R. (2015) Innovation, science and technology: regional networks for research and technology development in Africa. In K. T. Hanson (ed.) *Contemporary Regional Development in Africa*. Farnham: Ashgate, pp.139–58.

Robinson, M. (2017) Foreword. In Dodds *et al.* (2017) *Negotiating the Sustainable Development Goals: A Transformational Agenda for an Insecure World.* London and New York: Routledge, pp. xiv–xvi.

Sachs, J. D. (2012) From millennium development goals to sustainable development goals, *Lancet*, 379: 2206–11.

Saeed, A. M. and Masakure, O. (2015) The paradox of broadband access in sub-Saharan Africa. In E. Shizha and D. Diallo (eds) *Africa in the Age of Globalisation: Perceptions, Misperceptions and Realities*. Burlington, VT: Ashgate, pp. 83–99.

Shaw, T. M. (2015a) African agency? Africa, South Africa and the BRICS. *International Politics*, 52 (2): 255–68, doi:10.1057/ip.2014.48.

——. (2015b) Afterword: 'African agency' to maximise the continent's policy choices after a decade of the BRICS: beyond dependency? In K. T. Hanson (ed.) *Contemporary Regional Development in Africa*. Farnham: Ashgate.

Shizha E. and Abdi, A. (2014) (eds) *Indigenous Discourses on Knowledge and Development in Africa*. New York: Routledge.

Shizha, E. and Diallo, D. (2015) (eds) *Africa in the Age of Globalisation: Perceptions, Misperceptions and Realities*. Burlington, VT: Ashgate.

South Centre (2016) Development agenda at risk unless States honour political and financial commitments, United Nations experts warn, *South News*, 137 (5 December). Available at www.southcentre.int (accessed 5 January 2017).

Taylor, I. (2014) *Africa Rising?: BRICS – Diversifying Dependency*. Woodbridge: James Currey.

United Nations (2015a) *The Millennium Development Goals Report 2015*. New York: United Nations.

———. (2015b) *Taking Stock of the Global Partnership for Development Millennium Development Goal 8*. MDG Gap Task Force Report 2015. New York: United Nations.

———. (2016) *Declaration on the Right to Development*. Available at www.un.org/en/events/righttodevelopment/declaration.shtml (accessed 5 January 2017).

UNECA, AUC, AfDB (2015) *Africa Regional Report on the Sustainable Development Goals: Summary*. Addis Ababa: United Nations Economic Commission for Africa.

United Nations Development Programme (UNDP) (2003) *Human Development Report 2003 Millennium Development Goals: A compact among nations to end human poverty*. New York: Oxford University Press.

———. (2015) *Sustainable Development Goals*. New York: United Nations.

Wallis, W. (2016) Smart Africa: Smartphones pave way for huge opportunities. Available at www.ft.com/intl/cms/s/0/aba818a6-c392-11e5-808f-8231cd71622e.html#axzz3zRD581QC (accessed 26 January 2016).

Warner, J. and Shaw, T. M. (2017) (eds) *African Foreign Policy and International Organizations*. New York: Palgrave Macmillan.

Web references

Africa Mining Vision – www.africaminingvision.org
Africa Progress Panel – www.africaprogresspanel.org
African Capacity Building Foundation – www.acbf–pact.org
Centre for Conflict Resolution – www.ccr.org.za
Institute for Security Studies – www.issafrica.org
South African Institute of International Relations – www.saiia.org.za
Trade Law Centre – www.tralac.org

2 The African state and development initiatives

The role of good governance in the realization of the MDGs and SDGs

Peter K. Arthur

Introduction

When African countries attained independence in the 1950s and 1960s, their focus shifted from political self-rule to one of promoting socioeconomic development. To this end, a number of policy measures and initiatives littered the African continent in the immediate period after independence. Ayittey (2015: 345–6), however, states that while 'various mega-plans have been devised to boost aid and help pull Africa out of its economic mismanagement since the 1960s, they all came to naught and quietly faded from public discourse'. It is under these circumstances that the Millennium Development Goals (MDGs) were adopted by world leaders in 2000 to help address the numerous development challenges that had bedevilled the developing world (UNDP 2003). As Kwon and Kim (2014: 353) note, all 189 member states of the United Nations (UN), including 147 heads of state and government, adopted the MDGs to show their collective responsibility of addressing the challenges that the world's poor and vulnerable people had to contend with.

In terms of meeting some of the developmental targets outlined in the MDGs, according to the United Nations (2015), in the Latin America and the Caribbean region, the proportion of people suffering from hunger reduced from 15.3 per cent to 6.1 per cent between 1992 and 2014, while the proportion of people living on less than US$1.25 a day fell from 13 per cent in 1990 to 4 per cent in 2015. Similarly, Eastern Asia and South-Eastern Asia countries have met or are within reach of meeting most MDG targets. With the poverty rates in South-Eastern Asia falling from 45 per cent in 1990 to 12 per cent by the end of 2015, it is unsurprising that extreme poverty rates of people living on less than US$1.25 per day halved in Eastern Asia and South-Eastern Asia (United Nations 2015). In sub-Saharan Africa (SSA), although progress has been made, the region did not meet the target of eradicating poverty by half by the 2015 deadline – one of the daunting challenges in achieving the MDGs (Wakiaga 2016: 38–9). This has therefore raised a number of concerns and questions for actors involved in the development debate. This chapter focuses on what African countries need to do to ensure and attain its development goals, as well as contributing to the literature and ongoing debate over the importance of good governance. The following research questions are investigated: Why were African countries unable to attain the MDGs? How would its successor and alternative, embodied in the Sustainable Development Goals (SDGs), to continue the efforts to promote growth and improve human development, be attained by African countries?[1] Do African governments have the potential, political leadership and will to carry through the SDGs? What role would good governance play in the efforts to realize objectives outlined in the SDGs?

The chapter argues that with the crisis in good governance contributing to various development problems, attaining the objectives in development initiatives such as the SDGs in Africa would be dependent on the existence of certain good governance conditions. First, it would be necessary to have a political environment that is characterized by transparent, participatory and accountable decision-making processes. In addition, the political system must be grounded in the promotion of the rule of law, anti-corruption mechanisms that ensure the participation of civil society in decision-making. This argument is arrived at based on insightful discussions of the many varieties of African states, their nature and role in ongoing discussions on good governance and development. Apart from providing an analytical framework for understanding the structural sources of poverty, inequality and marginalization, it also maps out how African countries can negotiate their development challenges through the promotion of good governance. In doing so, it presents viable pathways and best practices, drawing from proven cases to illustrate how good governance can help African countries to attain the SDGs.

In terms of organization, the first section of this chapter operationalizes the concept of good governance, which is seen here as a crucial aspect of the efforts to realize the SDGs. The second section outlines the origins and significance of MDGs, and also highlights why they became the focus of attention by the international community in 2000. It provides a critical look at their conception and main elements. It also assesses the extent to which the MDGs impacted African countries in their efforts to promote socioeconomic development. The third section discusses options beyond 2015 as embodied in the SDGs, explores the elements of the SDGs, which has become the foundation for a new approach to promoting development in Africa and elsewhere, and shows how the promotion of good governance by African countries can help with the attainment of the SDGs.

Conceptualizing good governance: an overview

Although difficult to establish empirically, Lin and Monga (2012: 659) point out that there is theoretically compelling evidence and a wide consensus in academic and policy circles on the idea that good governance is a pre-condition to sustained growth and economic development. With a growing body of literature pointing to the positive relationship between good governance and economic growth, maintaining peace and poverty alleviation (Asefa and Huang 2015; Burnside and Dollar 2004; Hackenesch and Börzel 2013; Knoll and Zloczysti 2012; Lin and Monga 2012; Miyazawa and Zusman 2015), putting in place the right governance structures cannot be underestimated in ensuring that the SDGs are attained (Hulme *et al.* 2014). Without good governance, laws would not be applied and security upheld, and international investors would be deterred and local businesses would be unable to operate (World Bank 2002). Ineffective governance also leads to the loss of human lives, stunted human development, environmental degradation and waste of financial and organizational resources (Joshi *et al.* 2015: 286).

So what exactly constitutes 'good governance?' While problematic to measure (Hulme *et al.* 2014: 3), a review of the extant academic and policy literature reveals there are diverse and multiple conceptualizations and definitions in use for the term 'good governance' (Hackenesch and Börzel 2013; Joshi 2011: 341; Joshi *et al.* 2015: 287). For Hulme *et al.* (2014: 4), 'governance concerns the use of power: the effectiveness of rules, policies and the functioning of public bodies that affect the lives of the members of a community'. The United Nations Development Programme (UNDP 2002: 51) on the other hand sees good governance as 'democratic governance', which involves taking into consideration the needs of future generations, respect for human rights, participation in decision-making, accountability, poverty eradication, responsiveness, fairness, equal treatment and freedom from discrimination based on race, gender, and ethnicity, as well as inclusiveness. For the World Bank (2002: 271), good governance is epitomized by predictable, open and enlightened policy-making; a bureaucracy imbued with a professional ethos; an executive arm of government accountable for its actions; and a strong civil society participating in public affairs – and all behaving under the rule of law. Joshi (2011: 343) adds that from the perspective of the World Bank, the good governance agenda is based on: (1) protecting investors' property rights; (2) pro-market regulatory policies; (3) a stable macroeconomic situation; and (4) the absence of corruption.

Similarly, Sisay and Huang (2015: 131) state that the World Governance Indicators identify six core governance components: government effectiveness; regulatory quality; voice and accountability; political stability and absence of violence; rule of law; and control of corruption. Regulatory quality is measured by perceptions of the ability of the government to formulate and implement sound policies and regulations that permit and promote private sector development. Miyazawa and Zusman (2015: 5) stress that political stability and absence of violence or terrorism as a component of good governance measured perceptions of the likelihood that the government will be destabilized or overthrown by unconstitutional or violent means, including politically motivated violence and terrorism. Government effectiveness can be assessed by perceptions of the quality of public services, and the degree of its independence from political pressures, the quality of policy formulation and implementation, and the credibility of the government's commitment to such policies. According to McFerson (2010: 338), while transparency entails the low-cost access by citizens to relevant information – particularly on public service access and quality – accountability consists of the capacity to call public officials to task for their actions, especially in how public revenues are mobilized and how they are spent. This view is shared by Miyazawa and Zusman (2015: 4) who argue that accountability typically looks more broadly at the extent to which citizens are able to participate in selecting their government, as well as freedom of expression, freedom of association and a free media. Finally, the rule of law as an aspect of good governance is critical in ensuring that there is confidence in the courts, quality enforcement of contracts (Miyazawa and Zusman 2015: 5), and providing society and the private economic sector with predictability, which, in addition to formal laws, require regulatory provisions that are clear and uniformly enforced (McFerson 2010: 338).

In spite of the absence of an underlying consensus on what 'good governance' means (Joshi *et al.* 2015: 287), there is agreement that it is multi-dimensional in nature and practice. This chapter therefore combines the various arguments in the literature and conceptualizes good governance as entailing the creation of public structures that are legitimate, responsible, efficient, transparent and accountable to the general public who are supposed to be the targets and beneficiaries of government programmes. It also involves merit-based bureaucratic systems, the participation of civil society in political decision-making, the promotion of the rule of law, and transformational political leadership (Hackenesch and Börzel 2013; Knoll and Zloczysti 2012; Rotberg 2012; UNECA 2016).

MDGs: origins, objectives and impact

While there is some agreement on the nature of underdevelopment in Africa, the issue that often crops up centres on the factors responsible for the structural sources of poverty, inequality, marginalization, and the policies and strategies utilized to address them. Although the negative impact of colonial rule was a principal factor (Arthur 2015), Ayee (2013) contends that other structural factors including the absence of meaningful economic diversification and transformation, the lack of a facilitative environment for private sector growth and political economy vulnerabilities such as ineffective leadership, weak institutions and corruption have played a critical role in the lack of economic and political progress in Africa. Arthur (2015) notes that since the 1950s, various policies have been formulated and implemented in much of Africa to address the challenges of underdevelopment. The inability of these development policies and initiatives to promote growth and also help address the high incidence of poverty on the African continent account for the continuous search for alternative approaches to confront region's socioeconomic challenges (Arthur 2015). For Nayyar (2012: 5), the development experience of the preceding 50 years made 2000 an almost natural conjuncture for the birth of the MDGs. As a collection of goals, targets and indicators, Ayittey (2015: 347) stresses that the primary focus of the MDGs was to eradicate extreme poverty and hunger.

Despite the absence of a legally binding framework, Kharas and Zhang (2014) contend that one legacy of the MDGs is a history of international, multi-stakeholder partnerships among businesses, governments and civil society with a common interest in addressing specific global problems. Similarly, Higgins (2013: 1) argues that apart from setting the benchmarks against which development progress were measured, the MDGs united the international community around a global agenda for development, and also became the central reference point for aid and international cooperation, and for providing a compelling vision for international development. Higgins (2013: 4) also states that the MDGs devised as a selection of practical priorities, rather than an exhaustive list of all desirable outcomes, represented a political statement of what is feasible at the global level.

Some progress on the MDGs have been made when measured in both absolute and relative terms (Higgins 2013: 7). Wakiaga (2016: 32) confirms that the proportion of people living on less than US$1.25 a day, in Southern, East, Central and West Africa, decreased as a group from 56.5 per cent in 1990 to 48.5 per cent in 2010. Moreover, a UN report on the MDGs asserted that the poverty rate in the developing regions plummeted from 47 per cent in 1990 to 14 per cent in 2015 (UN 2015: 15 cited in Hickel 2016: 749). Also, projections on hunger indicated a drop of almost half in the proportion of undernourished people in the developing regions, from 23.3 per cent in 1990–1992 to 12.9 per cent in 2014–2016, which is very close to the MDG hunger target (UN 2015: 20, cited in Hickel 2016: 749).

Significantly, according to UNECA *et al.* (2015: xiv), since 2000, most African countries have shown accelerated progress in expanding access to basic education. In 2012, Algeria, Benin, Cape Verde, Cameroon, Congo, Mauritius, Rwanda, South Africa, Tunisia and Zambia recorded a net enrolment rate of over 90 per cent. Overall, most African countries made significant progress as a result of policy reforms using participatory approaches, improved service delivery and governance. The youth literacy rate for the population aged 15–24 years improved in Africa as a result of the increased access to universal primary education observed since 2000. In 2012, only Niger, Chad and Côte d'Ivoire recorded youth literacy rates below 50 per cent. Over 58.8 per cent of African countries achieved at least a 75 per cent youth literacy rate. Also, gender parity in primary education increased in most regions of the world, with several countries adopting universal primary education policies and implementing gender-responsive interventions that have helped increase girls' enrolment substantially over the years (UNECA *et al.* 2015: xiv).

Moreover, UNECA *et al.* (2015: xv) have noted that 43 countries in Africa, excluding those in North Africa, observed more significant decreases in child mortality during the 2000–2013 period than during the 1990–2000 period.

The infant mortality rate fell from 90 deaths per 1,000 live births in 1990 to 54 deaths per 1,000 live births in 2014 – an average decline of 40 per cent. Continent-wide, the under-five mortality rate reduced from 146 deaths per 1,000 live births in 1990 to 65 deaths in 2012 (i.e. a 55.5 per cent reduction). Finally, a downward trend was observed in the incidence, prevalence and death rates associated with HIV/AIDS, malaria and tuberculosis, especially since 2000 (UNECA *et al.* 2015: xvi).

MDGs in Africa: problems and challenges

Despite the successes, there were notable challenges with the efforts to realize the MDGs. Vandemoortele (2011: 13) argues that a major problem with the MDGs was that while it was meant to broaden the narrative beyond the narrow growth paradigm, the search for a broader interpretation of development failed because it simply reaffirmed the conventional view. By misconstruing and distorting development to make them fit with the orthodox policy framework, the global debate was dominated by the implicit argument that faster economic growth and more foreign aid, coupled with better governance, would lead to the realization of the MDGs. Hickel (2016: 749) also contends that while around four billion people remain in poverty today, and around two billion remain hungry – more than ever before in history, and between two and four times what the UN would have us believe. The MDGs have used targeted statistical manipulation to make it seem as though the poverty and hunger trends have been improving when in fact they have worsened. Through the use of definitions of poverty and hunger that dramatically underestimate the likely scale of these problems, the MDGs ignores the fact that the present model of development is not working and needs to be fundamentally rethought. Ayittey (2015: 360) asserts that in Africa, while only a handful of African countries had by 2014 achieved some of the MDGs, the absolute number of the poor increased from 389 million in 2005 to 413 million in 2014, about half the continent's population.

Apart from an increase in poverty levels in Africa since the adoption of the MDGs (Ayittey 2015; Hickel 2016), Makuta and O'Hare (2015) also note that progress in improving health status in SSA has been slow, as measured by progress in the MDG targets.

> The MDGs had set targets of reduction, between 1990 and 2015, of 67% in under-five mortality rate (U5M) (MDG number 4) and 75% in maternal mortality ratio (MDG number 5). With regard to these, the region had achieved, by 2013, only 45% reduction in U5M and 48% in maternal mortality ratio. At these rates of progress, SSA as a whole will miss the MDG targets on both of these goals. It has been estimated only nine countries in the region, out of a samples of 36, will achieve their targets on MDG number 4 at the current rates of reduction.
>
> (Makuta and O'Hare 2015)

Furthermore, as observed by the UNECA *et al.* (2015: xviii), only a quarter of the current African population (24 per cent) has gained access to an improved drinking water source since 2000, which is the lowest globally. Moreover, only 16 per cent of the population has access to piped drinking water, which is the lowest in the world. There are wide rural-urban disparities in access to safe drinking water that tend to pull down national aggregate figures in some countries. The weak initial conditions (low 1990 baseline), combined with high population growth relative to the rest of the world exacerbate the challenge of meeting the target in Africa. Similarly, the proportion of people with access to improved sanitation has increased only moderately in Africa excluding North Africa, from 24 per cent in 1990 to 30 per cent in 2012.

Moreover, while the promotion of good governance is not explicitly outlined in the MDGs, MDG 3 and its emphasis on gender equality and empowerment as well as ensuring that women are well represented in positions of power and decision-making can be seen as an important element in the efforts to promote good governance. Although from 2000 to 2014 Africa made the most progress on the target of women's representation in national parliaments with an increase of at least 15 per cent, according to UNECA *et al.* (2015), there are still uneven gains in the share of women in waged employment in the non-agricultural sector.

Similarly, Ghaus-Pasha (2007: 17) argues that a look at the MDGs, especially goal eight, immediately highlights the connection with issues of governance at the global, national and local levels. At the national and local levels, bringing about any change, such as achieving the MDGs, requires a conducive policy environment, adequate resources and an enabling institutional framework. These elements subsume the critical dimensions of good governance, which may be categorized as a pro-poor policy framework, public administration and civil services, and decentralization and delivery of services. The cross-cutting dimensions include accountability and transparency, rule of law, human rights and the role of civil society (Ghaus-Pasha 2007: 18). At the global level, issues of an open, rule-based, predictable, non-discriminatory trading and financial system, which form part of MDG 8, are all linked to good governance.

Also, how available resources would be mobilized and distributed among needy nations, and what would be the respective responsibilities of the donors and the recipients are issues of global governance. On this, UNECA *et al.* (2015) note that trade and related economic agreements are worrisome from an African perspective. Apart from intra-African trade, at 16.3 per cent of total trade in 2013, which is low compared with other regions, African share of global merchandise trade declined from 3.5 per cent in 2012 to 3.3 per cent in 2013, compared with 4.9 per cent in the 1970s. Likewise, Stein and Horn (2012: 670) point out that aid flows, which could facilitate attempts by developing countries to reduce poverty, still remained limited and many donor governments like the United States, Germany, the United Kingdom or Japan, have not increased their official development assistance to 0.7 per cent of their overall gross domestic product (GDP), a goal established in MDG 8.

Furthermore, other structural challenges and poor governance as epitomized in corruption, state fragility and violence produce other development challenges in Africa (Chimhowu and Hulme 2012). Chimhowu and Hulme (2012) argue that one of the greatest challenges facing Africa is the failure of its governments to formulate and implement strategies for inclusive growth. This means that growing national wealth are not equitably shared by the majority but only enjoyed by a few selected and well-connected political and bureaucratic elites, which as Kararach *et al.* (2016: 365) remind us has the potential to destabilize African societies.

In the Republic of Congo for example, McFerson (2009: 1535) points out that basic human development indicators have deteriorated for a majority of citizens, compared with 1990. Currently, the under-five mortality rate is 117 per 1,000 live births and infant mortality 75 per 1,000; malnutrition stands at 14 per cent; immunization coverage remains at a low 52 per cent; and maternal mortality remains at a high eight deaths per 1,000 live births. Despite these grim indicators, oil revenue is a personal cash cow for the ruling elites of society. Similarly, in Equatorial Guinea, McFerson (2009: 1538) points out that a small elite have virtually appropriated the entire oil revenue and wealth. Although average per capita income is in excess of US$14,000 a year, 60 per cent of the population earn below US$350 a year – under the absolute poverty line of US$1 a day. Equatorial Guinea ranked 35th out of 46 African countries for the quality of economic management and was perceived to be one of the world's most corrupt states.

To illustrate the elite's role in corruption, consider the case in Uganda. According to UNECA (2016: 19), in 2010 in Uganda, the firm Muehlbauer Technology Co. Ltd was awarded a contract to print national ID cards through a dubious single-source contracting process, even though the Public Procurement Authority had advised otherwise. The firm was allegedly given over US$100 million, but fewer than 500 cards had been issued by 2012.

Finally, UNECA (2016: 9–10) notes that evidence in 2015 of the Ibrahim Index of African Governance, which was created in 2007 and publishes annual data, shows that only six (Botswana, Cape Verde, Mauritius, Namibia, Seychelles and South Africa) of the 54 African countries have achieved progress in all four pillars and the sub-category components of the composite index: safety and rule of law (rule of law, accountability, personal safety, national security); participation and human rights (participation, rights, gender); sustainable economic opportunity (public management, business environment, infrastructure, rural sector); and human development (welfare, education, health).

In addition, inappropriate political governance continues to affect many countries on the continent, which incites civil unrest and violent uprisings (UNECA 2016: 12). Deterioration in safety, which stemmed from conflicts in countries such as South Sudan, Libya, Mali, Guinea-Bissau and the Central African Republic, coupled with the lack of economic opportunities have led to a general decline in governance in Africa. In fact, the report showed that of the ten countries that deteriorated the most between 2011 and 2014, five are previous top performers, including Botswana and Cape Verde (UNECA 2016). It is therefore reasonable to argue that poor governance makes it difficult for several African countries to make sustained progress in human development and poverty reduction. As Ghaus-Pasha (2007: 16) argues, when governance is characterized by lack of transparency, accountability or competence, the people suffer. When income inequality is high, the state is frequently captured by the ruling elite, which expropriates most of the resources; the poor do not have a 'voice' and are neglected. Consequently, if governments fail to invest adequately in the health and education of their people, economic growth will eventually taper off because of the lack of development of human capital. Thus, notwithstanding the gains achieved over the past few years in Africa, evidence in 2015 shows stalling progress in overall governance performance, threatening the very foundation and also efficacy of one of the drivers of structural transformation. (UNECA 2016: 9).

Post-2015 development agenda: the role of good governance

SDGs and governance

The foregoing has demonstrated that while contributing to a wide variety of development projects and programmes, helping alleviate the impacts of poverty and providing basic human needs to a substantial number of people in Africa, the targets and standards of the MDGs were not fully attained by 2015. It is against this backdrop that the 17 SDGs, with their focus of eradicating poverty and ensuring human development, and driving principles of improving health and human well-being, were launched. While the SDGs are seen as a means of addressing some of the concerns of the MDGs and building on the progress that had been realized, Le Blanc (2015: 1) states that the SDGs succeeded the MDGs as reference goals for the international community for the period 2015–2030, and also serve as guideposts for a difficult transition to the new development process. According to Fofack (2014: 58), in addition to the SDG framework emphasizing mutual accountability in the management and ownership of resources offered by the planet across space and over time, it also ensures that the success of every single SDG will be dependent on the commitment of all countries to align development policies and programmes to meet the growing challenges of the development process. With 169 targets covering and integrating economic, social development and environmental protection, and with poverty eradication as the overarching goal of the new agenda, Fofack (2014: 58) argues that the move towards the SDGs as the new development framework, can be partly explained by the increasing human and social costs of consumption and production patterns adopted by the majority of countries, especially the more advanced economies and, more recently, emerging market economies.

Thus, in Africa's post-2015 development agenda, Kararach, Besada and Shaw (2016: 366) argue that if the right policy and programmatic frameworks are put in place and bottlenecks are eliminated, then the goal of eliminating poverty could be achievable within the coming decade or so. However, notwithstanding several global initiatives, a recurring frustration in the efforts to promote overall socioeconomic development in Africa has been the lack of proper governance structures and the capacity to undertake and implement the necessary programmes and services (Arthur 2014; Hulme *et al.* 2014). Significantly, the UNECA (2016: 7) notes that although a number of requisites are important to achieve structural transformation, the application and practice of principles of good governance has a central place as it defines the interaction between actors of the public sector and those within other sectors. In fact, due to the widespread belief in the importance of good governance, Joshi *et al.* (2015: 286) note that two of the SDGs initially proposed by the High-Level Panel of Eminent Persons on the Post-2015 Development Agenda sought to advance 'good governance' (inclusion, transparency, access to information, freedom of association and participation), 'effective institutions' (state capacity, rule of law, property rights, reduced bribery and corruption), and 'stable and peaceful societies' (reduced violence and conflict, accountable and professional security forces, access to justice institutions). In sum, the observation that the generally low quality of governance in SSA is correlated to their level of economic development (Joseph 2013) is the reason behind the argument in this chapter that good governance in Africa can assist in the implementation and monitoring of progress towards the realization of the SDGs. Indeed, improved governance is not only a desirable end in itself but also a necessary means to accomplish the other SDGs (Joshi *et al.* 2015: 298).

So what kind of 'good governance' would it take to attain development initiatives like the SDGs in Africa? Fofack (2014: 59) argues that to achieve the desired development goals and increase development effectiveness under the SDG framework will require that African countries learn more from successful nations how to effectively align public and private sector interventions. Also, Sachs (2012: 2209) notes that a basic determinant of the world's ability to achieve SDGs will be the quality of governance at all levels, from local to global, and in the private sector as well as government. At every level, government and official agencies should be responsive to the citizenry. For Sachs (2012: 2209), in addition to the importance of governance being as close to the people as functionally possible – giving individuals and families maximum freedom of action, sharing information, exchanging ideas, encouraging meetings and brainstorming, and working in good faith across cultures – should all be important aspects of the efforts by governments to realize the SDGs. Equally, UNCTAD (2014: 49) is of the view that promoting development objectives and good governance means that African governments strive to maintain political stability, improve bureaucratic efficiency in state institutions and public-sector bodies to reduce the costs of doing business for investors, and also set up mechanisms between the state and private investors to encourage regular dialogue and consultations between the state and the private sector. In addition, there is the need to strengthen the judiciary apparatus, secure its independence in order to encourage respect for rule of law and promote peace and security.

Moreover, with the lack of capacity to implement programmes often seriously impeding delivery on well-intentioned poverty reduction policies in less-developed countries (Kwon and Kim 2014: 358), improving the capacity of bureaucratic institutions and public workers to enhance service delivery in Africa, as well as improving the quality of regulations so that the market economy runs smoothly in order to produce economic growth, would contribute to poverty reduction and also help attain the SDGs. Indeed, be it a state-led or market-friendly approach, a well-organized and functioning bureaucratic system as well as governance systems that recruit personnel and capacity based on merit are needed to ensure economic development in Africa. In other words, if African countries seek to improve their socioeconomic circumstances, then the patrimonial system that is very endemic needs to be replaced by a merit-based system of governance (Makinda 2012: 76). Joshi (2011: 349–350) makes a similar argument by suggesting that the importance of state capacity can be epitomized in the ability of the state to have the necessary revenue generation ability, qualified and trustworthy civil servants to implement policies, to enforce laws, to spend public money efficiently, as well as effectiveness on the part of the government in terms of the allocation of financial and human resources.

Transparency and accountability

Good governance in Africa through institutional quality can either lessen or aggravate uncertainties that arise from incomplete information about the behaviour of economic agents in the process of human interaction, and create incentives that advance socioeconomic opportunities. Better institutional quality can reduce information asymmetries by channelling information about market conditions. It helps to promote the development of human capabilities of a society, reduce risk as property rights are defined and contracts well-enforced, and make politicians accountable to citizens (Barry and Tacneng 2014: 4). Also, the existence of transparency and accountability – which involves exposing the truth, equal enforcement of the rules, openly and objectively discussing government transactions and procedures, as well as the right to access public information and records and government disclosure of information – results in a situation where political elites do not take advantage of their position to enrich themselves and family members while the rest of society is marginalized and impoverished (Arthur 2014; UNECA 2016). Moreover, through the existence of free and fair elections and a fully functioning legislature, decision-makers are held to account for their actions, and political institutions respond to the needs of citizens (Bauhr and Grimes 2014; Callamard 2010). The case of Ghana, which has experienced the successful change and transfer of power after close election results, is indicative of the importance of good governance, in the form of free and fair elections, for development. Of the six elections held in Ghana since 1992, two have produced power alternation in 2000 and 2008, making the country's democracy as firmly consolidated in the conceptual framework of Samuel Huntington (Debrah 2015).

Transparency can reveal improper or illegal government practices and potentially erode institutional confidence and the willingness of citizens to engage in the individual or collective actions needed to bring about the kind of gradual improvements hoped for (Bauhr and Grimes 2014: 309). At the same time, transparency 'grants political and public institutions greater insight into one another's operations, thereby increasing their capacity to hold one another accountable' (Bauhr and Grimes 2014: 293). In fact, Bauhr and Grimes (2014: 292) note that given that transparency increases the likelihood that principals will detect malfeasance on the part of agents and exact punishment, it represents the most compelling reason to realizing better practices in government operations and deterring the abuse of public power. In this regard, as part of the efforts to attain the SDGs, African governments should promote accountability and transparency.

Even though Botswana has (had) various challenges including lack of economic diversification, inequality, discrimination against minority ethnic groups, extreme poverty in the rural areas, high HIV/AIDS prevalence rate, drought and desertification (Sarkin and Cook 2010), one can cite it as a 'success story' in terms of the promotion of good governance, transparency, accountability and how that has positively impacted its economic development. As McFerson (2009: 1543) observes, Botswana, which has substantial political freedom, has been consistently ranked as 'free'; has the second highest possible rating in terms of political rights and civil liberties; and is fourth in Africa for regulatory effectiveness. It also has very low corruption, at levels comparable to those of well-managed developed countries, with a Transparency International score of 5.8 and a world integrity ranking of 36. Botswana has established strong and transparent governance structures, independent, professional and competent institutions, anti-corruption systems, and a well-functioning judicial system that respects property rights and the rule of law, which has contributed to its economic success (McFerson 2009). In sum, prudent fiscal policy; heavy government investment in infrastructure and human capital, collecting, efficiently managing the revenue and investing for development; rule of law; transparency and accountability; and a constitution that enshrines rights and freedoms, free and fair elections in Botswana demonstrate how good governance could address social inequities and improve the lives of citizens (McFerson 2009).

The role of CSOs and non-state actors

In terms of realizing the SDGs, the growing body of literature that has emphasized the role of non-state actors in governance is also of great importance.

Banks, Hulme and Edwards (2015) maintain that civil society and the space in which people mobilize to bargain, negotiate or coerce other actors in order to advance and promote their interests is key when it comes to safeguarding, protecting and promoting the position of marginalized or excluded groups. In fact, civil society organizations (CSOs) in various countries play a vital role in environmental conservation, raise ecological awareness, and help in service provision and community engagement. CSOs also engage in policy and advocacy, check on governments and public office holders, as well as foster debate to improve transparency and accountability through their watchdog and monitoring functions (Arthur 2014; Mercer and Green 2013). Zajontz and Leysens (2015), in assessing the potential of four CSOs – the Southern African Development Community (SADC) Council of NGOs, the Southern African Trade Union Co-ordination Council, the Economic Justice Network of the Fellowship of Christian Councils in Southern Africa, and the Southern African People's Solidarity Network – found that the CSOs have incrementally broadened their regional agenda, to bring it in line with the socioeconomic realities of the region. They note that the Council of NGOs, the Southern African Trade Union Co-ordination Council and the Economic Justice Network have developed a much-needed professional and technocratic understanding of regional policies, issues and institutions, and have established links with SADC policy-makers, while the Southern African People's Solidarity Network and the Economic Justice Network (to a lesser extent) have closer ties to local communities, workers and traders in the informal economy. Similarly, apart from CSOs being formidable actors in Ghana's democratic process, Debrah and Graham (2015) add that the Civil Society Platform on Oil and Gas, a group of 120 CSOs formed in 2009, including policy research think-tanks, human rights, environmental groups and community-based organizations, has helped prevent the 'resource curse' in Ghana by facilitating the creation of legislative frameworks, and checking and monitoring systems to keep government and oil companies on their toes.

In the context of realizing the SDGs, where the development and nurturing of active civil society groups and NGOs are important, many similar non-state actors often lack the capacity and resources to hold governments and business to account and thereby perform their watchdog functions. Debrah and Graham (2015) underscore that weak capacity, politicization and lack of access to information remain challenges to the effective mobilization of CSOs in Ghana. Zajontz and Leysens (2015) come to similar conclusions by noting that CSOs in Southern Africa are constrained by a lack of financial autonomy, and dependency on donor funding. Capacity is further hampered because the CSOs are managed by a small number of professional activists, and their representativeness and legitimacy among the regional populace tend to be limited. CSOs have different ideological and strategic orientations, lack of effective coordination and these factors have so far inhibited the creation of a broader, transformative regional civil society alliance. It is in this regard that Joshi (2011) notes that strong state capacity, which he perceives as a crucial aspect of good governance, is important in the realizing of various development initiatives. According to Joshi (2011: 347), sustaining services to the poor and the marginalized requires a permanent revenue source and a commitment to guaranteeing development initiatives as a human right. This entails adequate state capacity because NGOs and CSOs have limited resources and private businesses lack incentives to work with communities when there is no profit. This is especially the case in rural areas of the Third World and for investments such as education or basic infrastructure where the dividends may take decades to produce results.

Combating corruption and effective political leadership

Corruption is endemic in many parts of Africa and is measured by perceptions of the extent to which public power is exercised for private gain, including both petty and grand forms of corruption (UNECA 2016), as well as 'capture' of the state by elites and private interests (Miyazawa and Zusman 2015: 5). Besides the issues mentioned in the previous section, combating corruption is therefore crucial in the efforts to attain the SDGs. As a phenomenon closely linked to poor governance, Khan (2006: 216–244, cited in UNECA 2016: xi) argues that the 'pressure to reduce corruption and move towards good governance is both necessary and desirable, but these ends cannot be achieved unless attention is also given to other governance capacities required for accelerating and sustaining growth'. It is in this vein that for Joseph (2013) the solution to corruption is to create a policy environment and a development strategy that offers few opportunities for state capture and rent-seeking activities. Equally, the UNECA (2016) notes that for structural transformation and inclusive development in Africa, combating corruption should not only involve improving transparency and accountability, but also entail enhancing ownership and participation in development planning through the process of allowing citizens, including vulnerable groups, to participate in development planning and policy-making. It also calls for building credible governance institutions such as national planning authorities, independent oversight bodies (e.g. legislature, an independent judiciary), representative political institutions, effective central banks and other investment regulatory bodies, as well as improving the regional and global governance architecture.

The leak by a 'whistle-blower' in April 2016 and subsequent publication by an international consortium of investigative journalists of 11.5 million documents from the Panamanian law firm, Mossack Fonseca ('Panama Papers'), of the owners of anonymous offshore shell companies, demonstrate the need to stem massive and pervasive corruption in both developing and developed countries. While not all offshore bank accounts are necessarily illegal, the revelations in the 'Panama Papers' have shown how offshore tax havens are used to facilitate, divert and launder stolen and other illegally acquired money, and protect real owners from liability and accountability. It is therefore unsurprising that apart from the 'Panama Papers' resulting in a global discussion of how the elites of society evade taxes and hide their wealth and assets, it has also shed light on the importance of having a global and transnational approach to fight corruption.

Together with stemming the tide of corruption, effective and transformational leadership is a crucial piece and powerful agent in the efforts to attain development initiatives such as the SDGs. Historically, many African leaders have promoted clientelism by redistributing state assets to a few influential elites in return for political allegiance; abused state resources (Chimhowu and Hulme 2012); centralized power, and threatened or co-opted opposition leaders. Rotberg (2013) points out that leaders such as Presidents Robert Mugabe in Zimbabwe, Teodoro Obiang Nguema Mbasogo in Equatorial Guinea and Isaias Afewerki in Eritrea engage in activities that benefit the ruler and ruling class more than promoting the broader and collective social good.

Moreover, excessive and indiscriminate logging, poorly regulated extraction of resources such as gold, diamond, among others, by foreign companies in connivance with some corrupt politicians have caused serious environmental damage in most African countries (Tosam and Mbih 2015: 793). Thus, effective leadership and democratic management of environmental resources may help avoid violent conflicts, which are some of the main causes of environmental degradation, displacement of people and the disruption of social and economic activities (Tosam and Mbih 2015).

In this vein, the importance of enlightened and responsible leadership is an imperative to the overall development of a country including the efforts to attain the SDGs. As Rotberg (2012: 113) argues, individual leaders beget good governance, and the practice of good governance nurtures and enables robust institutions and strengthens the rule of law. The latter do not emerge in a vacuum, but only as a result of early and careful leadership attention to core values. For Rotberg (2012), transformative leaders who possess what he calls the 'critical competencies', emotional intelligence (which includes a capacity for empathy), vision, the ability to mobilize followers, integrity, prudence, courage, self-mastery and intellectual honesty, combine to give transformative leaders the ability to lead appropriately and with legitimacy.

In South Africa for example, Araia (2012) notes that Nelson Mandela's transformational leadership and approach to governance that was characterized by integrity, vision, reconciliation, the rule of law, commitment to fundamental reforms, promoting the welfare of all and 'willingness to work across racial and party lines and sit with his adversaries in the post-apartheid days showed that real leadership is collaborative, collective and inclusive – exactly the opposite of authoritative, corrupt or inflexible approaches'. Similarly, Rotberg (2012) demonstrates the role of Botswana's first President, Seretse Khama in helping to make the country what it is today in terms of preserving and strengthening a deliberative and democratic political culture. According to Rotberg (2012), Khama, who led Botswana from 1966 to 1980, embodied the virtues of transformative leadership that has contributed to a situation where despite its large deposits of diamonds, the country has not plunged into autocratic rule and corruption as is the case in many parts of Africa. Given the good precedent set by President Khama, it came as no surprise that he was followed by good leaders like President Festus Gontebanye Mogae, who won the 2008 Mo Ibrahim Prize for Achievement in African Leadership. President Festus Gontebanye Mogae stepped down as president in April 2008 in accordance with Botswana's constitution, having served two five-year terms in government.

Furthermore, there is the case of the former Namibian President, Hifikepunye Pohamba, who won the Mo Ibrahim prize in 2014, after leaving office after two terms (2005–2015) as president. Not only did he boost good governance by tolerating political opposition, promoting media freedom and human rights, but also he spearheaded his country's aggressive response to the AIDS crisis and promoted gender equality, as evidenced in the 48 per cent of Namibia's parliament being currently female (Mwakideu 2015).

Finally, one can also cite President Magufuli of Tanzania who came to power after elections in October 2015 and has been stamping his authority on the new government and society as a whole, which shows the importance of leadership in advancing good governance for development. As Mohammed (2015) comments, his 'new broom' approach, promise to root out corruption and anti-graft measures have set the right tone for Tanzania's efforts to promote development. Not only has President Magufuli banned ostentatious expenditure such as Independence Day celebrations, but also his government has removed more than 10,000 'ghost workers' from its public-sector payroll, and the focus on delivering essential public services shows his determination to fight corruption.

The lessons from the notable leaders in Botswana, Namibia, Tanzania and South Africa (under Nelson Mandela) can guide governments to perform effectively for their citizens by providing security and safety, the rule of law, open political participation, sustainable economic prospects and broader human development (Rotberg 2012, 2013). In sum, the transformation of African states will depend on the willingness of leaders to embrace new ideas and values embodied in new democratic governance (Makinda 2012: 58) as well as exhibit attributes such as knowledge, vision, determination, transparency and motivation to move their citizens towards positive societal transformations (Ukaegbu 2015: 24).

Concluding remarks

The focus of this chapter was to examine the role that good governance would play in the attempt by African countries to realize the SDGs. It noted that since independence in the 1950s and 1960s, African countries have formulated and implemented various policies and initiatives to promote socioeconomic development and alleviate poverty.

Despite substantive progress and economic transition in some African countries, it is still the case that not everyone has benefited from the improvements in living standards. It was to help promote development and alleviate poverty that the MDGs, and later the SDGs, were adopted by the international community. For Kwon and Kim (2014: 368), the MDGs led international organizations and governments in developing countries to focus on the poverty agenda. As a rallying point for the advancement of social development, the MDGs placed emphasis on poverty reduction and social development, in contrast to the structural adjustment agenda that had dominated in the 1990s. Also, as the UNECA, AU, AfDB and UNDP (2013: 3) argue, 'the overall aim of the SDGs is to provide guidance and contribute effectively to transformative changes in support of a rights-based, equitable and inclusive approach to sustainability at global, regional, national and local levels'.

This chapter has argued that despite the laudable objectives, efforts to realize development initiatives such as the SDGs would depend on the extent to which good governance is at the core of the process. UNCTAD (2014: 49) reiterates that the quality of governance has a direct bearing on private investment and the nature and productivity of that investment. Poor governance increases the costs of doing business for investors and entrepreneurs and introduces elements of risk and uncertainty in the decision-making calculus of investors which, in turn, affects their expected rate of return on investment. Poor governance can therefore create distortions in investment decisions and subsequent suboptimal outcomes for the economy (Joshi *et al.* 2015; World Bank 2002). Thus the importance of good governance cannot be disregarded in the efforts to attain development programmes like the SDGs in Africa. Through the existence of effective and transformational leadership, as well as ensuring that the principles of accountability, transparency, rule of law, participation and inclusion of non-state actors in the design and implementation of development activities are present, which are key aspects of good governance, then African countries have greater prospects of making progress on the realization of development initiatives like the SDGs.

Note

1 See Wall (2014) for details of the 17 SDGs.

References

Araia, S. (2012) Mandela Moments: My Observations on African Leadership, Peace and Development. Available at www.one.org/us/2012/07/18/mandela-moments-my-observations-on-african-leadership-peace-and-development/ (accessed 21 March 2016).

Arthur, P. (2014) Governance of natural resource management in Africa: contemporary perspectives. In K. T. Hanson, C. D'Alessandro and F. Owusu (eds) *Managing Africa's Natural Resources: Capacities for Development*. London: Palgrave Macmillan, pp. 39–65.

———. (2015) The state, infrastructure and capacity development as instruments for promoting socioeconomic development in contemporary Africa, *Global Development Studies*, 7, (3–4): 33–68.

Ayee, J. (2013) The developmental state experiment in Africa: the experiences of Ghana and South Africa, *Round Table*, 102 (3): 259–80.

Ayittey, G. (2015) Post-MDGs and Africa's development conundrum, *Journal of International Development*, 27 (3): 345–61.

Banks, N., Hulme, D. and Edwards, M. (2015) NGOs, states, and donors revisited: still too close for comfort? *World Development*, 66: 707–18.

Barry, T. and Tacneng, R. (2014) The impact of governance and institutional quality on MFI outreach and financial performance in sub-Saharan Africa, *World Development*, 58 (1): 1–20.

Bauhr, M and Grimes, M. (2014) Indignation or resignation: the implications of transparency for societal accountability, *Governance: An International Journal of Policy, Administration, and Institutions*, 27 (2): 291–320.

Callamard, A. (2010) Accountability, transparency and freedom of expression in Africa, *Social Research*, 77 (4): 1211–40.

Chimhowu, A. and Hulme, D. (2012) Africa and the MDGs: challenges and priorities. In R. Wilkinson and D. Hulme (eds) *The MDGs and Beyond: Global Development After 2015*. Abingdon: Routledge, pp. 146–57.

Debrah, E. (2015) Reforming Ghana's electoral process: lessons and the way forward, *Journal of Politics and Law*, 8 (1): 1–13.

Debrah, E. and Graham, E. (2015) Preventing the oil curse situation in Ghana: the role of civil society organisations, *Insight on Africa*, 7 (1): 21–41.

Fofack, H. (2014) RIP MDGs, arise SDGs, *African Business*, 414: 58–9.

Ghaus-Pasha, A. (2007) *Governance for Millennium Development Goals: Core Issues and Good Practices*. New York: United Nations. Available at www.publicadministration.un.org/publications/content/PDFs/E-Library%20Archives/2007%20Governance%20for%20the%20Millennium%20Development%20Goals.pdf (accessed 6 June 2016).

Hackenesch, C. and Börzel, T. (2013) Small carrots, few sticks: EU good governance promotion in sub-Saharan Africa, *Cambridge Review of International Affairs*, 26 (3): 536–55.

Hickel, J. (2016) The true extent of global poverty and hunger: questioning the good news narrative of the Millennium Development Goals, *Third World Quarterly*, 37 (5): 749–67.

Higgins, K. (2013) Reflecting on the MDGs and Making Sense of the Post-2015 Development Agenda. Available at www.nsi-ins.ca/wp-content/uploads/2013/05/2013-Post-2015.pdf (accessed 21 February 2016).

Hulme, D., Savoia, A. and Sen, K. (2014) *Governance as a Global Development Goal: Setting, Measuring and Monitoring the Post 2015-Development Agenda*. ESID Working Paper No. 32.

Joseph, R. (2013) Is Good Governance Necessary For Economic Progress in Africa? Available at africaplus.wordpress.com/2013/08/04/is-good-governance-necessary-for-economic-progress-in-africa/ (accessed 26 March 2016).

Joshi, D. (2011) Good governance, state capacity, and the millennium development goals, *Perspectives on global development and technology*, 10 (2): 339–60.

Joshi, D., Hughes, B. and Sisk, T. (2015) Improving governance for the post-2015 sustainable development goals: scenario forecasting the next 50years, *World Development*, 70: 286–302.

Kararach, G., Besada, H. and Shaw, T. (2016) African development, political economy and the road to Agenda 2063. In G. Kararach, H. Baseda and T. Shaw (eds) *Development in Africa: Reframing the Lens after the MDGs*. Bristol: Policy, pp. 365–92.

Khan, M. (2006) Determinants of corruption in developing countries: the limits of conventional economic analysis. In S. Rose-Ackerman (ed.) *International Handbook on the Economics of Corruption*. Cheltenham: Edward Elgar, pp. 216–44.

Kharas, H. and Zhang, C. (2014) New agenda, new narrative: what happens after 2015? *SAIS Review of International Affairs*, 34 (2): 25–35.

Knoll M. and Zloczysti, P. (2012) The good governance indicators of the Millennium Challenge Account: how many dimensions are really being measured, *World Development*, 40 (5): 900–15.

Kwon, H. and Kim, E. (2014) Poverty reduction and good governance: examining the rationale of the millennium development goals, *Development and Change*, 45 (2): 353–75.

Le Blanc, D. (2015) *Towards Integration at Last? The sustainable Development Goals as a Network of Targets*. DESA Working Paper No. 141. Available at www.un.org/esa/desa/papers/2015/wp141_2015.pdf (accessed 19 February 2016).

Lin, J. Y. and Monga, C. (2012) Solving the mystery of African governance, *New Political Economy*, 17(5): 659–66.

McFerson, H. (2010) Extractive industries and African democracy: can the 'resource curse' be exorcised? Extractive industries and African democracy, *International Studies Perspectives*, 11 (4): 335 53.

Makında, S. (2012) Africa's leadership malaise and the crisis of governance and transformative politics. In K. T. Hanson, G. Kararach and T. M. Shaw (eds) *Rethinking Development Challenges for Public Policy: Insights from Contemporary Africa*. London: Palgrave Macmillan, pp. 54–82.

Makuta, I. and O'Hare, B. (2015) Quality of governance, public spending on health and health status in sub-Saharan Africa: a panel data regression analysis, *BMC Public Health*, 15: 932. Available at bmcpublichealth.biomedcentral.com/articles/10.1186/s12889-015-2287-z (accessed 22 February 2016).

Mercer, C. and Green, M. (2009) Governance and hyper-corruption in resource-rich African countries, *Third World Quarterly*, 30 (8): 1529–48.

———. (2013) Making civil society work: contracting, cosmopolitanism and community development in Tanzania, *Geoforum*, 45: 106–15.

Miyazawa, I. and Zusman, E. (2015) *A Quantitative Analysis of the Effect of Governance on the Millennium Development Goals (MDGs): Implications for the Post-2015 Development Agenda*. Institute for Global Environmental Strategies (IGES) Discussion Paper No. 2014–02.

Mohammed, O. (2015) Tanzania's new President, John Magufuli, Inspires new Trend. Available at www.africa-ontherise.com/tanzanias-new-president-john-magufuli-inspires-new-trend/ (accessed 25 March 2016).

Mwakideu, C. (2015) Namibia's Pohamba Joins Africa's Best Leaders. Available at www.dw.com/en/namibias-pohamba-joins-africas-best-leaders/a-18289359 (accessed 5 April 2016).

Nayyar, D (2012) The MDGs after 2015: Some Reflections on the Possibilities. Available at www.un.org/en/development/desa/policy/untaskteam_undf/d_nayyar.pdf (accessed 23 February 2016).

Rotberg, R. (2012) *Transformative Political Leadership: Making a Difference in the Developing World.* Chicago and London: University of Chicago Press.

———. (2013) Good leadership is Africa's Missing Ingredient. Available at www.theglobeandmail.com/opinion/good-leadership-is-africas-missing ingredient/article9234496/ (accessed 13 March 2016).

Sachs, J. (2012) From millennium development goals to sustainable development goals, *Lancet*, 379 (9832): 2206–11.

Sarkin, J. and Cook, A. (2010) Is Botswana the miracle of Africa? Democracy, the rule of law, and human rights versus economic development, *Transnational Law & Contemporary Problems*, 19 (2): 453–89.

Sisay, A. and Huang, W.-C. (2015) The challenges of good governance and leadership in developing countries: cases from Africa and China. In A. Sisay and W.-C. Huang (eds) *The Political Economy of Good Governance*, Kalamazoo, MI: W. E. Upjohn Institute for Employment Research, pp. 131–53.

Stein, A. and Horn, P. (2012) Asset accumulation: an alternative approach to achieving the MDGs, *Development Policy Review*, 30 (6): 663–80.

Tosam, M. J. and Mbih, R. (2015) Environment, development and sustainability: a multidisciplinary approach to the theory and practice of sustainable development, *Environment, Development and Sustainability*, 17 (4): 787–800.

Ukaegbu, C. (2015) Leadership and African agency for development in post-fifty Africa, *Journal of Retracing Africa*, 2 (1): 1–28.

UNCTAD (2014) *Economic Development in Africa Report 2014: Catalysing Investment for Transformative Growth in Africa*. New York and Geneva: United Nations. Available at unctad.org/en/PublicationsLibrary/aldcafrica2014_en.pdf (accessed 28 February 2016).

United Nations (no date) Sustainable Development Goals: 17 Goals to Transform our World. Available at www.un.org/sustainabledevelopment/peace-justice/ (accessed 26 March 2016).

———. (2015) *Millennium Development Goals Report 2015*. New York: United Nations.

United Nations Development Programme (UNDP) (2002) *Human Development Report 2002: Deepening Democracy in a Fragmented World*. New York: Oxford University Press.

———. (2003) *Human Development Report 2003 Millennium Development Goals: A Compact Among Nations to End Human Poverty*. New York: Oxford University Press for UNDP.

United Nations Economic Commission for Africa (UNECA) (2016) *Measuring Corruption in Africa: The International Dimension Matters – African Governance Report IV*. Addis Ababa: UNECA.

United Nations Economic Commission for Africa (UNECA), Africa Union (AU), African Development Bank Group (AfDB) and United Nations Development Programme (UNDP) (2013) Outcome Document of the Regional Consultations on the Post-2015 Development Agenda. Available at www.regionalcommissions.org/africa2015.pdf (accessed 1 March 2016).

———. (2015) *MDG Report 2015: Lessons Learned in Implementing the MDGs: Assessing Progress in Africa Toward the MDGs*. Addis Ababa: UNECA.

Vandemoortele, J. (2011) If not the millennium development goals, then what? *Third World Quarterly*, 32 (1): 9–25.

Wakiaga, J. (2016) The post-2015 development agenda: building a global convergence on policy options. In G. Kararach, H. Baseda and T. M. Shaw (eds) *Development in Africa: Reframing the Lens after the MDGs*. Bristol: Policy, pp. 25–46.

Wall, T. (2014) Sustainable Development Goals: New Targets Hold Promise for Africa. Available at www.un.org/africarenewal/magazine/december-2014/sustainable-development-goals-new-targets-hold-promise-africa (accessed 23 February 2016).

World Bank (2002) *A Sourcebook for Poverty Reduction Strategies. Vol. 1: Core Techniques and Cross-Cutting Issues*. Washington, DC: World Bank.

Zajontz, T. and Leysens, A. (2015) Civil society in Southern Africa – transformers from below? *Journal of Southern African Studies*, 41 (4): 887–904.

3 Conflict and sustainable development goals in Africa

Damilohun D. Ayoyo and Temitope B. Oriola

Introduction

Despite significant progress made on many of the Millennium Development Goals (MDGs) worldwide, there are serious gaps in many developing societies (UN 2015), particularly Africa. These gaps led to reappraisal of the MDGs and the subsequent birth of the Sustainable Development Goals (SDGs) in 2015. The SDGs consist of 17 goals built from the lessons of the MDGs and emerging global issues. One key lesson from the end-report of the MDGs is that conflict and insecurity prevented many nation states and regions from attaining the MDGs at end of 2015. For instance, at the end of 2014, conflicts forced almost 60 million people to abandon their homes, the highest level recorded since the Second World War (UN 2015). The report states that conflicts forced an average of 42,000 persons globally to seek refugee outside their homes every day (*ibid.*).

Conflict remains the biggest threat to sustainable development (Bissio 2016: 21–23; UN 2015). This suggests conflict and development are inversely related (Ismail 2015; Mentan 2014; Samad 2016: 116–17; UN 2015; Zuber 2016: 115, 118–21). For instance, Mentan (2014) argues that conflict-ridden spaces generally have economic, political, environmental, health, cultural, personal and food insecurity. Conflict often increases poverty rates and the proportion of out-of-school children (UN 2015). By the end of the MDGs era in 2015, conflict-prone regions in Africa and the Middle East performed relatively poorly in the human development index when compared to other regions with relative stability. Many areas in Africa that recorded low performance in ending extreme poverty appeared engrossed in conflicts before and after the MDGs were put forward in 2000. African countries with relative stability seemed to make more progress towards the MDGs than those that were politically unstable at the end of 2015.

Since year 2000, no part of Africa has been spared conflicts (ethnic, religious, civil and terroristic). It is well documented in the development, conflict and security literature that conflicts contribute to hunger, famine, poverty, maternal and child mortality, human rights abuses, sexual and gender-based violence against women and children, high number of out-of-school children, diseases, environmental degradation, business disruption and unemployment, crime and humanitarian crisis (Bugnacki 2015; Mentan 2014; United Nations High Commission for Refugees (UNHCR) 2016a, 2016b). In its 2015 final report, the UN transitional committee on MDGs notes the interrelatedness of the MDGs and therefore recommended an integrated approach in meeting the SDGs. This is an indication that conflicts and insecurity can prevent Africa from attaining SDGs by 2030 (UN 2015).

Given the continuing security concerns across many parts of Africa, it appears the continent is yet to learn any lessons from the end-report of the MDGs, which suggests the continent is still lagging in poverty eradication. Thus, it is important to take urgent and serious steps to address the current conflict and insecurity situation on the continent in order to achieve the SDGs. Meeting the MDGs and SDGs is significant for Africa's development (Nayyar 2012; Sachs 2012) and, as a result, it is imperative to put the relationship between development and conflict, and by extension, (in)security in proper perspective, especially as it relates to the success and failure of MDGs and SDGs in Africa.

This chapter interrogates the connection between MDGs/SDGs, conflict and insecurity in Africa, and argues that the poor performance of many African states during the MDGs era is strongly linked to conflict and insecurity situations on the continent. Particular attention is given to the multiple conflicts in Nigeria. The choice of Nigeria is by no means whimsical: (1) Nigeria is the largest country in Africa; (2) it is Africa's economic powerhouse; (3) it has historically played a major role in crisis intervention in Africa through the Economic Community of West African States Monitoring Group (ECOMOG), the African Union (AU) and the UN; and (4) it is the country that the authors have extensively researched. The chapter also surveys the conflict and insecurity situation in East African countries such as Kenya, Somalia, South Sudan and Sudan, as well as in North Africa. The chapter concludes that resolving the conflicts and security challenges on the African continent is pivotal to achieving the SDGs by 2030.

Conflict, insecurity and SDGs in Africa: lessons from the MDGs years and beyond

According to Mentan (2014), there is a fundamental connection between human security on the one hand and political, economic, environment, food, health, personal and community security on the other. This suggests that the ability of any human being to successfully engage in productive activities is primarily hinged on whether she or he is safe to do so. The widespread unrests, civil wars and insurgencies in Africa made human lives unsafe and undermine efforts towards attaining the MDGs (Bugnacki 2015; Frontier Economics 2015). In 2016, a report by UNHCR states that over 18 million people in sub-Saharan Africa (26 per cent of the world refugee population) are facing refugee-like conditions largely due to major conflicts on the continent (UNHCR, 2016a). The report indicates that conflicts often deny displaced people access to services such as education, health care, safe environments, and create risks of sexual and gender-based violence (*ibid.*).

With the Boko Haram, Niger Delta and Mali insurgencies in West Africa; Arab Spring and Islamic insurgency in North Africa; Sudan, South Sudan and Somalia conflicts in East Africa; and ethnic and sectarian conflicts in Central Africa, Africa occupies the epicentre of global insecurity and humanitarian crises. The question is not whether these conflicts had/have impacts on the continent's capacity to meet the MDGs and SDGs, but rather how much do the conflicts impede the achievement of these developmental goals. The Center for Strategic and International Studies (2016) observes that Islamist terrorism has attracted the most attention among African conflicts and found expression in the actions of Boko Haram in West and Central Africa, Islamic State of Iraq and the Levant (ISIL) and Al Qaeda in the Maghreb, and Al-Shabaab in the eastern Horn of Africa. Some of the major conflicts in Africa and their impact on the continent's capacity to achieve the MDGs and by extension SDGs are analysed below.

a) Nigeria

Nigeria has witnessed a series of risks and vulnerabilities which have collectively reduced the country's capacity to implement MDGs (Office of the Senior Special Assistant to the President on MDGs End-Report 2015: 2). These risks and vulnerabilities include the Boko Haram and Niger Delta insurgencies, repression of Shi'ites by state forces, the Fulani herdsmen–farmer crisis and Biafra agitation. These conflicts have had debilitating impacts on Nigeria and neighbouring countries.

According to the 2015 Nigeria end-report on MDGs, even though the country made progress in reducing under-five mortality, maternal deaths, the spread of HIV/AIDS, hunger, gender disparity in education, out-of-school children enrolment and lack of access to cell phones and internet, many of the MDGs successes have been upturned by conflicts and insecurity. Consequently, Nigeria still faces huge challenges in tackling poverty, hunger, malnutrition, maternal health, sanitation, water shortages and environmental sustainability. The report further states that Nigeria only met one of the eight goals at the end of 2015 – development of a global partnership. The assertion that Nigeria met one of the MDGs is debatable considering the high level of insecurity in the country since year 2000. Insecurity undermines international partnership. Therefore, the more stability a country experiences, the greater the level of global (economic) relationship (Bugnacki 2015). Some of Nigeria's main conflicts and their impacts are analysed below.

Boko Haram insurgency

The Boko Haram insurgency has grown from a localized Nigerian crisis in the early 2000s to a regional security threat with dire consequences for attainment of any developmental goals. Boko Haram, which means western education is forbidden, is an Islamic terror group, committed to the establishment of an Islamic Caliphate in northern Nigeria. The violence perpetrated by the organization became exacerbated following the assassination of its leader, Mohammed Yusuf, by state police in July 2009 (Oriola 2017). The organization has committed war crimes and crimes against humanity in north-eastern Nigeria (Amnesty International 2014), including killing of over 20,000 civilians and triggering one of the worst humanitarian crises in recent African history. Boko Haram's activities spread from one state (Borno) in 2009 to 17 states in 2014 (Oriola 2017). By January 2015, the group had captured swaths of territory including Baga and Monguno in Borno State. Boko Haram has killed hundreds of civilians and destroyed more than 3,700 buildings during the attack on Baga (Amnesty International 2015a, 2016a; Bugnacki 2015). This attack is considered the organization's deadliest to date (Amnesty International 2016a).

Thousands of civilians, mostly women and children, were abducted and forced to live under Boko Haram's Sharia rule in camps and captured towns between 2009 and 2015 (Amnesty International 2016a). Women and girls continue to be disproportionately victimized by Boko Haram in gender-based violence, and they risk contracting sexually transmitted infections such as HIV/AIDS. Many of the girls and women were constantly raped, forced into marriage and/or killed. Boko Haram's attacks on markets, schools, transportation hubs, bars, restaurants and places of worship in cities across north-east Nigeria have undermined human safety and business activities (Amnesty International 2016a). In addition, Boko Haram has been using young women and girls as suicide bombers. In April 2014, over 200 girls were abducted by Boko Haram from the government secondary school Chibok, Borno State. This act attracted global condemnation. Although 105 of the 219 Chibok schoolgirls believed to be under Boko Haram captivity have been released or managed to escape (Vanguard 2017), the fate of the remaining girls is unknown. Boko Haram admitted that some of these girls have been killed during counter-insurgent operations by the Nigerian armed forces. This was confirmed by some of the girls who escaped or were released in 2016.

The Nigerian military has been accused of human rights abuses, including arbitrary arrests and extrajudicial killing of civilians in the war against Boko Haram (Amnesty International 2014). Arrests were made in many cases without investigation or due process (Amnesty International 2016a). By September 2015, more than two million people were internally displaced in northern Nigeria. Most of them have been living in host communities and the remainder in camps (The International Organization for Migration cited in Amnesty International 2016a). By August 2016, the UNHCR corroborated this report arguing that the majority of more than two million internationally displaced persons (IDPs) are women and children (UNHCR 2016b). There are reports from international humanitarian organizations that the IDP camps are overcrowded, with inadequate access to food and sanitation as well as reported cases of human trafficking and sexual violence against women. Women and young girls are coerced to offer sex in exchange for food and accommodation in the IDP camps (Amnesty International 2016a).

A report published in December 2016 by *Vanguard*, a Nigerian newspaper, indicates that 5,000 IDPs in the north-east are infected with HIV/AIDS. Most of the victims are women who were rescued from Boko Haram. About 512 new cases of HIV/AIDS were recorded among Borno IDPs, including two children (Borno Agency for the Control of HIV/AIDS 2016 cited in *The Punch* 2016).

Oriola (2017) describes sexual and gender-based violence against women as a weapon used by Boko Haram to prosecute its war against Nigeria and neighbouring countries of Niger, Cameroon and Chad. Oriola (2017) identifies three categories of women who are deployed by Boko Haram: young girls below 14 years; women and girls 14 to 45 years; and those above 45 years. Boko Haram targets women within the reproductive ages of 14 and 45 for their reproductive capacity and sexual satisfaction of male operatives. These women and girls are considered by Boko Haram as 'spoils of war' (United States Department of State Bureau of Diplomatic Security 2015: 9) who are essential to the future plans of Boko Haram (Oriola 2017). The gendered violence against women and girls by Boko Haram has severe consequences for the sustainable development goals of promoting gender equality and maternal health, preventing the spread of diseases and reducing maternal mortality.

The World Health Organization (WHO), in a recent report on the impact of Boko Haram on the condition of human lives in Nigeria, states that 64 per cent of the 743 health facilities in Borno State, Nigeria (the main theatre of Boko Haram's activities) that existed in the pre-Boko Haram crisis era have either been partially or completely destroyed by Boko Haram insurgents. According to the report, of the 481 health facilities that were not destroyed, 31 per cent are not in good condition, almost 60 per cent have no access to safe water; 32 per cent do not have water at all while 73 per cent do not have sufficient chemicals to purify water (WHO 2016 cited in *Reuters* 2016). The report notes that the UN and partners need US$94 million (28.7 billion naira) to provide health services to six million people, more than half of whom are children (WHO 2016 cited in *Reuters* 2016).

The Food and Agriculture Organization (cited in *The Nation* 2016) reported in November 2016 that the Boko Haram insurgency in Nigeria had left more than five million returnees, IDPs and host communities in the north-eastern states of Borno, Adamawa and Yobe with acute food insecurity. FAO describes the situation as urgent, and thus requiring action to restore food security and combat severe hunger and malnutrition especially among women and children. A report by the National Emergency Management Agency (NEMA) (cited in Ajayi 2016) in November 2016 indicates that the Boko Haram insurgency has created a refugee population of 239,834 Nigerians. According to NEMA, there were 20,804 displaced Nigerians living in the Republic of Chad; 80,709 in Cameroon and 138,321 in Niger Republic. The Boko Haram insurgency has contributed to human displacement, food insecurity and consequently, undermines the potential to achieve SDGs of poverty eradication, and healthy living and well-being.

One of the goals of both the MDGs and SDGs is universal access to quality education. However, attacks on educational institutions and the abduction of girls are part of Boko Haram's agenda to stop Western-style education in Nigeria (Oriola 2017). This is aimed to deny both sexes, particularly girls in north-east Nigeria, access to education. The Boko Haram insurgency can be viewed as a war against the MDGs and SDGs in Africa given that it has contributed to the large numbers of out-of-school children, maternal and infant mortality, hunger, famine and malnutrition, poverty, HIV/AIDS, gender-based violence, human displacement and other humanitarian problems, as well as business disruption in north-east Nigeria and parts of Niger, Chad and Cameroon. The foregoing suggests that ending the Boko Haram insurgency is pivotal to achieving SDGs in Africa.

Shi'ites and state violence

There has been a resurgence of violence between the Nigerian security agencies and members of the Islamic Movement of Nigeria (IMN), the largest Shia Muslim minority group in Nigeria. The group is led by Sheik Ibrahim Al-Zakzaky. In December 2015, the Nigerian armed forces killed hundreds of IMN supporters in Zaria, Kaduna State for allegedly blocking the convoy of the Chief of Army Staff, the country's highest army authority. The Nigerian army accused the group of attempted assassination of the country's Army Chief. The IMN has vigorously denied the accusation.

Although there have been attempts by the Nigerian government to cover up the killings, Amnesty International (2016b) in its report titled 'Unearthing the truth: Unlawful killings and mass cover-up in Zaria', published evidence of military atrocities against the group, particularly how the Nigerian military burned alive members of the group and dumped their bodies in mass graves. The report accused the Nigerian army of war crimes including the unlawful killing of more than 350 men (including three sons of Al-Zakzaky), women and children, who were supporters of IMN, with many more allegedly missing (Amnesty International 2016b).

The egregiousness of state-sponsored terror against the group in the form of continuing arrests and detention of the group members and its leader,

Al-Zakzaky, has raised concerns about the possible emergence of another Boko Haram-like insurgency in northern Nigeria. This is because the circumstances that led to the Boko Haram insurgency in 2009 are similar to the manner in which the Nigerian state is currently treating the Shi'ites group. The title of a newspaper editorial succinctly captures the situation: 'Nigeria must not transform the Shi'ites into enemies'. The Boko Haram insurgency started under similar circumstances with the killing of hundreds of Boko Haram members and its leader, Mohammed Yusuf, in 2009 by the Nigerian state. Mohammed Yusuf's successor, Abubakar Shekau, has consistently accused the Nigerian state of killing their leader and members in cold blood.

Although the report of the Commission of inquiry to look into the causes and impact of the Army-Shi'ite clashes in 2015 admitted excessive use of military force and killing of the group's members, the report describes the group as insurgent and unlawful while its activities have since been banned by the Kaduna State government (Amnesty International 2016b; Tukur 2016). The continued repression of the group is considered by human rights groups and security experts as constituting human rights abuse and security threat (Gaffey 2016). The group may resort to violent response against the Nigerian state if state-sponsored violence continues against the group. The situation is capable of throwing the region into another humanitarian catastrophe that can undermine the implementation of SDGs in Nigeria.

Fulani herdsmen–farmer crisis

The conflict between Fulani herdsmen and farmers poses danger to the attainment of SDGs in Nigeria. The Fulani are primarily cattle herders who follow their livestock along migratory patterns (Gaffey 2016). Although this crisis has been happening for decades in Nigeria (Hagher 2013), cases were either underreported or unreported (Campbell 2016) and treated with levity by the Nigerian state. The issue, however, assumed an unprecedented public condemnation when in February 2016, ten Agatu communities in the Middle Belt region of Nigeria were razed and over 300 people including women, children and the elderly were massacred by suspected Fulani herdsmen (Gaffey 2016; Mayah *et al.* 2016). Thousands of people were also displaced. Though no part of Nigeria is spared the herder-farmer crisis (Hagher 2013), the hottest spot is the Middle Belt region of Nigeria (Campbell 2016; Gaffey 2016).

Fasona and Omojola (2005) note in a study of conflicts in Nigeria between 1991 and 2005 that herdsmen–farmer clashes accounted for 35 per cent of major crises reported by some selected Nigerian newspapers (cited in Adisa and Adekunle 2010). During these clashes, sophisticated weapons are freely used, communities destroyed, people are displaced and killed while farmlands, economic trees, houses, food barns and domestic animals are destroyed. According to the Institute for Economics and Peace Global Terrorism Index (2015), Fulani herdsmen were responsible for the deaths of 1,229 persons in 2014 in Nigeria (cited in Gaffey 2016).

The Fulani herdsmen–farmer crisis is land resource-based and driven by environmental, political and cultural stressors (Hagher 2013). Fulani herdsmen have been driven ever more southwards in Nigeria and hence increasingly compete for grazing land with farmers, due to the impact of desertification and deforestation, occasioned by drought and fewer rainfall in the Sahel and Sudan regions of Nigeria and other parts of West Africa (Adisa and Adekunle 2010; Campbell 2016; Hagher 2013; Odoh and Chigozie 2012; Taiwo 2010). In several parts of West Africa, including Nigeria, Mali, Guinea, Senegal, Ghana and Niger, Fulani herders-farmers' crises are commonplace (Tonah 2006; Hagher 2013).

The role of agriculture in the development of African economies and eradication of poverty is socially significant (Eastwood *et al.* 2006). Consequently, the herdsmen–farmers' conflict has negative socioeconomic consequences for SDGs. The conflict constitutes a major source of insecurity, low agricultural output, poverty, food shortages and high prices of staples, violence against women, displacement of farmers and herdsmen, arms proliferation, land degradation, cattle rustling and loss of human lives (Adisa and Adekunle 2010; Cotula *et al.* 2004; Fasona and Omojola 2005; Fiki and Lee 2004; Gaffey 2016; Hagher 2013). The Nigerian Security Tracker, a portal of the United States Council on Foreign Relations, reports that between January and April 2016, farmer–herdsmen conflict cost the Nigerian economy billions of naira and was responsible for 438 deaths compared to 208 deaths caused by Boko Haram (Gaffey 2016).

The Middle Belt of Nigeria is the major food production zone in the country and has the capacity to drive not only Nigeria's national food security but also that of West Africa (Campbell 2016; Hagher 2013). For instance, Benue State, in the Middle Belt, is known as the 'food basket of Nigeria' but is the site of the most serious incidents of herdsmen–farmer clashes. In most cases, these clashes are sectarian conflicts between Fulani Muslim herdsmen against non-Fulani Christian farmers (Campbell 2016). A growing number of scholarly works (Fiki and Lee 2004; Folami 2010; Ofuoku and Isife 2009; Olabode and Ajibade 2010; Van't Hooft *et al.* 2005) show a correlation between poor farmers' output and grazing challenges vis-à-vis the Fulani herdsmen–farmer crisis. In 2015, Mercy Corps reported that if the menace of the Fulani herdsmen–farmer conflict is reduced to near-zero in four problematic states in Nigeria, the country would annually gain an additional US$13.7 billion macroeconomic benefit (cited in Gaffey 2016).

The herdsmen–farmer crisis undermines the sustainable development goal of ending poverty, food shortages and hunger. Many herdsmen and farmers have lost their means of livelihood as a result of the conflict, while many farmers are scared of going to their farms for fear of being attacked by Fulani herders. Stable farming and agriculture are central to ending poverty by year 2030. However, insecurity on account of the conflict between Fulani herdsmen and farmers implies that SDGs are already being jeopardized. This also implies that the issue of climate change needs to be taken seriously since it is believed that the crisis is caused by environmental factors such as deforestation and desertification (Olagunju 2015).

The Niger Delta insurgency

The Niger Delta insurgency has undergone three waves (Egbe and Oriola, forthcoming). The first wave was led by Isaac Adaka Boro and involved a secessionist struggle aimed at excising the Niger Delta region from Nigeria. A 'Niger Delta Republic' was declared on 23 February 1966 but was quashed within 12 days by the superior firepower of the Nigerian forces. The end of the first wave of insurgency in 1966 was succeeded by non-violent advocacy in the 1980s to 1990s. The Movement for the Survival of the Ogoni People (MOSOP) led by Ken Saro-Wiwa garnered significant international attention in an attempt to put an end to the environmental degradation caused by oil extraction in Ogoni land specifically and the Niger Delta in general (Oriola 2013). This period of non-violent advocacy ended with the hanging of Ken Saro-Wiwa and eight other Ogoni leaders by Nigerian government in 1995. This heralded the second wave of insurgency in the Niger Delta. Dozens of insurgent groups were formed by youth in the Niger Delta. The Movement for the Emancipation of Niger Delta (MEND) emerged in late 2005 as the clearing house of the insurgency (Okonta 2006; Oriola 2013). Militant and pirate groups in the Niger Delta from the late 1990s to 2009 engaged in a range of insurgent activities such as kidnapping, robbery, attacks on oil infrastructure, hijacking of ships and trawlers. These activities had dire consequences on the attainment of MDGs and are poised to pose similar problems to SDGs. The Niger Delta insurgency is generally acknowledged as a fallout of agitation for resource control and development in a region with high level of poverty, social exclusion and unemployment. The amnesty programme introduced by the government of President Umaru Yar'Adua led to a period of respite between late 2009 and 2015.

The Niger Delta crisis has escalated in recent times despite intervention and control efforts such as the establishment of the Niger Delta Development Commission in 2000, the Joint Task Force in 2004, the Ministry of Niger Delta in 2008 and the Amnesty Programme in 2009. Following major changes in Nigeria's political process, including the electoral loss of President Goodluck Jonathan, an indigene of the Niger Delta, a realignment of forces led to the birth of what Egbe and Oriola (forthcoming) call 'insurgency 3.0'. This wave began in February 2016. It is led by the Niger Delta Avengers and has as its cardinal methodology - the destruction of oil infrastructure and minimization of the capacity of the Nigerian petro-state to produce oil.

Several studies (Andersen *et al.* 2009; Gibson 2009; International Maritime Bureau, 2008, 2009; Potgieter 2008; Vrey 2009) have shown that the Niger Delta insurgency undermines human safety and security, environmental sustainability and economic activities. Katsouris and Sayne (2013) have indicated that an average of 100,000 barrels of crude oil are stolen daily from oil pipelines in the Niger Delta. This undermines not only government revenue and environmental sustainability but also the capacity of the country to provide basic social infrastructure for its people, including millions of women and children of IDPs camps in north-east Nigeria who are in desperate need of food, water, schools and hospitals. The Niger Delta crisis has compounded environmental pollution (as a result of oil spills from damaged pipelines) and the current economic recession and poverty in Nigeria through dwindling oil production and declining revenue from crude oil.

Pro-Biafra agitation

Nigeria continues to be entangled in the labyrinth of the proposed 'Biafra Republic'. The earliest struggle for Biafra Republic was led by its late founder and leader Emeka Odumegwu and resulted in the Civil War between 1967 and 1970. The war led to the deaths of millions of people, mostly women and children, human displacement, widespread hunger and malnutrition, and lack of medical care (Amamkpa and Mbakwe 2015). The agitations for Biafra and state efforts to control such protests have consequences for the attainment of SDGs.

The Movement for the Actualization of Sovereign State of Biafra (MASSOB) led by Ralph Uwazuruike has intensified its efforts in the last several years. The struggle, however, assumed a new dimension on President Muhammadu Buhari's assumption of office in 2015. The change in Nigeria's political leadership coincided with the emergence of the Indigenous People of Biafra (IPOB) led by Kanu Nnamdi (Amamkpa and Mbakwe 2015). These groups are part of a broader movement for the self-determination of the Igbo-speaking people of south-east Nigeria. The two groups have accused the Nigerian government of deliberate historical marginalization of the Igbo ethnic group in political positions and economic infrastructure. The groups also believe that the idea of Nigeria has outlasted its relevance to the ethnic nationalities in the country.

Although both MASSOB and IPOB are largely non-violent groups, disproportionate state violence is often directed at the group members. Amnesty International reports that the Nigerian security forces killed an estimated 150 members and supporters of IPOB; hundreds have also been arrested and injured in the course of demonstrations and meetings that were non-violent between August 2015 and May 2016 (Amnesty International 2016c, 2016d). IPOB, however, believe the actual figure of members killed by the Nigerian security agencies within the period is higher than the Amnesty International estimates (Nwaiwu 2016). There are also reports of torture, extrajudicial killings, use of excessive force by security agencies, and arbitrary arrests and detentions including the arrest of wounded victims in hospitals (Nwaiwu 2016). Since the IPOB leader and Radio Biafra director Nnamdi Kanu was arrested on 14 October 2015, demonstrations calling for his release by supporters and human rights violations by the military have increased (Amnesty International 2016c).

The IPOB movement has received increasing popularity in Igbo-speaking areas in Nigeria despite state-sponsored violence against the group. While the Nigerian federal government is averse to MASSOB and IPOB's demand for Biafra Republic, it has a weak conflict management system to douse the tension created by the Biafra question. Austin (2004) notes that when the level of tension rises in a conflict, it is an early sign of a growing conflict. If nothing is done to resolve the situation, the rising tension on the demand for Biafra in eastern Nigeria is an early warning sign of a larger conflict to come (Amamkpa and Mbakwe 2015). State-sponsored violence against Biafra agitation in Nigeria is capable of undermining business and food security, and engenders poverty and hunger. Another civil unrest in eastern Nigeria can prevent government and development partners from implementing policies aimed at achieving SDGs.

b) Somalia

The Somali conflict, which started during the 1990s, has become one of the worst humanitarian crises on the continent. Though the Somali conflict started between rival warlords and clan-based militia groups, since 2006 it has taken new dimensions between the internationally backed Somali government and an Al Qaeda-linked group, Al-Shabaab (BBC 2011; Bugnacki 2015). According to Global Development (2012), the Somali conflict has led to a major humanitarian crisis with tens of thousands of people (mostly women and children) suffering from hunger, starvation, famine and death. There were one million Somali refugees in the Horn of Africa and around 1.3 million displaced people within Somalia, out of an estimated population of 7.5 million as of 2012 (Global Development 2012). The conflict has produced a battered economy, people, social institutions and environment (Social Watch Report 2014), and made it a difficult place for aid agencies to carry out their work (Global Development 2012; UNICEF 2007).

In 2007 it was reported that children in southern Somalia were being recruited and/or abducted by militia groups (UNICEF 2007). They were also experiencing displacement from their villages and other effects of violence and instability. UNICEF further notes that the Somali conflict increased the rate of out-of-school children and led to the suspension of its critical activities and programs in the country (UNICEF 2007). The conflict in Somalia has contributed to deteriorating social conditions for children and women, leading to one of the worst cases of under-five mortality (146 per 1,000 live births), early child school enrolment, maternal health, HIV/AIDS treatment, sanitation, water, hunger and poverty in Africa (UNICEF Data 2013).

At the regional level, the Somali conflict has contributed largely to the refugee crisis in countries such as Djibouti, Uganda, Kenya, Ethiopia, Egypt, Tanzania, Eritrea and even Yemen with a combined registered refugee population of 904,096 (UNHCR 2016c). Today, Somalia remains poor in relation to most African countries and health facilities remain rudimentary in most parts of the country. The impact of piracy has further isolated the country from global partnership and no country or corporation would want to do business in a chaotic environment.

c) Kenya

Kenya continues to be a prime victim of the spillover effect of regional conflicts, particularly in East Africa (Human Rights Watch 2002). Apart from the post-election crisis in 2007 which left over 1,000 people killed and 600,000 people displaced including women, children and infants (Aljazeera 2008; BBC 2008; Yedioth 2008;), major conflicts and insecurity situations in Kenya since 2000 are externally induced, particularly from Sudan, South Sudan and Somalia. The country has been dragged into the Somali conflict with occasional clashes with the Islamic group, al-Shabaab. In 2013, Al-Shabaab carried out a terrorist attack on the Westgate Mall in Nairobi, killing at least 67 people. As one of the countries affected by regional conflicts, Kenya is host to one of the world's largest refugee camps, Dadaab, with a population of 471,000 (Global Development 2012). These refugees were displaced in the Sudan and South Sudan conflicts and have lost almost their entire means of livelihood in their home country.

d) Sudan and South Sudan

Sudan and South Sudan remain the deadliest flash point of violence and humanitarian crisis in Africa since the turn of the twenty-first century. The ethnic and sectarian violence in the old Sudan lasted for many years before South Sudan gained independence from Khartoum through a historic referendum in 2011. Earlier in 2003, the Sudan Liberation Movement/Army and Justice and Equality Movement took up arms against the Arab-led Sudanese government of Oman Bashir, accusing it of historic marginalization of non-Arab population (Insight on Conflict 2015). In 2004, the conflict led to genocide against the non-Arab Darfur people in which thousands of people including women and children were killed and raped. By 2015, more than three million civilians were reported to have been internally displaced and more than half a million lived in refugee camps due to the Sudan conflict (Insight on Conflict 2015). The UN also estimated that about seven million people are in need of civilian assistance in Sudan, with far-reaching consequences for the MDGs and SDGs (Insight on Conflict 2015).

Ottaway and El-Sadany (2012) note that the splitting of Sudan into the Republics of Sudan and South Sudan in 2011 did not end the Sudan crisis but rather marked the beginning of new, multiple conflicts. After independence from Sudan in 2011, civil war broke out between South Sudanese rival groups in 2013. The South Sudan conflict has produced sexual violence, killings and regional humanitarian crises (Astill-Brown 2014; Bugnacki 2015). The conflict which broke out between government forces loyal to President Salva Kiir and former Vice-President Riek Machar has caused the death of thousands of people, food shortages and famine, recruitment of child soldiers, destruction of livelihoods, environmental pollution, sexual violence against women and girls, refugee crisis and a drop in school enrolment of children (Frontier Economics 2015). There were also reports by aid agencies that as many as four million people face serious food shortages while attacks on hospitals, churches, mosques and United Nations bases continue (Frontier Economics 2015).

The conflict situations in both Sudan and South Sudan continue to cause regional humanitarian crisis in Uganda, Kenya, Sudan and Ethiopia. The cost of Sudan and South Sudan to the international community, especially UN aid agencies, is huge. For instance, in early 2014 the United Nations declared South Sudan a level-3 emergency country – the highest emergency classification with the estimated humanitarian needs valued at US$1.4 billion and standing at US$1.8 billion in 2015 (Frontier Economics 2015). In a situation report released in May 2015 on the South Sudan crisis, Amnesty International (2015b) notes with grave concern that

> the spike in fighting between the parties to the conflict is a clear indication that South Sudan's leaders have little interest in a cessation of hostilities, while the region and the rest of the international community are reluctant to take bold steps towards addressing repeated atrocities..
>
> (Amnesty International 2015b)

e) North Africa

The 2011 Arab Spring is central to the insecurity situation in northern Africa, particularly in Tunisia, Egypt and Libya. The year 2011 was marked by a wave of massive demonstrations in several countries in North Africa (Bugnacki 2015). The Arab Spring impacted negatively on the humanitarian situation in the region. The activities of public institutions responsible for the implementation of MDGs were disrupted. During the Arab Spring, the governments in the region were busy with the business of maintaining law and order rather than funding projects related to MDGs. Enrolment of children in schools declined, many schools were shut down and parents were more concerned with the safety of their children.

The Libyan crisis is of particular interest. After the civil war and killing of Muammar Gaddafi by NATO-backed rebel groups in October 2011, the country degenerated into another civil war in 2013 (Bugnacki 2015) with the emergence and growth of Al Qaeda and ISIL linked groups. The Libyan crisis continues to have humanitarian ramifications in the region. Many people have been displaced and killed. The number of out-of-school children increased, businesses and investment especially in the oil industry (the mainstay of Libya economy) were disrupted in places where violence occurred. Many countries and international organizations have already moved out of Libya thereby undermining global partnership and worsening the economic conditions of the people.

f) Elsewhere on the continent

Regional Islamic terrorism remains a significant threat to West African stability (United States Department of State Bureau of Diplomatic Security 2015). The Boko Haram insurgency has spillover effect in Cameroon, Chad and Niger, causing humanitarian crises in the three countries with large numbers of displaced persons and refugees from Nigeria (Bugnacki 2015). Although a Multinational Joint Task Force has been formed, the Boko Haram insurgency continues to unsettle the region with dire consequences for public expenditure and safety particularly for women and children.

In Central African Republic, the sectarian crises between Seleka, Anti-Balaka, and government-backed groups (Bugnacki 2015) continue to ravage the country. The post-election violence in Côte d'Ivoire between supporters of Laurent Gbagbo and Alassane Ouattara in 2011 left thousands of people dead with severe humanitarian crisis. Laurent Gbagbo is currently facing war crimes against humanity at the International Criminal Court in Hague. In 2012, the Mali crisis started between government forces and Tuareg rebel groups in the north of the country. By late 2012, the Tuareg rebels had gained control of major cities in the Azawad region until the French and African Union forces intervened to check their offensive. Today, the Mali crisis continues to unsettle Africa and constitutes part of the larger threat of Islamic insurgency in the Maghreb, and West and Central Africa.

In 2015, xenophobic attacks against foreign nationals in South Africa left many people dead and injured while businesses were disrupted. The attacks raised concerns about the safety of lives and businesses of foreign nationals living in South Africa. Ethnic and sectarian violence continue to undermine development and human security in Burundi and Democratic Republic of Congo (DRC). The impacts of these conflicts and concomitant humanitarian crises on African development particularly with regard to the attainment of MDGs, and by extension SDGs, are undeniably huge. The social condition of refugees and IDPs across Africa is dehumanizing. These conflicts need to be addressed if Africa is to end poverty by year 2030.

Conclusion and moving forward: lessons for SDGs

The 2015 MDGs end-report views the implementation of MDGs as unfinished business that needs to be rolled over to the SDGs framework. As Africa navigates the SDGs era, the continent continues to experience major conflicts and situations of insecurity. The continent still has many ongoing ethnic conflicts and activities of violent non-state actors, particularly religiously inspired terrorist groups. These are capable of undermining the attainment of the SDGs. These conflicts are spread across Africa: The Boko Haram, Fulani herdsmen–farmer conflict, Niger Delta and Mali insurgencies in West and Central Africa, the ongoing Libyan civil war and growth of Islamic jihad in the Maghreb region, and Sudan, South Sudan and the activities of al-Shabaab in East Africa.

Beyond 2015, the Boko Haram and Niger Delta insurgencies, state violence against Shi'ites' religious group, Fulani herdsmen and farmers' clashes and Biafra/IPOB-Nigerian state imbroglio remain serious regional concerns in Africa. Even though Boko Haram's activities have been degraded with the takeover of Sambisa Forest (their de facto headquarters) by the Nigerian military, the group still constitutes a major threat in West and Central Africa with continued suicide attacks on soft targets such as markets, schools, mosques, churches and public parks especially in north-eastern Nigeria. Many women and children are still under Boko Haram's captivity. About 113 of the abducted Chibok girls remain in the organization's custody: several were reported to have been killed, forced into marriage and/or under constant sexual violence. Many schools, businesses and hospitals in places (in)directly affected by the insurgency in north-east Nigeria and parts of Chad, Niger and Cameroon largely remain closed and under constant threat of attacks. Millions of children are out of school. Hunger and food shortages remain severe because farmers cannot go to their farms for fear of being attacked by insurgents. Women and girls continue to be sexually abused by Boko Haram and IDP camp officials (Human Rights Watch 2016). Investors are scared of setting up businesses in north-east Nigeria and other affected parts of Niger, Chad and Cameroon. Thousands of men, women and children affected by the Boko Haram insurgency are still scattered in different IDP camps in Nigeria, and refugee camps in Niger, Chad and Cameroon. The situation remains dire and requires urgent assistance for returnees, IDPs and host communities in the region.

In addition, the conflict between the Shi'ites and the Nigerian state has the capacity to produce another Islamic insurgency in northern Nigeria; the Fulani herdsmen–farmer clashes, particularly in the Middle Belt of Nigeria continue to undermine food security in Nigeria and other parts of West Africa; the Niger Delta insurgency has worsened the current economic recession in Nigeria and remains a source of concern for the Nigerian government and people. The renewed pro-Biafra movement led by IPOB with continued state-sponsored violence against, and arrests and detention of MASSOB and IPOB members has made eastern Nigeria volatile. The conditions on the ground in Nigeria are not conducive for implementation of SDGs.

The Somali conflict between al-Shabaab and the internationally backed Somali government lingers with regional spillover in Kenya, Eritrea, Tanzania, Djibouti, Uganda, Egypt, Ethiopia and Yemen (in the Middle East). The Maghreb region of Africa remains volatile with the continuation of the Mali and Libyan insurgencies. The Sudan conflict between rebels and the Sudanese government remains unresolved particularly in Blue Nile, Darfur, Abyei and South Kordofan regions with thousands of people still displaced and in need of humanitarian assistance. The South Sudan conflict between government and rival groups has degenerated into full-blown civil war with increasing humanitarian catastrophe and lack of concern for human lives on both sides. Countries such as Democratic Republic of Congo (DRC), Central African Republic (CAR), and Burundi continue to experience major sectarian violence.

Islamic terrorism, sectarian violence and their accompanying humanitarian consequences remain the greatest threat against the attainment of developmental goals in many parts of Africa. The continued failure of African leaders to find workable solutions to various conflicts across the continent undermines the capacity to attain SDGs. Insecurity and conflict situations across the continent exacerbate poverty, hunger and famine, number of out-of-school children, maternal death, infant mortality, gender inequality, environmental degradation (resulting from the use of explosives such as improvised explosive devices and ammunitions), the spread of HIV/AIDS and other diseases. Such situations deny Africa and Africans the benefits of development and global partnerships as war zones are rarely conducive to legitimate businesses. In the words of Zuber (2016: 115): 'There can be no sustainable development without peace and no peace without sustainable development.' These are huge challenges for the attainment of the SDGs in Africa by 2030.

Meeting the SDGs in Africa hinges on the resolution of existing conflicts, preventing new ones and guaranteeing the security of people, communities and businesses. Allowing the current conflict situation across the continent to persist into the future would mean Africa is abandoning the SDGs from the start. Finally, the signals emanating from each state in Africa are fundamental to the attainment of SDGs, how it polices protests, resolves conflicts, its capacity to provide basic social services, and eschew official corruption, among others.

References

Adisa, R. S. and Adekunle, O. A. (2010) Farmer-herdsmen conflicts: a factor analysis of socio-economic conflict variables among arable crop farmers in north central Nigeria, *Journal of Human Ecology*, 30 (1): 1–9.

Ajayi, O. (2016) Boko Haram: Nigerian refugees rise to 240,000, Vanguard, 29 November. Available at www.vanguardngr.com/2016/11/boko-haram-nigerian-refugees-rise-240-000/ (accessed 10 April 2017).

Aljazeera (2008) Kenya Ethnic Clashes Intensify, 29 January. Available at www.aljazeera.com/news/africa/2008/01/200852514155386432.html (accessed 3 January 2017).

Amamkpa, A. W. and Mbakwe, P. U. (2015) Conflict early warning signs and Nigerian Government response dilemma: the case of increasing agitations for statehood by indigenous people of Biafra and Movement for the Actualization of Sovereign State of Biafra (MASOB), *African Journal of History and Archaeology*, 1 (8): 26–36.

Amnesty International (2014) *Nigeria: More Than 1,500 Killed in Armed Conflict in North-Eastern Nigeria in Early 2014.* London: Amnesty International.

———. (2015a) 'Our Job is to Shoot, Slaughter and Kill': Boko Haram's Reign of Terror in North-East Nigeria. London: Amnesty International.

———. (2015b) South Sudan: Escalation of Violence Points to Failed Regional and International Action. Available at paanluelwel2011.wordpress.com/2015/05/22/south-sudan-escalation-of-violence-points-to-failed-regional-and-international-action/?iframe=true&preview=true (accessed 27 December 2016).

———. (2016a) *Nigeria 2015/2016.* London: Amnesty International.

———. (2016b) *Nigeria– 'Unearthing the Truth': Unlawful Killings and Mass Cover-up in Zaria.* London: Amnesty International.

———. (2016c) *Nigeria: 'Bullets Were Raining Everywhere': Deadly Repression of Pro-Biafra Activists.* London: Amnesty International.

———. (2016d) *Nigeria: Killing of Unarmed Pro-Biafra Supporters by Military must be Urgently Investigated.* London: Amnesty International.

Andersen, E., Brockman-Hawe, B. and Goff, P. (2009) *Suppressing Maritime Piracy: Exploring the Options in International Law.* A report from the workshop convened through the efforts of One Earth Future Foundation, the Academic Council on the United Nations System, and the American Society of International Law in Washington, USA in 2009.

Astill-Brown, J. (2014) South Sudan's Slide into Conflict: Revisiting the Past and Reassessing Partnerships. The Royal Institute of International Affairs: Chatham House. Available at www.cmi.no/file/3187-20141203SouthSudanConflictAstillBrown.pdf (accessed 10 April 2017).

Austin, A. (2004) Early Warning and the Field: A Cargo Cult Science? Available at www.berghof.handbook.net (accessed 28 December 2016).

BBC (2008) Key Points: Kenya Power-sharing Deal. (28 February). Available at news.bbc.co.uk/2/hi/africa/7269476.stm (accessed 3 January 2017).

———. (2011) Somalia: Counting the Cost of Anarchy, 26 January. Available at www.bbc.com/news/world-africa-12285365 (accessed 30 December 2016).

Bissio, R. (2016) Reports from the bottom up: 'The road is hazy and full of obstacles'. Report by Global Policy Forum, *Spotlight on Sustainable Development 2016: A Report by the Reflection Group on the 2030 Agenda for Sustainable Development*, Bonn, Social Watch, Global Policy Forum, Development Alternatives with Women for a New Era, Third World Network, and Arab NGO Network for Development, pp. 16–25.

Bugnacki, J. (2015) Critical issues facing africa: terrorism, war, and political violence. *American Security Project*, 17 January. Available at www.americansecurityproject.org/critical-issues-facing-africa-terrorism-war-and-political-violence/ (accessed 27 December 2016).

Campbell, J. (2016) What is new about sectarian fighting in Nigeria's middle belt? *Africa in Transition*, 5 May. Available at blogs.cfr.org/campbell/2016/05/

05/what-is-new-about-sectarian-fighting-in-nigerias-middle-belt/ (accessed 27 December 2016).

Center for Strategic and International Studies (2016) Religious Extremism in Africa, CSIS (Event), 1 August. Available at www.csis.org/events/religious-extremism-africa (accessed 28 December 2016)

Cotula, L., Toulmin, C. and Hesse, C. (2004) Land Tenure and Administration in Africa: Lesson of Experience and Emerging Issues, International Institute for Environmental Development (IIED). Available at www.pubs.iies.org/pdfs/9305IIED.pdf (accessed 30December 2016).

Eastwood, R., Kirsten, J. and Lipton, M. (2006) Premature de-agricuturalization? Land inequality and rural dependency in Limpopo Province, South Africa, *Journal of Development Studies*, 42 (8): 1325–49.

Fasona, M. J. and Omojola, A. S. (2005) *Climate Change, Human Security and Communal Clashes in Nigeria*. Paper at International Workshop in Human Security and Climate change, Holmen Fjord Hotel, Oslo, 21–23 October.

Fiki, C. and Lee, B. (2004) Conflict generation, conflict management and self-organizing capabilities in drought-prone rural communities in north-eastern Nigeria: A case study, *Journal of Social Development in Africa*, 19 (2): 25–48.

Folami, O. M. (2010) Climate change and inter-ethnic conflict between Fulani herdsmen and host communities in Nigeria. Climate Technology Centre and Network. Available at www.eldis.org/go/display&type=Document&id=56108 (accessed 27 December 2016).

Frontier Economics (2015) *South Sudan: The Cost of War – An Estimation of the Economic and Financial Costs of Ongoing Conflict*. A report prepared by Frontier Economics in collaboration with the Center for Conflict Resolution (CECORE) and the Centre for Peace and Development Studies (CPDS).

Gaffey, C. (2016) Nigeria's herdsmen and farmers are locked in a deadly, forgotten conflict, *Newsweek*, 20 April.

Gibson, J. (2009) Maritime Security and International Law in Africa, Institute of Security Studies, *African Security Review*, 18 (3): 60–70.

Global Development (2012) Somalia famine a year on: effects of al-Shabaab conflict and hunger persist, *The Guardian*, 20 July. Available at www.theguardian.com/globaldevelopment/2012/jul/20/al-shabaab hunger-displacement-somalis (accessed 27 December 2016).

Hagher, I. (2013) The Fulani-Tiv at War in Nigeria, as President Jonathan Helplessly Looks On (1), *Premium Times*, 10 January. Available at www.premiumtimesng.com/opinion/114532-the-fulani-tiv-at-war-in-nigeria-as-president-jonathan-helplessly-looks-on-1-by-iyorwuese-hagher.html (accessed 27 December 2016).

Human Rights Watch (2002) Weapons Inflows and the Impact of Regional Conflict. Available at www.hrw.org/reports/2002/kenya/Kenya0502-03.htm (accessed 27 December 2016).

———. (2016) Nigeria: Officials Abusing Displaced Women, Girls Displaced by Boko Haram and Victims Twice Over, 31 October. Available at www.hrw.org/news/2016/10/31/nigeria-officials-abusing-displaced-w (accessed 6 December 2016).

Insight on Conflict (2015) Sudan: Conflict Profile, online journal *Peace Direct*. Available at www.insightonconflict.org/conflicts/sudan/conflict-profile/ (accessed 11 December 2016).

International Maritime Bureau (2008) *Piracy and Armed Robbery Against Ships*. Annual Report, 1 January – 31 March.

———. (2009) *Piracy and Armed Robbery Against Ships*. Annual Report, 1 January – 31 December.

Ismail, O. (2015) The Boko Haram Insurgency and the Changing Patterns of Regional Security Arrangements in Africa. In K. T. Hanson (ed.) *Contemporary Regional Development in Africa*. Farnham: Ashgate, pp. 201–24.

Katsouris, C. and Sayne, A. (2013) *Nigeria's Criminal Crude: International Options to Combat the Export of Stolen Oil*. The Royal Institute of International Affairs. London: Chatham House.

Mayah, E., Sani, T. and Hassan, A. (2016) Why we struck in Agatu — Fulani herdsmen, *Premium Times*, 19 March. Available at www.premiumtimesng.com/news/headlines/200426-exclusive-struck-agatu-fulani-herdsmen.html (accessed 27 December 2016).

Mentan, T. (2014) *Africa: Facing Human Security Challenges in the 21st Century*. Oxford: African Books Collective.

Nayyar, D. (2012) *The MDGs after 2015: Some Reflections on the Possibilities*. Background paper prepared for the UN System Task Team on the Post-2015 UN Development Agenda. New York: United Nations.

Nwaiwu, C. (2016). Nigeria: IPOB commends amnesty international's report on killing of Biafra agitators. *Vanguard*, 26 November.Available atallafrica.com/stories/201611250578.html (accessed 26 April 2017).

Office of the Senior Special Assistant to the President on MDGs (2015) *Millennium Development Goals End-Point Report*. Published by the Federal Government of Nigeria with support from UNDP. Available at www.ng.undp.org/content/nigeria/en/home/post-2015/mdgoverview.html (accessed 28 December 2016).

Odoh, S. I. and Chigozie, C. F. (2012) Climate change and conflict in Nigeria: a theoretical and empirical examination of the worsening incidence of conflict between Fulani herdsmen and farmers in northern Nigeria. *Arabian Journal of Business and Management Review*, (Oman Chapter), 2 (1): 110–24.

Ofuoku, A. O. and Isife, B. I. (2009) Causes, effects and resolution of farmers-nomadic cattle herders conflict in Delta State, Nigeria, *International Journal of Sociology and Anthropology*, 1 (2): 47–54.

Okonta, I. (2006) *Behind the mask: Explaining the Emergence of the MEND Militia in Nigeria's Oil-Bearing Niger Delta*. Niger Delta Economies of Violence, Working Paper No. 11, Institute of International Studies, University of California, Berkeley.

Olabode A. D. and Ajibade, L. T. (2010) Environment-induced conflict and sustainable development. A case of Fulani-farmers' conflicts in Oke-Ero LEDs, Kwara State, *Journal of sustainable Development in Africa*, 12 (5): 289–66.

Olagunju, T. E. (2015) Drought, desertification and the Nigerian environment: A review, *Journal of Ecology and the Natural Environment*, 7 (7): 196–209.

Oriola, T. B. (2013) *Criminal Resistance? The Politics of Kidnapping Oil Workers*. Farnham: Ashgate.

———. (2017) 'Unwilling cocoons': Boko Haram's war against women, *Studies in Conflict and Terrorism*, 40 (2): 99–121.

Ottaway, M. and El-Sadany, M. (2012) Sudan: From Conflict to Conflict. Carnegie Endowment for International Peace. Available at www.CarnegieEndowment.org/pubs (accessed 30 December 2016).

Potgieter, T. (2008) The Maritime Security Quandary in the Horn of Africa Region: Causes, Consequences and Responses. East African Human Security Forum. Hanns Seidel Foundation, Kenya.

Premium Times (2016) Nigeria Must not Transform the Shiites into Enemies, 21 October. Available at www.premiumtimesng.com/news/headlines/213295-editorial-nigeria-must-not-transformshiites-enemies.html (accessed 27 December 2016).

Reuters (2016) A third of health facilities in Nigeria's insurgency-hit Borno state destroyed: WHO, 14 December. Available at www.reuters.com/article/us-nigeria-security-who idUSKBN1431IM?il=0 (accessed 30 December 2016).

Sachs, J. D. (2012) From millennium development goals to sustainable development goals, *Lancet*, 379: 2206–11.

Samad, Z-A. (2016) Implementation of SDG 16 vital for the Middle East and North Africa. Report by Global Policy Forum, *Spotlight on Sustainable Development 2016: A Report by the Reflection Group on the 2030 Agenda for Sustainable Development*, Bonn: published by Social Watch, Global Policy Forum, Development Alternatives with Women for a New Era, Third World Network, and Arab NGO Network for Development, 116–17.

Social Watch Report (2014) Somalia: Progress towards the MDGs. Available at www.socialwatch.org/node/15979 (accessed 28 December 2016).

Taiwo. A. (2010) Terror in their land, *The Nation*, Sunday 7 March.

The Nation (2016) Five million in Nigeria's northeast need food – FAO, 25 November. Available at thenationonlineng.net/five-million-in-nigerias-northeast-need-food-fao/ (accessed 2 December 2016).

The Punch (2016) Borno records 512 new HIV cases in IDPs' camps. 4 December. Available at punchng.com/borno-records-512-new-hiv-cases-in-idps-camps/ (accessed 2 December 2016).

Tonah, S. (2006) Managing farmers-herders' conflicts in Ghana's Volta basin, *Ibadan Journal of Social Sciences*, 4 (1): 33–45.

Tukur, S. (2016) Kaduna Govt. labels Shiite IMN an 'insurgent group', vows to prosecute El-Zakzaky, *Premium Times*, 5 December. Available at www.premiumtimesng.com/news/headlines/217107/breaking-kaduna-government-declares-war-shiite-imn-officially-labels-group-insurgent.html (accessed 28 December 2016).

United Nations (2015) *The Millennium Development Goals Report 2015*. New York: United Nations.

UNHCR (2016a) Sub-Saharan Africa Hosts More Than 26 Per Cent of the World's Refugee Population. New York: The United Nations Refugee Agency.

———. (2016b) Nigeria Military Advances Uncover Vast Humanitarian Needs. New York: The United Nations Refugee Agency. Available at reliefweb.int/report/nigeria/nigeria-military-advances-uncover-vast-humanitarian-needs (accessed 28 December 2016).

———. (2016c.) Refugees in the Horn of Africa: Somali Displacement Crisis, *Information Sharing Portal*. Available at data.unhcr.org/horn-of-africa/regional.php (accessed 28 December 2016).

UNICEF Data (2013) Monitoring the Situation of Children and Women: Somalia. Available at data.unicef.org/country/som/ (accessed 27 December 2016).

United States Department of State Bureau of Diplomatic Security (2015) *Nigeria 2015 Crime and Safety Report*. Lagos: Overseas Security Advisory Council.

Uwaiwu, C. (2016) Nigeria: IPOB Commends Amnesty International's Report on Killing of Biafra Agitators, *Vanguard*, 26 November. Available at allafrica.com/stories/201611250578.html (accessed 28 December 2016).

Van't Hooft, K., Millar, D. and Django, S. (2005) Endogenous Livestock Development. Report from the Workshop in Cameroon, *Campus Magazine*, pp. 38–39.

Vanguard (2017) Rescued Chibok Girls: This is a pleasant 2nd anniversary gift to Nigerians – Buhari, 7 May. Available at: http://www.vanguardngr.com/2017/05/rescued-chibok-girls-pleasant-2nd anniversary-gift-nigerians-buhari/ (Accessed June 2, 2017).

Vanguard (2016) 5,000 IDPs infected with HIV/AIDS, 1 December. Available at www.vanguardngr.com/2016/12/5000-idps-infected-hivaids/ (accessed 28 December 2016).

Vrey, F. (2009) Bad order at sea: from the Gulf of Aden to the Gulf of Guinea, Institute of Security Studies, *African Security Review*, 18 (3): 17–30.

Yedioth, A. (2008) Report: Up to 1,000 killed in Kenyan crisis. Available at www.ynetnews.com/articles/0,7340,L-3491386,00.html (accessed 30 December 2016).

Zuber, R. (2016) There can be no sustainable development without peace and no peace without sustainable development. Report by Global Policy Forum, *Spotlight on Sustainable Development 2016: A Report by the Reflection Group on the 2030 Agenda for Sustainable Development*, Bonn: Social Watch, Global Policy Forum, Development Alternatives with Women for a New Era, *Third World Network, and Arab NGO Network for Development*, pp. 115, 118–21.

4 From MDGs to SDGs

The policy and institutional dynamics of African agriculture

Korbla P. Puplampu and George O. Essegbey

Introduction

The World Food Programme (WFP) update on world hunger in March 2016 flagged the worsening food situation in several African countries. From Angola, Cameroon, Ethiopia, Malawi, Nigeria to South Sudan and Zimbabwe, the food problem is a combination of conflict and drought conditions. Sub-Saharan Africa, with a population of 950 million people which is projected to reach 2.1 billion or 22 per cent of the global population by 2050, suffers from the food crisis more than any other part of the world with about 218 million undernourished people (OECD/FAO 2016). Not only is the inclusion of Ethiopia revealing, given the country's historical experience of the food crisis in the 1980s, but also the presence of supposedly successful African agricultural countries such as Malawi and Zimbabwe and oil-rich countries such as Angola and Nigeria. Equally puzzling is how to reconcile the economic growth in several African countries in the last decade, with some recording impressive growth rates, even after the 2008 global depression, with the failure of the agricultural sector to respond to broader social forces, especially increasing urbanization (Ncube *et al.* 2014; World Bank 2016).

African agriculture has been the focus of several policy and institutional initiatives in the past two decades. The African Union (AU) has spearheaded two significant agricultural initiatives. First was the launch of Agenda 2063, an ambitious continent-wide strategic plan for inclusive growth and sustainment development with plans for a thematic working group on agriculture (African Union 2013). Second, the AU declared 2014 as the 'Year of Agriculture and Food Security', a declaration that marked the ten-year anniversary of the adoption of the Comprehensive Africa Agriculture Development Program (CAADP) (African Union 2014a). When African heads of state and governments endorsed CAADP, a framework by the New Partnership for African Development (NEPAD), in the 2003 Maputo Declaration, it represented a high-profile continent-wide political and policy commitment to African agriculture (African Union 2003). The African Capacity Building Foundation (ACBF) (2012), a pan-African institution, undertook an authoritative study on the capacity as well as related policy and institutional traits of African agriculture. The continental policy initiatives were consistent with other global activities.

The World Bank (2007) study on agriculture was followed by the Group of Eight (G8) industrialized countries making specific comments on agriculture, via food security and nutrition, particularly at the L'Aquila and Camp David Summits in 2009 and 2012 respectively. There is growing awareness by several global development partners of the enormous potential of agribusiness for African development and a source of innovation and inspiration for the reinvigoration of African agriculture (Adenle *et al.* 2016; Amanor and Chichava 2016; Juma 2011; Larsen *et al.* 2009). Finally, the United Nations-sponsored Millennium Development Goal (MDG) 1 is to eradicate extreme poverty and hunger, a goal that could be attained by improving the agricultural sector. The MDG 8 indirectly impacts on agriculture by calling for global partnerships for development (UNDP 2003).

The MDGs formally ended in 2015, although the United Nations (2015) launched the Sustainable Development Goals (SDGs) as a successor plan to them. Specifically for agriculture, SDG 1 (to end poverty in all its forms everywhere) and 2 (to end hunger, achieve food security and improved nutrition, and promote sustainable agriculture), 16 (peace, justice and strong institutions) alongside 17 (strengthen the means of implementation and revitalize the global partnership for sustainable development) are significant, and extensions of the MDGs (UNDP 2015). Generally, most of the SDGs have bearings on agriculture and their achievement will remarkably contribute to the specific agriculture-related SDGs. The common theme in the initiatives within and beyond the continent has been to establish a viable system for policy initiation and an institutional framework in a sustainable manner with an eye on transforming African agriculture.

The significance of the interest in and focus on African agriculture is not so much its contribution to gross domestic product (GDP). In terms of the three main sectors of the African economy – agriculture, industry and services – the contribution of agriculture to the GDP has been falling in the last decade, particularly due to significant transformations in the sector (ACBF 2012; OECD/FAO 2016). Currently, the contribution of agriculture to GDP ranges from about 3 per cent in South Africa; to about 20 per cent in Zambia, Nigeria and Ghana; and to more than 50 per cent in Chad (OECD/FAO 2016). However, the sector, in terms of employment and poverty reduction, remains a vital part of the African political economy and thus essential in any discussions on food security (Africa Progress Panel 2014; International Food Policy Research Institute (IFPRI) 2015; Li and Wang 2016).

This chapter is about the MDGs and the SDGs, their relationship and implications for policy and institutional performance of African agriculture. We analyse the specific policy and institutional aspects of the MDGs and offer an assessment of the performance of African countries relative to MDGs 1 and 8. Such an exercise is helpful to better contextualize the extent to which the SDGs, as a follow-up programme, are able to attain desirable policy and institutional outcomes in the agricultural sector. Fundamental to the enquiry is to identify barriers and obstacles in implementing global, continental, regional or national agricultural policies as well as the institutional prerequisites and requirements for desirable outcomes in African agriculture. We contend that underpinning policy and institutional performance are problems relating to the availability and access to resources. Understandably, the success of agriculture, like any other form of economic activity, depends on how policies and institutions condition agricultural resources to support the sector.

Agricultural resources include land, labour, water supply and inputs, such as pesticides and fertilizers. Other resources include knowledge, technological innovations and diffusion, agricultural credit, infrastructural support (research, communications and market networks). The state of these tangible (physical) and intangible (human) resources are essential for any programme to transform agriculture.

The chapter is divided into three sections. The first will provide a brief overview of African agriculture, placing the key agricultural dimensions of both the MDGs and SDGs in the policy and institutional environment. The second section examines and accounts for the performance of African agricultural within the MDGs and beyond. And the final section presents remarks on policy and institutional imperatives for the future and planning priorities of African agriculture.

The state, MDGs, SDGs and African agriculture: an overview

Given the importance of the agricultural sector to Africa's political economy the role of the state in agriculture from both a historical (colonial) and a contemporary (postcolonial) perspective has been the focus of several studies (Rauch 2011; Taeb and Zakri 2008). Two significant issues have to be stressed. First, the state has concentrated on agricultural exports to raise revenue as well as to address food security and nutrition since the dawn of colonial rule (Devereux 2016). The state accumulated revenue mainly from its role in agricultural pricing policies and the marketing of export crops. It was therefore not surprising that the state and its role in agricultural pricing and marketing institutions were the focus of criticism and policy reforms during the height of the 1980s African agricultural crisis (Cooksey 2011; Tschirley 2010). While the impact of the policy reforms has been mixed, the African state continues to assume a role in agriculture, even if a minimal one.

Second, consistent with forces of neoliberal globalization, there is a changing role of the state in African agriculture, even though the changes do not align with the theoretical claims of neoliberal globalization (Jayne *et al.* 2002; Kaminski *et al.* 2011; Puplampu 2006, 2014). Consequently, the contemporary African state continues to assume some measure of presence in the policy and institutional aspects of agricultural organization.

MDG 1 sought to eradicate extreme poverty and hunger (UNDP 2003). Under MDG 1, the focus on eradicating extreme poverty and hunger translated to two specific targets and related indicators (Andrews *et al.* 2015; UNDP 2013). The two targets were aimed to reduce the proportion of people with a daily income of less than a one dollar as well as hunger by 50 per cent between 1990 and 2015. These targets translated into specific indicators such as the number of people below the one dollar daily income or poverty level and the nutritional and dietary needs of children (Khlalema *et al.* 2015). MDG 8, in terms of a global partnership for development, called for the establishment of an open, rule-based, predictable and non-discriminatory trading and financial system, and a tariff and quota free access for exports from less-developed countries. These targets gave rise to the renewed focus on development financial assistance and market access.

The ambitious goals, notwithstanding, the volume and value of major agricultural export crops (coffee, cotton, cocoa, coffee, palm oil and groundnuts) continue to experience price fluctuations due to the marketing structure, particularly the flow of price information about agricultural exports from the global to national markets (Musumba and Gupta 2013; World Bank 2015). The instability in world commodity prices coupled with the decline in the volume of agricultural exports, affected the foreign exchange reserves of many African countries. With shortfalls in foreign exchange and producers receiving less than their fair share of export prices, there are problems in sustaining production of export and domestic food crops and an increased reliance on imported food crops such as maize, rice and wheat (World Bank 2013).

While food production in Africa has improved, high food prices and volatile food prices amid rapid urbanization continue to impact the ability to secure food for a sizeable number of Africans. This highlights the effects of food insecurity and hidden hunger in the region, especially since the 2007/2008 global food crisis (Berazneva and Lee 2013; UNDP 2013; Von Grebmer *et al.* 2014). Thus, in the post-2015 development landscape, 'food security in Africa remains a daunting challenge that could substantially affect the continent's economic transformation' (UNDP 2013: 102). Food security is essential to manage risks and uncertainties engendered by headwinds such as falling commodity prices, weakening terms of trade, conflict or security concerns, and the incidence of disease epidemics (World Bank 2015, 2016). In this environment, the extent to which the agricultural dimensions of both the MDGs and SDGs can shore up the outcomes of African agricultural policy and outcomes is of critical importance.

By the time the United Nations launched the MDGs in 2003, African agricultural policy and institutions were already under the influence of neoliberal globalization (Chuhan-Pole and Angwafo 2011; Havnevik *et al.* 2007; World Bank 2007). Beginning with the agricultural crisis in Africa in the 1980s, the policy response was to remove subsidies on agricultural inputs as a strategy to reduce state expenditure and intervention as well as encourage private sector participation in the market for input supply. However, the policy outcomes on both subsidies on agricultural inputs and private sector participation in the distribution were poor (ACBF 2012; Banful 2011; Chinsinga and Poulton 2014; Cooksey 2011; Poulton and Kanyinga 2014).

In both cases, the state continues to play a role in the agricultural sector and is concerned about agricultural production. The state's interest can best be placed in the context of the politics of democracy and agricultural policies in Africa (Poulton 2014). In terms of institutions, explicitly marketing reform, the state had to 'free' the agricultural market, and the restructuring of state-owned agricultural marketing boards in Africa has given rise to different outcomes (ACBF 2012; World Bank 1994, 2013). A common feature in the outcomes for the restructuring of agricultural marketing and input supplies is the absence of full-blown privatized agricultural markets. At play is how the national or local environment, including resource endowments and institutional capacity, impinge upon agricultural policy and outcomes in Africa (Berhanu and Poulton 2014; Booth and Golooba-Mutebi 2014; Chinsinga and Poulton 2014; Poulton and Kanyinga 2014).

In effect, the success of policy and institutional initiatives calls for attention to context. This is the environment that awaits the SDGs. The initiatives from the MDGs and essential to the SDGs are as follows: the Alliance for an African Green Revolution (AGRA); the Fourth Assessment Report of the Intergovernmental Panel on Climate Change (IPCC); and the NEPAD-led Comprehensive Africa Agriculture Development Programme (CAADP) (ACBF 2012; Africa Progress Panel 2015). AGRA was premised on a multi-sector and partnership approach with the aim to deepen the agriculture value chain, critical with rapid urbanization and an emerging middle class (Reardon *et al.* 2015; Toenniessen *et al.* 2008; World Bank 2007). In the processing aspect of the value chain, the weaknesses of African agriculture are well exhibited.

The infrastructure for post-harvest processing remains fragile and food processing and value addition are major challenges for most African countries. This is regrettable since 80 per cent of the value in the global food industry is in the value-added components in the 'buyer-driven' aspects of the value chain (World Bank 2013: 56). These components include simple post-harvest practices such as sorting, cleaning and packaging as well as agro-processing in industrial parks and export zones. However, for many African countries, there are inefficient agro-industries, poor road networks to link agricultural production and processing sites as well as inadequate communication facilities; in sum, the infrastructure to support agricultural productivity (Mhlanga 2013, Torero 2015).

Furthermore, African agriculture cannot be oblivious to the issue of climate change. The IPCC report reinforces the argument of the vulnerability of African agriculture in a context of reduced growing seasons and high temperatures (Africa Progress Panel 2015). With drought as a perennial problem of African agriculture, the increasing realization of the importance of climate in agriculture is not only timely, but will offer the required impetus for worthy initiatives to better adjust to agriculture (see Kedir in this volume).

The NEPAD-inspired CAADP is pivotal in the sense that it has received large-scale continent-wide political support from the African Union via the Maputo Declaration. Two significant aspects of CAADP and the Maputo Declaration were the commitment to reenergize the food and agriculture sector, improve 'productivity to attain an average annual growth rate of 6 per cent' and the urgent call on all African countries to 'adopt sound policies for agricultural and rural development, and commit … to allocating at least 10 per cent of their national budgetary resources for their implementation within five years' (NEPAD 2003: 9). The programme represented a watershed document in the sense that it comes after the mixed outcomes of policy reforms of African agriculture since the 1980s (Anseeuw 2010; Cooksey 2011; Devèze 2011; NEPAD 2001). CAADP therefore represents a bold 'collective action both among African countries and among donor countries that has never before been experienced in the history of Africa's post-independence development' (Kolavalli *et al.* 2012: 2).

CAADP revolves around four main pillars with a requisite lead institution that spearheads the operational aspects of each pillar. The four pillars are: sustainable land and water management; improving market access through rural infrastructure and other trade-related initiatives; increasing food supply and reducing hunger; and improving agricultural research, technology dissemination and adoption systems (NEPAD 2003). Land and water management, the focus of pillar one, are two essential resources in agricultural organization and finite in nature. The importance of this pillar cannot be overemphasized with the evolving significance of natural resources in Africa's development, climate change and the green economy (ACBF 2013; Hanson *et al.* 2014).

The thematic focus of pillar two is rural infrastructure and trade-related activities for improved market access. This pillar complements and deepens the significance of the first pillar because production is never complete until goods and services get to the market. A functional infrastructure 'will be required to support the anticipated growth in agricultural production and improve the competitiveness of production, processing and trade in the crop, livestock, forestry or fishery sub-sectors' (NEPAD 2003: 13). The infrastructure requirements include roads, railway, ports and harbours as well as airports (AfDB 2010; Foster and Briceno-Garmendia 2010). Improvements in infrastructure will address supply-side agricultural constraints such as storage and regulatory concerns of sanitary and phytosanitary standards and technical barriers to trade. The AU is signalling a recognition of the importance of infrastructure and the need to address what has become known as the 'infrastructure gap or deficit in Africa' (Mafusire *et al.* 2011).

Pillar three is concerned about food supply and reducing hunger. The pillar advances the argument that African agriculture has to 'develop a diversified agricultural sector with commercial as well as smallholder farming', having the ultimate aim to 'attain a higher level of food security' (NEPAD 2003: 15). With food security as an underpinning factor, the pillar draws attention to the preparedness of emergency-related food security activities that are able to withstand natural and human-inspired calamities in addition to safety nets (feeding programmes, food for work or training initiatives) to deal with food insecurity.

The theme of the final pillar – agricultural research, knowledge dissemination and adoption – underscores the need for 'increasing investment in research and technology development; increasing the share of private sector funding of agricultural research; institutional and financial reforms aimed at making national agricultural research systems more sustainable' (NEPAD 2003: 17). This pillar is led by the Forum for Agricultural Research in Africa (FARA), an AU-created agency. Although this pillar ties together knowledge production and dissemination, the practical implications would entail a renewed attention to the role and nature of policy and institutions on agricultural education and the link between the agricultural research system and farmers, in particular, as end-users of research (Eicher 2006).

One global development partner has been the Consultative Group on International Agricultural Research (CGIAR) and its valuable support to African agricultural research in general and FARA specifically (FARA 2015). The foregoing lays bare the nature and form of African agriculture, the policy and institutional dimensions in an era of globalization of agriculture (ACBF 2012; Bruntrup 2011; Haggblade 2013; Puplampu 2014; Sasson 2012). The global imperatives at play relevant for the subsequent analysis are the policy and institutional outcomes with regard to the historical role of the state in the agricultural sector and the continued relevance of global development partners, particularly in the area of foreign aid.

African agriculture, policy and institutional performance: MDGs, SDGs and beyond

It is common to attribute the failure of development programmes in Africa, including those in agriculture, to a lack of political will. The same cannot be said of the range of initiatives following the launch of the MDGs. CAADP, for instance, received considerable and the highest form of political support for any continental agricultural development programme in recent years (Nhamo 2016). Consequently, it was reasonable to expect that the high-level political support for CAADP, following the 2003 Maputo Declaration, would lead to effective implementation and outcomes. The Declaration called for a 10 per cent budgetary allocation to agriculture within five years, that is by 2008, and only Rwanda had signed the compact document and completed the technical review in 2009 (NEPAD 2010). In any case, by July 2015, 42 out of the 54 AU member states had signed the CAADP compact, and 30 of these countries had completed the related plans (Bahiigwa *et al.* 2015).

Even though a sizeable number of African states have signed the CAADP, the agriculture share of public expenditure 'has been less than 4 per cent for Africa as a whole, thus failing to reach the CAADP target of 10 per cent' (Bahiigwa *et al.* 2015: 187). Indeed, lack of investment resources have been the bane of African agriculture. Investment in agriculture in Africa is rather low. Commercial bank lending to the pure agricultural sector is less than 10 per cent of the total lending for most SSA countries (Mhlanga 2013).

Nevertheless, the indications in recent times are pointing to an upsurge. The impact, though, has been that the 'pace of growth of agricultural expenditures decreased markedly for the continent after the Maputo target date of 2008. The continent as a whole saw an annual decrease in the rate of agricultural expenditure of -1.34 per cent from 2008 to 2013' (Bahiigwa *et al.* 2014: 72). These outcomes reflect the fact that only seven countries (Burkina Faso, Ethiopia, Guinea, Malawi, Mali, Niger and Senegal) have surpassed the CAADP 10 per cent target in several years since 2003, while 13 (including the above seven and another six: Burundi, Ghana, Madagascar, Republic of Congo, Zambia and Zimbabwe) have surpassed the target in a single year (Benin and Yi 2013: xii).

The performance of African countries in agricultural expenditure relative to the Maputo target date of 2008 has therefore varied among countries. While the achievement of the CAADP target is significant, it does not sufficiently address the rather inadequate performance of Africa's agriculture. The striking manifestation of the poor performance is the increasing food imports into African countries, which generally have all the natural resources to be net food exporters. Yet, since the mid-1970s, most African countries have to contend with food deficits (Rakotoarisoa *et al.* 2012). Several analytical themes can be gleaned for agricultural policy and institutions analysis in Africa within the MDGs, SDGs and beyond.

The first theme is the letter and spirit of policy and institutional initiatives and how internal and external social forces frame the performance of agricultural policy and institutions. In terms of the former, African governments do not hesitate to launch or announce new policy documents and establish institutions, mostly amid much fanfare. However, the mechanics and processes for successful outcomes do not receive commensurate attention. In discussing the relationship between agricultural policy performance and the democratic dispensation in several African countries within a political economy framework, Poulton (2014) and Booth and Golooba-Mutebi (2014) provide some useful insights into agricultural policy performance in Rwanda.

The Government of Rwanda, in the immediate post-genocide 1994 era, was cognizant of the simmering divide between the Tutsis and the Hutus, with the former in government and the latter as the majority group. In the choice between ethnic-based politics or policy outcomes that would have a broad-based appeal to all Rwandans, the government sought to pursue agricultural policies that would have a positive demonstrable effect on the larger society. As Poulton astutely observes, the

> logic seems to be that, if enough people benefit from growth and gain a sufficient stake in economic prosperity, then eventually elections will be fought on the basis of policy, rather than ethnicity, as voters recognize the cost of a return to ethnic conflict.
>
> (Poulton 2014: S117)

Rwanda not only embraced the CAADP, the country also enacted other agricultural policies and demonstrated a certain degree of seriousness about policy implementation; a practice not common in other African countries (Booth and Golooba-Mutebi 2014).

Furthermore, agricultural policy and institutions are confronted with organizational legitimacy, especially in terms of political leadership (Makinda 2012; Obi 2001; Taylor 2011; Tettey 2012; Wanasika *et al.* 2011). Several African leaders tend to use their signature and implied commitment to continental agreements to secure legitimacy of their leadership (Franke 2007; Taylor 2011). These practices have led to the condition in which many political leaders do not 'put in any more effort than was absolutely necessary in order to maintain influence and credibility on the African stage' (Franke 2007: 43–4) or what Söderbaum (2004) calls 'sovereignty-boosting governance'. In other words, the state uses commitment to agreements as a conduit for legitimation and pays lip service to outcomes or performance. State behaviour in this context reflects both the neopatrimonial character of the African state and the pragmatism of African leaders (Owusu 2003; Van de Walle 2001). Consequently, the capacity of agricultural institutions in African countries has varied since the commencement of institutional restructuring in the 1980s.

SDG 9 (industry, innovation and infrastructure) and SDG 16's emphasis on strong institutions find expression in the promise of renewal in African agriculture, certainly in the realm of value chain and agribusiness (Larsen *et al.* 2009; World Bank 2013). The significance of agribusiness is part of a strategy of diversification and carving a niche in the agro global markets for agricultural exports including cassava, maize, sunflowers and banana (Essegbey 2009; Kibwika *et al.* 2009; Mpagalile *et al*. 2009; Odame *et al.* 2009; World Bank 2013). Even though value chain agriculture has received well-deserved attention, the focus is not problem free. It is becoming increasingly clear that quality should be an integral part of the entire value chain, enlarging the range of beneficiaries to include smallholder farmers and a more strategic role of the state in forging innovation, particularly through public-private partnerships. The policy dilemma in operationalizing the relevant aspects of the SDGs would be how to manage these challenges with prioritization and investment of available resources.

In terms of the spirit, the question is whether the goals of policy and institutions are realistic, in view of the historical role of foreign aid in African agricultural development, an issue that is central MDG 8 and SDG 17: the call for partnership for development. Thus, the second major analytical theme is the place of foreign aid in Africa's agricultural development programme. Several African countries adopted a lukewarm attitude towards CAADP, the continental initiative, until the emergence of the Global Agriculture and Food Security Program (GAFSP) in 2010 following the 2009 G8 L'Aquila Summit. GAFSP was to support national and regional agriculture and food security investment plans that have been developed or aligned with CAADP (table 4.1).

Table 4.1 GASFP awards to selected African countries

Country	*(US$ million)*
Burundi	30.0
Ethiopia	51.5
Liberia	46.5
Malawi	39.6
Niger	33.0
Rwanda	11.5
Senegal	40.0
Sierra Leone	50.0
Tanzania	22.9
The Gambia	28.0
Togo	19.0

Source: Adapted from GAFSP (2015: 40–65)

The role of foreign aid in the development process has worrisome implications for African agriculture, in light of the emerging discussions on aid coherence, coordination and effectiveness (Asongu and Nwachukwu 2016; Birdsall and Khraras 2010; Brown 2012; Brown *et al.* 2014; OECD 2008). There are extremist views where aid is completely abhorred; for example the views of Moyo (2009) who argues that aid fosters corruption, impedes growth and leads to a vicious cycle. However, even without going to extremes, an important concern is that non-aid policies in trade and investment have consequences for development outcomes (Ashoff 2005; OECD 2009).

The European Union and governments in many developed countries in the global north continue to provide subsidies to their farmers, undermining the competitiveness of African cotton farmers; for example, against their counterparts in the global north (Anderson and Masters 2009; Delpeuch and Leblois 2013; Jobodwana 2011; Moseley and Gray 2008). Subsidies for farmers in the global north have led to situations where their governments, through foreign aid, seek to improve the competitiveness of farmers in the global South in global commodity markets. Foreign aid demonstrates that 'incoherence exists between developed countries' goals of support farmers at home and in the developing world' (Bülles and Kindornay 2013: 8).

To be sure, the global aid community has acknowledged the multiple forms of incoherence (intended and unintended, structural or institutional or political) (Barry *et al.* 2010). Addressing these problems and renewed commitments to aid effectiveness are central in the 2005 Paris Declaration on Aid Effectiveness, the 2008 Accra Agenda for Action and the 2011 Busan Partnership for Effective Development Cooperation (Cabral 2008; Faust and Messier 2007; Rogerson 2011). Notwithstanding the changes in the architecture of aid from Paris, Accra to Busan, incoherence of aid remains, especially since the 2008 financial crises in advanced capitalist economies and the associated calls by their domestic audience for greater accountability of foreign aid.

Thus, on one hand, the above analysis demonstrates the tensions and inherent contradictions of SDG 17, specifically how to balance competing domestic (the donor) and foreign (recipient) interests when it comes to foreign aid. On the other hand, global partnership can also improve the competitiveness of farmers in the global south and might serve the interests of consumers in the global North. For example, in cases where African farmers have produced agricultural commodities that meet the European Good Agricultural Practices (EUROGAP), consumers have better confidence in what they consume and that would serve as an incentive to boost production and address SDGs 1 and 2.

The foregoing does not suggest that the presence or absence of foreign aid per se is the major feature for desirable policy and institutional outcomes. Rather, the performance of aid has to factor in the primacy of the domestic policy and political environment, as illustrated by the cases of Kenya and Malawi (Chinsinga and Poulton 2014; Poulton and Kanyinga 2014). The donor community, as Poulton and Kanyinga (2014) contend, backed Kenya's 2004 Strategy for Revitalizing Agriculture, yet not much was achieved against the backdrop of competitive politics and other contextual constraints. In the case of Malawi, the donor community was ambivalent to the Farm Input Subsidy Programme, but the government was keen, in view of domestic politics, to pursue the programme in President Mutharika's first term in office between 2005 and 2009 (Chinsinga and Poulton 2014). Thus the issue is the need for institutional mechanisms 'that at least partially insulate policymaking from short-term political pressures, so as to place more emphasis on the public-goods investments necessary to stimulate broad-based agricultural growth in Africa' (Poulton 2014: S119). One indispensable public-goods investment is the agricultural research system.

The third focus of analysis is agricultural research; precisely the role of knowledge creation and dissemination in the African development process. This layer brings into sharp focus the significance of the Forum for Agricultural Research in Africa (FARA), the AU's designated lead institution for 'matters concerning agricultural science, technology and innovation' (2015: 7). In terms of its strategic priorities, FARA is engaging with 'emerging sciences, technology and risk mitigation ... [i]ntegrating capacities for change [and using] evidence-based advocacy, communication and stakeholder engagement to generate enabling policies and institutions ... required for the sustainable implementation of programmes for African agricultural innovation' (2015: 7). There has therefore been an increasing call to utilize new technologies, specifically biotechnology, to transform agricultural production systems for African development (AU 2006; Holt-Gimenez 2008; NEPAD 2006; Schurman 2016; Thompson 2007; UNDP 2003). While the call for infusing biotechnology into African agriculture predates the MDGs, the role of industry, innovation and infrastructure are the focus of SDG 9. Despite the enthusiasm for biotechnology through policy pronouncements and the establishment of institutions, many African countries have not enacted biosafety rules that will govern the infusion of biotechnology into agricultural development (AU 2006; Ayele *et al.* 2006; Essegbey 2008; NEPAD 2001, 2003; Puplampu 2010; World Bank 1989).

Beyond South Africa and Burkina Faso, who have engaged biotech crops for over a decade, few countries including Cameroon, Egypt, Ghana, Kenya and Malawi, Nigeria, Swaziland and Uganda have recently conducted field trails (James 2015). Nigeria and Ghana have confined field trials specifically of biotechnology cowpea and bio-fortified staples. In Ghana, there are other crops undergoing confined field trials such as the genetically modified rice, NEWEST: the variety of rice modified for nitrogen efficiency, water efficiency and salt tolerance. In Kenya, field trials are ongoing for genetically modified cotton and cassava. All these constitute an important step in the application of modern biotechnology in improving Africa's agricultural systems. Nevertheless, the pursuit of biotech crops in a policy vacuum places not only a great deal of institutional responsibility on the FARA, but also calls for public policy debates on biotechnology and other emerging agricultural technologies.

FARA, as other institutions in the region, is confronted with the major challenge of effective linkage between farming systems and agricultural research systems in Africa. The fact is that research does not take place in a vacuum and, to be successful, it has to critically engage with fundamental problems of how citizens and society at large relate to scientific knowledge claims, derive meanings from, attach values and learn about the practices associated with science, particularly the risk and uncertainty of agricultural technology (Entine 2006; Scoones 2006). The perennial difficulty has been the place of farmers in the research agenda of national agricultural research systems, a situation exacerbated by their institutional set-up and the high funding dependency on external multilateral agencies and institutions (Asare and Essegbey 2016; Beintema and Stads 2014; Lyman *et al.* 2012; Spielman *et al.* 2011). The problematic place of farmers persists, even as examples abound of how the effective engagement with farmers account for the successful outcomes in rice production in West Africa (Diagne *et al.* 2011; IFPRI 2006). FARA's own concept of Integrated Agricultural Research for Development (IAR4D) demonstrates some solutions for addressing the dichotomy between farmers and agricultural research (Adekunle *et al.* 2013; FARA 2015). This approach is essential for African national agricultural research systems to create the capacity in order to assume a place in emerging trends in global science, especially collaboration, which is fundamental towards the effective transformation of agriculture and society (FARA 2015).

The agricultural research system in Africa is the most dependent on donor funding compared to other developing regions of the world (Beintema and Stads 2014). There is a high variation in funding capability across African countries, with countries like Burkina Faso and Madagascar deriving 'between

60 and 70 per cent of their total funding from donors and development banks in 2011' (Beintema and Stads 2014: 18). Donor funding is often tied to specific projects and short-term in nature. In view of aid incoherence, a mismatch between the priorities of donor and recipient countries or groups is not a theoretical possibility. The theoretical problems are further compounded when the funding period expires, accelerating uncertainties about the long-term commitments required for policy and institutional effectiveness. Amid the above problems, it stands to reason that FARA's regional nodal centres like the African Agricultural Technology Foundation would not have the capacity required for effective collaboration within the African continent and beyond with global institutions. Collaboration between Africa-based research institutions with their global counterparts calls for a certain level of consistency in terms of standards of operation.

Conclusion and planning for the future

In this chapter we have examined the policy and institutional aspects of African agriculture within the context of the MDGs and the just launched SDGs. There is the diversity of approaches to support and investment. Yet such initiatives have to be scrupulously analysed to fine-tune sound investment approaches. Successful outcomes in the agricultural sector would be consistent with several SDGs, particularly SDG 1 (no poverty), SDG 2 (zero hunger) and SDG 16 (justice, peace and strong institutions). Given the range of new policies and institutions aimed at advancing African agriculture, the blight of African agriculture is not the paucity of policies or institutions. The problem remains desirable policy and institutional outcomes in the face of available resources, because political commitment, although necessary, is not a sufficient condition.

Perhaps, the following suggestions are worth stressing if only to reinforce the salient aspects of the planning required for Africa's agricultural agenda. First, while enacting policies and establishing institutions are important, it is equally important to pay attention to outcomes. This is because, without any record of implementation or the resources to back up policies and institutions, African political leaders and their policy-makers can be accused of sloganeering. Such an accusation, definitely, will not serve the interests of the citizenry. Usually the issue of resources boils down to the scheme of prioritization. Given the inflows of some resources at least from their traditional exports, no African country can claim not to have some resources for allocation to priority sectors of the economy, which must include agriculture. Policy-makers should be aware that the creation of institutions, while desirable, is the easy part of the process. Indeed, the 23rd Ordinary Session of the African Union in Malabo in June 2014 rightfully reiterated a commitment to African agriculture, having declared 2014 as the year of African agriculture and food security (AU 2014b). Keeping the momentum from Malabo requires investment in several areas of agriculture, from improving market access to the agricultural value chain (Badiane and Makombe 2015).

Second, it is necessary for African policy-makers to finally engage and deal with farmers in a bold and innovative manner. For such an engagement to attain sustainable success, policy will have to pay serious attention to the conditions of access to resources, for example the plight of women in agriculture (Drafor-Amenyah and Puplampu 2013). The need to engage women farmers, stems from SDG 5 (gender equality) and their integral role in any credible programme to deal with food security and the nutrition problem in Africa (IFPRI 2016; Lartey 2013; Lokosang *et al.* 2015; Von Grebmer *et al.* 2014). This is also the justification for the increasing calls for African countries to pay greater attention to strengthening the social safety network and insurance for farmers (Africa Progress Panel 2014).

Third, there is the need to rethink the role of regional agricultural institutions in Africa. The Forum for African Agricultural Research can be commended for the regional nodal centres and similar initiatives, for instance, the African Agricultural Technology Foundation; but such activities should not be seen as ends in themselves (FARA 2006; Mignouna *et al.* 2008). As FARA (2015: 19) correctly states, the 'Malabo Declaration presents a perfect opportunity to leverage on agricultural research for the evidence to inform policy-making and investment in technology adoption and innovation to meet the poverty alleviation, nutrition and food security goals' of the African continent. For that to happen, the politics at the heart of the development process has to be replaced by the politics that seeks to address the collective welfare of the nation and citizens at large, particularly farmers as the key producers of the agricultural and national wealth.

References

Adekunle, A. A., Ayanwale, A. B., FatunbI, A. O., Kwesiga, F. and Jones, M. P. (2013) *Maximizing Impact from Agricultural Research: Potential of the IAR4D Concept*. Accra: Forum for Agricultural Research in Africa (FARA).

Adenle, A. A., Manning, L. and Azadi, H. (2016) Agribusiness innovation: a pathway to sustainable economic growth in Africa. *Trends in Food Science & Technology*, 59, 88–104.

Africa Progress Panel (2014) *Grain Fish Money – Financing Africa's Green and Blue Revolutions*. Geneva: Africa Progress Panel.

———. (2015). *Power People Planet: Seizing Africa's energy and climate opportunities*. Geneva: Africa Progress Panel.

African Capacity Building Foundation (ACBF) (2012) *Africa Capacity Indicators 2012 – Capacity Development for Agricultural Transformation and Food Security*. Harare: Africa Capacity Building Foundation.

———. (2013) *Africa Capacity Indicators 2013 – Capacity Development for Natural Resource Management*. Harare: Africa Capacity Building Foundation.

African Development Bank (AfDB) (2010) *African Development Report 2010*. Oxford: Oxford University Press for African Development Bank.

African Union (AU) (2003) Assembly of the African Union, Second Ordinary Session, 10–12 July, Maputo (Assembly/AU/Decl.4–11 (II), Addis Ababa: African Union.

———. (2006) *African Strategy on Biosafety*. Addis Ababa: African Union.

———. (2014a) *2014 Year of Agriculture and Food Security in Africa, Marking 10th Anniversary of the Adoption of CAADP*. Department of Rural Economy and Agriculture (Briefing Note). Addis Ababa: African Union.

———. (2014b) *The 23rd Ordinary Session of the African Union ends in Malabo*, Press Release N°18/23rd AU Summit. Addis Ababa: African Union.

Amanor, K. S. and Chichava, S. (2016) South–south cooperation, agribusiness, and African agricultural development: Brazil and China in Ghana and Mozambique, *World Development*, 81, 13–23.

Anderson, K. and Masters, W. A. (eds) (2009): *Distortions to Agricultural Incentives in Africa*. Washington, DC: World Bank.

Andrews, N., Khalema, N. E. and Assié-Lumumba, N. T. (2015) (eds) *Millennium Development Goals (MDGS) in Retrospect: Africa's Development Beyond 2015*. Cham, ZG: Springer.

Anseeuw, W. (2010) Agricultural policy in Africa – renewal or status quo?: A spotlight on Kenya and Senegal. In V. Padayachee (ed.) *The Political Economy of Africa*. New York: Routledge.

Asare, R. and Essegbey, G. O. (2016) Funding of agricultural research and development in Ghana: The case of Council for Scientific and Industrial Research (CSIR). *Technology and Investment*, 7, 40–50. Available at dx.doi.org/10.4236/ti.2016.72006.

Ashoff, G. (2005) *Enhancing Policy Coherence for Development: Justification, Recognition and Approaches to Achievement*. Bonn: German Development Institute.

Asongu, S. A. and Nwachukwu, J. C. (2016) Foreign aid and inclusive development: updated evidence from Africa, 2005–2012, *Social Science Quarterly*. doi:10.1111/ssqu.12275.

Ayele, S., Wield, D. and Chataway, J. (2006) Partnerships in African crop biotech, *Nature Biotechnology*, 24 (6): 619–21.

Badiane, O. and Makombe, T. (eds) (2015) *Beyond a Middle Income Africa: Transforming African Economies for Sustained Growth with Rising Employment and Incomes*. Resakss Annual Trends and Outlook Report 2014. International Food Policy Research Institute (IFPRI).

Badiane, O., Makombe, T. and Bahiigwa, G. (eds) (2014) *Promoting Agricultural Trade to Enhance Resilience in Africa: ReSAKASS Annual Trends and Outlook Report 2013*. Washington, DC: IFPRI.

Bahiigwa, G., Benin, S., Tefera, W. and Jemaneh, S. (2015) Tracking key CAADP indicators and implementation. In O. Badiane and T. Makombe (eds) *Beyond a Middle Income Africa: Transforming African Economies for Sustained Growth with Rising Employment and Incomes. Resakss Annual Trends and Outlook Report 2014*. Washington, DC: IFPRI, pp. 180–6.

Bahiigwa, G., Collins, J., Makombe, T., Jemaneh, S. and Tefera, W. (2014) in Badiane, O., Makombe, T. and Bahiigwa, G. (eds) *Promoting Agricultural Trade to Enhance Resilience in Africa: ReSAKASS Annual Trends and Outlook Report 2013*. Washington, DC: IFPRI, pp. 70–7.

Banful, A. B. (2011) Old problems in the new solutions? Politically motivated allocation of program benefits and the 'new' fertilizer subsidies, *World Development*, 39 (7): 1166–76.

Barry, F., King, M. and Matthews, A. (2010) Policy coherence for development: five challenges, *Irish Studies in International Affairs*, 21: 207–23.

Beintema, M. and Stads, G. J. (2014) *Taking Stock of National Agricultural R&D Capacity in Africa South of the Sahara*. Washington, DC: IFPRI and ASTI.

Benin, S. and Yu, B. (2013) *Trends in Public Agricultural Expenditures in Africa*, (Issue Note No. 22), Washington, DC: IFPRI.

Berazneva, J. and Lee, D. R. (2013) Explaining the African food riots of 2007–2008: an empirical analysis, *Food Policy* 39: 28–39.

Berhanu, K. and Poulton, C. (2014) The political economy of agricultural extension policy in Ethiopia: economic growth and political control, *Development Policy Review*, 32 (S2): S199–S216.

Birdsall, N. and Khraras, H. (2010) *Quality of Official Development Assistance Assessment 2009: Is Aid Quality Improving?* Washington, DC: Brookings Institute and Center for Global Development.

Booth, D. and Golooba-Mutebi, F. (2014) Policy for agriculture and horticulture in Rwanda: A Different Political Economy? *Development Policy Review*, 32 (S2): S173–S198.

Brown, S. (ed.) (2012) *Struggling for Effectiveness: CIDA and Canadian Foreign Aid*. Montreal and Kingston: McGill-Queen's University Press.

Brown, S., Heyer, M. D. and Black, D. R. (eds) (2014) *Rethinking Canadian Aid*. Ottawa: University of Ottawa Press.

Bruntrup, M. (2011) The comprehensive Africa agriculture development – an assessment of a pan-African attempt to revitalise agriculture, *Quarterly Journal of International Agriculture*, 50 (1): 79–106.

Bülles, A. and Kindornay, S. (2013) *Beyond Aid: A Plan for Canada's International Cooperation*. Ottawa: The North-South Institute.

Cabral, L. (2008) Accra 2008: the bumpy road to aid effectiveness in agriculture natural resource, *Perspectives*, 114, 1–4 (Overseas Development Institute).

Chinsinga, B. and Poulton, C. (2014) Beyond technocratic debates: the significance and transience of political incentives in the Malawi Farm Input Subsidy Programme (FISP), *Development Policy Review*, 32 (S2): S123–S150.

Chuhan-Pole, P. and Angwafo, M. (eds) (2011) *Yes Africa Can: Success Stories from a Dynamic Continent*. Washington, DC: World Bank.

Comprehensive Africa Agriculture Development Programme (2010) *The Comprehensive Africa Agriculture Development Programme (CAADP) in Practice – Highlighting the Successes*. Midrand: NEPAD Planning and Coordinating Agency.

Cooksey, B. (2011) Marketing reform? The rise and fall of agricultural liberalisation in Tanzania, *Development Policy Review*, 29 (Supplement): S57–S81.

Delpeuch, C. and Leblois, A. (2013) Sub-Saharan African cotton policies in retrospect, *Development Policy Review*, 31 (5): 617–42.

Devereux, S. (2016) Social protection for enhanced food security in sub-Saharan Africa, *Food Policy*, 60, 52–62.

Devèze, J-C (ed.) (2011) *Challenges for African Agriculture*. Washington, DC: World Bank.

Diagne, A., Gnonna, S-K., Wopereis, M. and Akintayo, I. (2011) Increasing rice productivity and strengthening food security through new rice for Africa (NERICA). In P. Chuhan-Pole and M. Angwafo (eds) *Yes Africa Can: Success Stories from a Dynamic Continent*. Washington, DC: World Bank.

Drafor-Amenyah, I. and Puplampu, K. P. (2013) *Women in Agriculture: An Assessment of the Current State of Affairs in Africa.* ACBF Working Paper No 24. Harare: African Capacity Building Foundation.

Eicher, C. (2006) *The Evolution of Agricultural Education and Training: Global Insights for Relevance for Africa.* Washington, DC: World Bank.

Entine, J. (ed.) (2006) *Let Them Eat Precaution: How Politics Is Undermining the Genetic Revolution in Agriculture.* Washington, DC: American Enterprise Institute.

Essegbey, G. O. (2008) Biotechnology policy: the myth and reality in sub-Saharan Africa. In G. Ruivenkamp, S. Hisano and J. Jongerden (eds) *Reconstructing Biotechnologies – Critical Social Analyses.* Wageningen: Wageningen Academic Publishers.

———. (2009) Ghana: cassava, cocoa, and poultry. In K. Larsen, R. Kim and F. Theus (eds) *Agribusiness and Innovation Systems in Africa.* Washington, DC: World Bank.

Faust, J. and Messier, D. (2007) *Organizational Challenges for an Effective Aid Architecture – Traditional Deficits, the Paris Agenda and Beyond.* Discussion Paper 20/2007, Bonn: German Development Institute.

Forum for Agricultural Research in Africa (FARA) (2006) *Framework for African Agricultural Productivity.* Accra: Forum for Agricultural Research in Africa.

———. (2011) *Transforming African Agriculture through Research, Advisory Services, Education and Training.* Accra: Forum for Agricultural Research in Africa.

———. (2014) *Science Agenda for Agriculture in Africa (S3A): Connecting Science to Transform Agriculture in Africa.* Accra: Forum for Agricultural Research in Africa.

———. (2015) *Seeding Science for the Transformation of African Agriculture.* Annual Report. Accra: Forum for Agricultural Research in Africa.

Foster, V. and Briceno-Garmendia, C. (2010) *Africa's Infrastructure – A Time for Transformation*: Washington, DC: Agence Française de Développement and the World Bank.

Franke, B. F. (2007) Competing regionalisms in Africa and the continent's emerging security architecture, *African Studies Quarterly*, 9 (3): 31–64.

Global Agriculture and Food Security Program (GAFSP) (2015) *2015 Annual Report.* Washington, DC: Global Agriculture and Food Security Program.

Haggblade, S. (2013) Unscrambling Africa: regional requirements for achieving food security, *Development Policy Review*, 31 (2): 149–76.

Hanson, K. T., D'Alessandro, C. and Owusu, F. (eds) (2014) *Managing Africa's Natural Resources: Capacities for Development.* New York: Palgrave Macmillan.

Havnevik, K., Bryceson, D., Birgegård, L., Matondi, P. and Beyene, A. (2007) *African Agriculture and the World Bank: Development or Impoverishment?* Uppsala: Nordic Africa Institute

Holt-Gimenez, E (2008) Out of AGRA: the green revolution returns to Africa, *Development*, 51 (4): 464–71.

International Food Policy Research Institute (IFPRI) (2005) *Africa Without Borders: Building Blocks for Regional Growth*, Policy Brief No. 38. Washington, DC: International Food Policy Research Institute.

———. (2006): *Annual Report, 2005–2006.* Washington, DC: International Food Policy Research Institute.

———. (2015) *Global Food Policy Report, 2014–2015.* Washington, DC: International Food Policy Research Institute.

———. (2016) *Global Nutrition Report 2016: From Promise to Impact: Ending Malnutrition by 2030*. Washington, DC.: International Food Policy Research Institute.

James, C. (2015) *Global Status of Commercialized Biotech/GM Crops: 2015*. ISAAA Brief No. 51. Ithaca, NY: ISAAA.

Jayne, T. S., Govereh, J., Mwanaumo, A., Nyoro, J. K. and Chapoto, A. (2002) False promise or false premise: the experience of food and input market reform in Eastern and Southern Africa, *World Development*, 30 (11): 1967–85.

Jobodwana, Z. N. (2011) WTO African cotton wars: the intractable agriculture policy reforms, *US-China Law Review*, 8 (2): 87–120.

Juma, C. (2011) *The New Harvest: Agricultural Innovation in Africa*. New York: Oxford University Press.

Kaminski, J., Headey, D. and Bernard, T. (2011) The Burkinabè cotton story 1997–2007: sustainable success or sub-Saharan mirage? *World Development*, 39 (8): 1460–75.

Kibwika, P., Kyazze, F. B. and Musoke, M. N. (2009) Uganda: fish, bananas, and vegetables. In K. Larsen, R. Kim and F. Theus (eds) *Agribusiness and Innovation Systems in Africa*. Washington, DC: World Bank.

Kolavalli, S., Birner, R. and Flaherty, K. (2012) *The Comprehensive Africa Agriculture Program as a Collective Institution.* Discussion Paper 1238 – Development Strategy and Governance Division. Washington, DC: IFPRI.

Larsen, K., Kim, R. and Theus, F. (eds) (2009) *Agribusiness and Innovation Systems in Africa*. Washington, DC: World Bank.

Lartey, A. (2013) Nutrition in Sub-Saharan Africa: Setting the Stage for a Post-2015 Take-Off, *IDS Bulletin*, 44 (5–6): 49–54.

Li, G. and Wang, W. (2016) *Investing in Africa's Agriculture: Solidifying Foundation for Sustainable and Inclusive Development.* Washington, DC: World Bank. Available at openknowledge.worldbank.org/handle/10986/25188 (accessed 24 April 2017).

Lokosang, L., Osei, A. and Covic, N. (2015) The African Union policy environment toward enabling action for nutrition in Africa. In N. Covic and S. L. Hendriks (eds) *Achieving a Nutrition Revolution for Africa: The Road to Healthier Diets and Optimal Nutrition*. Resakss Annual Trends and Outlook Report 2015. IFPRI, pp. 5–11.

Mafusire, A., Anyanwu, J., Brixiova, Z., Mutambatsere, E., Mubila, M. and Dhib, A. (2011) Closing Africa's infrastructure gap. In K. Mlambo, A. B. Kamara, A. Kateeto and C. Lufumpa (eds) *Telling Africa's Development Story.* Tunis: African Development Bank.

Makinda, S. M. (2012) Africa's leadership malaise and the crisis of governance. In K. T. Hanson, G. Kararach and T. M. Shaw (eds) *Rethinking Development Challenges for Public Policy: Insights from Contemporary Africa*. New York: Palgrave Macmillan.

Mhlanga, N. (2013) *Private Sector Agribusiness Investment in Sub-Saharan Africa*. Rome: FAO.

Mignouna, H. D., Abang, M. M., Omanya, G., Nan'ayo, F., Bokanga, M., Boadi, R., Muchiri, N. and Terry, E. (2008) Delivery of agricultural technology to resource-poor farmers in Africa, *Annals of the New York Academy of Sciences* 1136: 369–76.

Moseley, G. and Gray, L. C. (eds) (2008) *Hanging by a Thread: Cotton, Globalization, and Poverty in Africa*. Athens, OH: Ohio University Press.

Moyo, D. (2009) *Dead Aid – Why Aid Makes Things Worse and How There is Another Way for Africa*. London: Pengiun.

Mpagalile, J., Ishengoma, R. and Gillah, P. (2009) Tanzania: sunflower, cassava, and dairy. In K. Larsen, R. Kim and F. Theus (eds) *Agribusiness and Innovation Systems in Africa*. Washington, DC: World Bank

Musumba, M. and Gupta, R. S. (2013) Transmission of world prices to Ugandan coffee growers in a liberalised economy, *Development Policy Review*, 31 (2): 219–34.

Ncube, M., Brixiova, Z. and Bicaba, Z. (2014) *Can Dreams Come True? Eliminating Extreme Poverty in Africa by 2030*. Discussion Paper No. 8120. Bonn: Institute for the Study of Labour (IZA).

New Partnership for Africa Development (NEPAD) (2001) *NEPAD Policy Document*. Midrand: New Partnership for Africa Development.

———. (2003) *Comprehensive Africa Agriculture Development Programme*. Midrand: New Partnership for Africa Development.

———. (2006) *Africa's Science and Technology Consolidated Plan of Action*. Lynnwood, Pretoria: New Partnership for Africa Development Office of Science and Technology

———. (2010) CAADP *Review – Renewing the Commitment to African Agriculture*. Midrand: NEPAD Planning and Coordinating Agency.

Nhamo, G. (2016) New global sustainable development agenda: a focus on Africa, *Sustainable Development*, doi: 10.1002/sd.1648.

Obi, C. (2001) Reconstructing Africa's development in the new millennium through NEPAD: Can African Leaders Deliver the Goods? *African Journal of International Affairs*, 4 (1 and 2): 142–75.

Odame, H., Musyoka, P. and Kere, J. (2009) Kenya: maize, tomato and dairy. In K. Larsen, R. Kim and F. Theus (eds) *Agribusiness and Innovation Systems in Africa*. Washington, DC: World Bank.

OECD/FAO (2016) Part 1 – Chapter 2 Agriculture in Sub-Saharan Africa: Prospects and Challenges for the next Decade. *OECD/FAO Agricultural Outlook 2016–2025*. Paris: OECD.

Organization for Economic Co-operation and Development (OECD) (2008) *Accra Agenda for Action*. Paris: OECD.

———. (2009) *Building Blocks for Policy Coherence for Development*. Paris: OECD.

Owusu, F. (2003) Pragmatism and the gradual shift from dependency to neoliberalism: the World Bank, African leaders and development policy in Africa, *World Development*, 31 (10): 1655–72.

Poulton, C. (2014) Democratisation and the political incentives for agricultural policy in Africa, *Development Policy Review*, 32 (S2): S101–S122.

Poulton, C. and Kanyinga, K. (2014) The politics of revitalising agriculture in Kenya, *Development Policy Review*, 32 (S2):S151–S172.

Puplampu, K. P. (2006) The World Trade Organization, global trade and agriculture. In M. S. Smith (ed.) *Beyond the 'African tragedy': Discourses on Development and the Global Economy*. Aldershot: Ashgate, pp. 233–45.

———. (2010) Bureaucratic politics and the search for biotechnology policy in Ghana. In K. P. Puplampu and W. J. Tettey (eds) *The Public Sphere and the Politics of Survival: Voice, Sustainability and Public Policy in Ghana*. Accra: Woeli Publishing Services.

———. (2014) The shifting boundaries of the African state in agricultural institutions and policies in an era of globalization. In E. Shizha and A. A. Abdi (eds) *Indigenous Discourses on Knowledge and Development in Africa*. New York: Routledge.

Rakotoarisoa, M. A., Lafrate, M. and Paschali, M. (2012) *Why has Africa Become a Net Food Importer*. Rome: FAO.

Rauch, T. (2011) Fundamentals of African agriculture, *Quarterly Journal of International Agriculture*, 50 (1): 9–27.

Reardon, T., Tschirley, D., Minten, B., Haggblade, S., Liverpool-Tasie, S., Dolislager, M., Snyder, J. and Ijumba, C. (2015) Transformation of African agrifood systems in the new era of rapid urbanization and the emergence of a middle class. In O. Badiane and T. Makombe (eds) *Beyond a Middle Income Africa: Transforming African Economies for Sustained Growth with Rising Employment And Incomes.* Resakss Annual Trends and Outlook Report 2014. International Food Policy Research Institute (IFPRI), pp. 62–74.

Rogerson, A. (2011) *Key Busan Challenges and Contributions to the Emerging Development Effectiveness Agenda Background Note*, 1–8 November, Overseas Development Institute.

Sasson, A. (2012) Food security for Africa: an urgent global challenge, *Agriculture and Food Security*, 1 (2): 1–16.

Schurman, R. (2016) Building an alliance for biotechnology in Africa. *Journal of Agrarian Change*, doi: 10.1111/joac.12167.

Scoones, I. (2006) *Science, Agriculture and the Politics of Policy: The Case of Biotechnology in India*. New Delhi: Orient Longman.

Söderbaum, F. (2004) Modes of regional governance in Africa: neoliberalism, sovereignty boosting, and shadow networks, *Global Governance*, 10: 419–43.

Spielman, D. J., Zaidi, F. and Flaherty, K. (2011) *Changing Donor Priorities and Strategies for Agricultural R&D in Developing Countries – Evidence from Africa.* Washington, DC and Accra: IFPRI and FARA.

Taeb, M. and ZakrI, A. H. (eds) (2008) *Agriculture, Human Security, and Peace: A Crossroad in African Development*. West Lafayette, IN.: Purdue University Press.

Taylor, I. (2011) South African 'Imperialism' in a region lacking regionalism: a critique, *Third World Quarterly*, 32 (7): 1233–53.

Tettey, W. J. (2012) Africa's leadership deficit: exploring pathways to good governance and transformative politics, K. T. Hanson, G. Kararach and T. M. Shaw (eds) *Rethinking Development Challenges for Public Policy: Insights from Contemporary Africa.* New York, Palgrave MacMillan, pp. 18–53.

Thompson, C. B. (2007) Africa: green revolution or rainbow evolution, *Review of African Political Economy*, 34 (113): 562–5.

Tschirley, D. L. (2010) Institutional diversity and performance in African cotton sectors, *Development Policy Review*, 28 (3): 295–323.

Toenniessen, G., Adesina, A. and Devries, J. (2008) Building an alliance for a green revolution in Africa. *Annals of the New York Academy of Sciences*, 1136: 233–42.

Torero, M. (2015) Infrastructure challenges and potential for Africa south of the Sahara. In Badiane, O. and Makombe, T. (eds) Beyond a Middle Income Africa: Transforming African Economies for Sustained Growth with Rising Employment and Incomes. *Resakss Annual Trends and Outlook Report 2014*. International Food Policy Research Institute (IFPRI), pp. 157–79.

United Nations Development Program (UNDP) (2003) *Human Development Report 2003 Millennium Development Goals: A compact among nations to end human poverty*. New York, Oxford University Press for UNDP.

———. (2013) *Millennium Development Goals Report 2013, Assessing Progress in Africa Towards the Millennium Development Goals*. New York: Oxford University Press for UNDP.

———. (2015) *Sustainable Development Goals*. New York: United Nations Development Programme.

Van de Walle, N. (2001) *African Economies and the Politics of Permanent Crisis*. New York: Cambridge University Press.

Von Grebmer, K., Saltzman, A., Birol, E., Wiesman, D., Prasai, N., Yin, S., Yohannes, Y., Menon, P., Thompson, J. and Sonntag, A. (2014) *2014 Global Hunger Index: The Challenge of Hidden Hunger*. Bonn, Washington, DC and Dublin: Welthungerhilfe: IFPRI and Concern Worldwide. Available at dx.doi.org/10.2499/9780896299580.

Wanasika, I. H., Littrell, J. P. and Dorfman, P. (2011) Managerial leadership and culture in sub-Saharan Africa, *Journal of World Business*, 46 (2): 234–41.

World Bank (1989) *Sub-Saharan Africa: From Crisis to Sustainable Growth – A Long Term Perspective Study*. Washington, DC: World Bank.

———. (1994) *Adjustment in Africa Reforms, Results and the Road Ahead*. Washington, DC: World Bank.

———. (2007) *World Development Report, 2008 – Agriculture for Development*. Washington, DC: World Bank

———. (2013) *Growing Africa: Unlocking the Potential of Agribusiness*. Washington, DC: World Bank.

———. (2015) *Africa's Pulse: An Analysis of Issues Shaping Africa's Economic Future*. October, Vol. 11, Washington, DC: The World Bank (Office of the Chief Economist for the Africa Region).

———. (2016) *Africa's Pulse: An Analysis of Issues Shaping Africa's Economic Future*. October, Vol. 14, Washington, DC: The World Bank (Office of the Chief Economist for the Africa Region).

5 South–South cooperation, SDGs and Africa's development

A study of China's development intervention in Ghana

Isaac Odoom

Introduction

The Millennium Development Goals (MDGs) brought together the international community in an effort to reach set targets. Goal 8, in particular, called for a global partnership for development involving both developing and developed countries (UNDP 2015). Similarly, since the 2000s, South–South Cooperation (SSC) has become an important feature of international development and therefore critical for attaining some of the MDGs (Chun 2015; Grimm and Zhang 2013). While partnership with traditional donors such as the Organization for Economic Co-operation and Development (OECD) members remains important for achieving the MDGs and its successor Sustainable Development Goals (SDGs), other platforms such as SSC and triangular cooperation have become fundamental in achieving the broader goals of African development (D'Alessandro and Zulu 2016: 6). In terms of the SDGs, goal number 17 directly calls for revitalizing global partnership and embracing arrangements such as SSC and welcoming private sources of finance.

The emerging economies on the international scene have led to power shifts in the international development landscape. Over the last decade, countries such as China, Brazil and India, among others, have shown significant increases in their respective cooperation activities with African countries. For example, under the framework of SSC in general and the Forum on China–Africa Cooperation (FOCAC) in particular, China and Africa have had some fruitful results in MDG implementation cooperation, laying the foundation for cooperation on the post-2015 development agenda (Aurégan, 2016; Chun 2015; Grimm and Zhang 2013). While global partnership for sustainable development including SSC remains crucial for African economies, there are questions about the extent to which Africa's 'new' and growing partnership with emerging powers such as China will facilitate the achievement of the SDGs and whether such relationships will be any different from the historical partnership with traditional donors (Andrews *et al.* 2015; Taylor 2014).

There is no consensus on the impact of new forms of South–South partnerships (Alden *et al.* 2010; Amanor and Chichava 2016). Africa, however, continues to deal with many development challenges including a huge deficit in the infrastructure sector. According to the World Bank, sub-Saharan Africa lags behind other developing regions on most standard indicators of infrastructure development (Foster *et al.* 2009). The infrastructure gap in Africa is estimated at about US$10 billion a year for minimum investment needs, and US$22 billion is required to meet the MDGs (Bosshard 2007; see also Foster *et al.* 2009). Significantly, power is Africa's largest infrastructure challenge, the least developed and most costly to operate, compared to any region of the world (Foster *et al.* 2009) While China's engagement in Africa cuts across various sectors (e.g. education, agriculture and health) the noticeable focus has been on the role of Chinese firms constructing roads, bridges, hydrodams, sewage systems and telecommunication services across the continent.[1] In several countries such as Nigeria, Ethiopia, Angola, Kenya and Tanzania, Chinese government and multinationals have taken the approach of bundling together business and development assistance packages in funding projects. This integrated approach to development cooperation is presented by Chinese officials as a win-win model, but has both positive and negative implications for achieving the SDGs in Africa.

Focusing on the role of SSC and infrastructure development practices of China, this chapter reveals some key features of the development practice in Africa and draws attention to some of the dynamics that will shape the future of Africa's post-MDGs political economics. The chapter examines the development cooperation practices of China in Africa, and evaluates how such practices limit or contribute to the achievement of the SDGs on the continent.[2] The rest of the chapter is organized into three parts.

The following section situates China's increasing engagement with Africa within the framework of SSC, and interrogates the origin and use of SSC as an analytical framework to examine the strategic relations between African states and China. Next, there is an overview of Beijing's development cooperation practices in Ghana's energy infrastructure sector using the Chinese-funded Atuabo Gas project in Ghana as a case study. The Atuabo Gas project is a good example of China's approach to development cooperation; it also reveals important features of that approach in Ghana and Africa in general.

This chapter concludes by highlighting some implications of China's development practices and how they contribute to or detract from achieving the SDGs. I argue that while Chinese infrastructural investment in Africa is critical for achieving SDGs, the developmental benefits of Chinese engagement will require responsible African agency. African actors need to ensure that they engage China within a framework, consistent with their own strategic development plans including the SDGs.

China in Africa: a model of South–South cooperation?

China's increasing interaction with African countries is recasting Africa's international relations and changing the continent's development landscape.

Although some analysts express concern about China's motives and practices, others are optimistic about the opportunities presented by such an arrangement (Brautigam 2009; French 2014; He 2007; Manji and Marks 2007; Moyo 2009; Tull 2009). Some observers, mostly Chinese officials and academics, present China as 'the largest developing country in the world' and an 'all-weather-friend' of Africa, by emphasizing, among other things, the value of China's development experience and cooperation for transforming Africa through South–South collaborative efforts (GOV 2010). As DeHart (2012: 1360) explains, while Western governments and pundits (negatively) depict Chinese involvement with terms such as the 'China model' or the 'Beijing consensus', China 'has rejected these models ... offering instead South-South cooperation to describe its goal'. As with other Southern countries,[3] the Chinese government premises its presence on the African continent on historical relations and as part of the broader discourse on SSC (Mawdsley 2007; Vickers 2012).Other analysts fail to see China's engagement in Africa as a form of South-South cooperation (Alden 2005; Manji and Marks 2007; Melville and Owen 2005;). How should Africa–China relations be analysed within the changing development landscape?

The idea of SSC emerged when the newly independent Asian and African states, or what was then called 'Third World', begun to institutionalize their solidarity. This solidarity was based on shared struggles against (neo) colonialism, imperialism and concerns regarding a global political and economic structure that, they argued, was tilted in favour of developed countries (also referred to as the 'West' or the 'North'). Therefore, as DeHart (2012: 1367) explains, at the root of the concept of SSC is the understanding of a shared history, experience with colonialism and desire for sovereignty and equality. In this vein, the concept of 'South' has more to do with an understanding of the global divide between developed and developing countries than geographical regions. Other scholars go further, seeing in SSC, suspicions of the 'hegemonic' character of North–South relations, and a wish to promote more 'mutuality' in exchanges among developing countries of the global South (Vickers 2012).

Two important historical events that account for the emergence of the SSC concept are: the Asian–African Conference held in Bandung, Indonesia, in April 1955[4] which led to the creation of the Non-Aligned Movement in 1961; and the 1978 United Nations Conference on Technical Cooperation among Developing Countries held in Buenos Aires (UN 2009; UNCTAD 2010). Significantly, the Buenos Aires conference took place during a decade when the Western[5] world felt vulnerable due to the increase in oil prices by Southern oil producers and the sustained pressure by increased Southern societies for a new international economic order (Cohn 2012). The 1978 conference was also significant because the Buenos Aires Plan of Action was adopted, which gave a strategic framework for South–South collaboration (UNCTAD 2009: 7).

Although its substance has changed over time, SSC is recognized today as a framework for developing countries 'to strengthen their economic, social and political interdependence, accelerate development and correct distortions in international systems caused by the asymmetrical power relations of the colonial era' (UN 2009: 4). SSC is seen as a mechanism for enhancing growth, reducing poverty and integrating into the global economy (Shaw 2010; UNCTAD 2010). Tejasvi (2007) defines SSC as 'developing countries working together to find solutions to common development challenges'. SSC thus refers to the processes, institutions and arrangements designed to promote political, economic and technical cooperation among developing countries in pursuit of common development goals. It is multi-dimensional in scope, encompassing cooperation in areas such as trade, investment, as well as the exchange of knowledge and technical expertise between developing countries. SSC is also a mobilizing symbol for a diverse group of developing nations and serves as a strategy for these sets of states to manage their relations with the countries of the global North (Alden *et al.* 2010: 3).

The SSC framework is a useful concept for understanding aspects of China's relations with African countries. However, the growing economic and political diversity between China and African states calls for a more critical understanding of Africa–China relations even within this context. Wallerstein's 'semi-periphery' and 'periphery' formulations help to delineate China's role and position *vis-à-vis* its African counterparts (Shaw 1979; Wallerstein 1974, 1976, 1997). In its relations with African countries, China could be described as a 'semi-periphery' state that engages its peripheral African states in seemingly 'similar' yet unexpectedly 'different' ways (Mohan and Power 2011: 46). China's approach to politics and development intervention, to borrow Bhabha's (1994: 86) words, are 'almost the same [as the West] but not quite'.

Although the asymmetrical relations (particularly in trade) between African countries and China could be understood from the 'core-periphery' dichotomy, at the same time this notion seems insufficient at explaining the complex dialectic relations between China and its African partners. China's developing country status and its development challenges at home as well as its development practices and the rhetoric it employs in its engagements with African countries requires a more nuanced, complex conceptual model. In its economic and trade relations with Africa, China does not seem to fit the theoretical concept of a 'core' country, nor does it any longer fit the standard 'periphery' nation. Unprecedented growth in China (Breslin 2005, 2007; Jiang 2009) over the past decade, and subsequently its export of manufactured goods to Africa, has meant that its trade with African countries is markedly unfavourable for the latter. However, China's own struggle from underdevelopment and its ambiguous status as a developing country (Sautman 2006) affords Beijing a historical legitimacy resulting in a distinct culture of SSC (see China Africa Policy 2006).

China, unlike other European actors, does not have a history of colonization in Africa. China thus has a specific position among African countries; but, this position is ambiguous. China's economic and social structure defines a 'dual position' as a developing country on the one hand, and 'donor' in its external relations on the other (Six 2009: 1110). Consequently, the framing and conduct of China's engagement is informed by a discourse of difference and similitude: in Africa, China is considered different from other external powers based fundamentally on China's own experience as a developing country (Alden and Large 2010: 1).While China's status as a developing country and its political claim to speak for Southerners is questionable, China shares certain commonalities with African countries coming from similar development experiences and shared interests (China Africa Policy 2006; He 2007). The 'China way' of engagement in Africa purports to promote mutual benefit and win-win outcomes, so that while its relations with Africa may remain asymmetrical in economic content, the two can be almost equal in recognition of economic gains and political standing (Alden and Large 2010).

In its development cooperation, China actively mobilizes the historical discourse of geopolitics (respect for sovereignty, non-interference in political affairs, anti-hegemony) and the language of commonality and mutuality (solidarity, friendship, anti-imperialism) in order to justify and legitimize its Africa policy. Consequently, China is 'different' and conducts its economic relations with Africa in somewhat distinctively different ways to Western countries (Mohan and Power 2011: 487). The rapidly changing setting with substantially increasing financial volumes and a multiplication of actors under an umbrella approach to SSC, creates administrative and policy challenges, not least also for SSC 'providers' such as China and 'recipients' like African countries (Grimm 2015: 33; see also Chaturvedi *et al.* 2012; Pérez *et al.* 2014).

In examining Africa's engagement with China, this chapter hopes to depart from unproblematic normative assumptions about China's place within Africa. Instead, the goal is to flesh out the complexity of the relationship. While in many ways China exhibits a different relationship with its African counterpart (Six 2009) and is therefore perceived as different from other European powers, we should nonetheless interrogate ways in which China exercises hegemony in its relations (Power *et al.* 2012).

Financing infrastructure development in Africa: the China approach[6]

Although China's economic and political objectives in Africa are similar to those of other foreign actors, the approach, terms of engagement and the tools used to develop and leverage these relations differ from those of other actors – particularly Western actors. In its interaction with African countries, China seems to recognize a particular complementarity between Africa's endowment as well as its needs and China's capacity to meet these needs. Most African countries are rich in natural resources, but poor infrastructure remains one of the key stumbling blocks to their development. At the same time, China needs Africa's oil and minerals to fuel its growing economy and has developed one of the world's largest and most competitive infrastructure construction industries (Habiyaremye 2013; Jiang 2009).

This economic complementarity between resource-rich Africa, faced with infrastructure challenges, and manufacturing giant China, which is proficient with infrastructure construction firms but also confronted with the need for oil and minerals, informs the dynamics of China's role in Africa. China offers its African partners an integrated system of development cooperation that bundles trade and investment instead of only offering foreign aid (Moyo 2009). China's integrated aid strategy and scheme of financing provides Chinese firms with export credits, securitized by access to an African country's resources through agreement with the government of the African economy, and has been termed 'infrastructure for resources' or 'Angola Mode'.[7] (Chen 2010; Corkin 2013).

This type of natural resource-backed financing deal has become embedded in China's policy of engagement with resource-rich countries in Africa. However, the approach did not originate in China and it is not unprecedented. As Brautigam explains: 'China learned from Japan the current system of using commodities as security for a commercial line of credit that enables a country to finance a specific investment today, and pay for it later with future earnings' (Brautigam 2011: 5). China believes its experience with Japan was premised on mutual benefit and thus has adopted a similar strategy in Africa.

There are incentives associated with this arrangement for both China and the recipient African nation since 'securing the investment with a resource flow reduces the risk and allows the interest rate to be lower, and the loan to be cheaper' (Brautigam 2011: 5). Under this arrangement, the funds earmarked for specific projects are not directly transferred to the recipient government. Instead, China signs a framework agreement with the recipient government covering a certain programme of infrastructure investments. The projects are then contracted to a Chinese construction firm. At the same time, a Chinese company is awarded rights to begin procurement or production of the natural resource in question. The Chinese contractor undertakes infrastructure works supported by a credit from a Chinese bank; usually Exim Bank. As a guarantee, repayment is in the form of the natural resources (Foster *et al.* 2009). A commodity-backed mode of financing has been used across Africa (e.g. oil in Congo-Brazzaville, sesame in Ethiopia and tobacco in Zimbabwe) (Brautigam 2011).

This Chinese approach to development assistance and economic cooperation differs from the methods of other economic actors in Africa. Key principles espoused under China's support include mutual benefit, reciprocity and complementarities, and the stipulations are grounded in bilateral agreements among states (Foster *et al.* 2009). Unlike traditional official development assistance, Chinese infrastructure financing is channelled not through a development agency but through state-supported institutions such as the Exim Bank (Foster *et al.* 2009).

Influenced mainly by its own development experience and by the requests of recipient countries, Chinese aid and economic cooperation programmes emphasize infrastructure development at a time when traditional donors, including Washington and other Western countries and organizations, have downplayed these arrangements. While Western development assistance has rarely focused on infrastructure in recent times, Chinese assistance focuses on the infrastructure sector because China sees infrastructure development as a key prerequisite for mutually beneficial economic development.[8] As one analyst observes, since Africa's independence, 'there rarely has been such rapid and intense investment in African infrastructure as is going on today' (Reisen 2007: 8).

As discussed further below, Chinese assistance for infrastructure is not entirely positive for Africa's development. The Angola Mode deals typically favour the Chinese. As long as the borrowing countries have not covered their debts, their obligations to China rise. Chinese authorities may extend the length of the loans instead of writing off part of the principal. This approach means countries will have to hand over their natural resources for additional years, limiting their governments' subsequent abilities to borrow money and pursue other development opportunities. Along with steep interest payments, borrowers are largely required to use Chinese companies and technologies on the projects. Many loans and grants are tied to considerable use of Chinese inputs. For example, China may be entitled to secure reliable sources of oil from Africa and elsewhere; however, the worry is that Beijing's approach encourages oil-producing countries to mortgage their long-term future through oil-backed loans. This arrangement has adverse effect on natural resource sustainability in Africa. Thus, it is important for African counties to be wary and critical of China's extraction of natural resources through the Angola Mode mechanism.

China's practice of bundling together aid, trade and investment makes it difficult for researchers to determine their respective effects. This problem is also complicated by the lack of transparency in Chinese deals in Africa. Consequently, some analysts lump loans, investment and aid into one category, which may project an inaccurate image of Chinese influence in Africa. As Brautigam (2009) rightly points out, the amount of Chinese aid reported is often inaccurate, including the confusion of Chinese renminbi (RMB) for US dollars.

However, problems associated with China's infrastructure investment do not negate the fact that such projects are crucial and make significant contributions to infrastructure development and the broader development agenda in Africa. SDG 9 shows that investment in infrastructure and innovation are crucial drivers of economic growth and development in many countries. Investment in infrastructure such as transportation, irrigation, energy, and information and communication technology have long been recognized as crucial to achieving sustainable development and empowering communities around the world. Indeed, any growth in productivity and incomes, and improvements in health and education require an appreciable level of investment in infrastructure. Investment in transport services and infrastructure, for example, is important and indeed an enabler for achieving a number of the SDGs. Certainly, without investment in infrastructure, it is difficult to envision most African countries attaining goal 2: 'Ending hunger, achieving food security, improving nutrition, and promoting sustainable agriculture'. In parts of Africa, large quantities of produce including fruits and vegetable are lost annually due to lack of reliable transportation from rural farms to markets.[9]

Similarly, adequate investment in transport is key for the achievement of SDG 3: ensuring healthy lives and promoting well-being for all at all ages. For example, in the area of maternal mortality, research shows that referral and transport strategies, together with other interventions, can contribute close to an 80 per cent reduction in maternal mortality.[10] In Uganda, an integration of transport initiatives into maternal health programmes country-wide significantly increased hospital or institutional deliveries.[11]

The importance of transport infrastructure in achieving the SDGs goes beyond health and agriculture. In order to ensure inclusive and equitable quality education and promote lifelong learning opportunities for all (goal 4), children and teachers need to get to school. To achieve gender equality and empower all women and girls (goal 5), and promote sustained, inclusive and sustainable economic growth, full and productive employment and decent work for all (goal 8), citizens need to be able to travel safely. It is against this backdrop of increasing importance of infrastructure development that many African governments, including Ghana, have welcomed China's new role as a partner and a source of infrastructure finance.

Atuabo Gas project and Chinese infrastructure development in Ghana: an overview

Over the past decade, China's infrastructure funding and projects are considered to be critical to the success of governments in Ghana (Aidoo 2010; Amoah 2014). Ghana has more than an estimated US$2 billion financing gap for necessary infrastructure (Foster and Pushak 2011). To overcome this infrastructural shortfall, Ghana has relied on China for financing roads, energy and telecommunication infrastructure, which have been largely neglected by Ghana's traditional partners in recent times. As in most African countries, Ghana has long been battling the problem of supply of consistent energy. An inconsistent electricity supply not only affects the domestic or household level, but has led to a drastic scale back and even shut down of large industrial operations over the last several years.

While unreliable access to electricity is not new (Ghana suffered energy crises in 1983, 1998 and 2006/7), the recent energy crisis has taken on a persistent pattern unknown in previous years (Rupp 2013: 106). The nation has attempted to boost its supply of energy over the past few years by considering other sources of energy, yet as far back as the mid-1990s Ghana's consumption of electricity outstripped supply as a result of the increase in consumption and the ambitious National Electrification Programme, which aimed to bring electricity to rural communities.[12] The demand for power is now estimated to be growing in excess of 10 per cent per annum with the electricity supply gap in Ghana oscillating between 300 and 600 MW.[13] This shortage and the resulting electricity fluctuations are detrimental to businesses, individuals and the nation as a whole.

Ghana has relied principally on hydroelectricity. However, this dictates that a consistent power supply depends on availability of rainwater to fuel hydro-dams, such as the Akosombo, Kpong and the recently completed Bui Dam. Due to low rainfall in the catchment area of the Volta River in recent years, the water level of all three dams, especially the Akosombo reservoir, has fallen critically. This scarcity has led to attempts to look for other sources of power such as solar, wind, tidal wave and biomass, as well as gas fired thermal power following the oil discovery in 2007 in Ghana. All of these developments have made it even more crucial for the Ghanaian government to target prospective partners interested in such sectors of Ghana's economy. In terms of Ghana's reliance on China for its energy infrastructure needs, the Atuabo Gas project is notable for its scope and as an illustration of China's unique approach to development financing.[14]

Following Ghana's discovery of oil in commercial quantities in 2007 at the Jubilee Field and subsequent production of oil, then President Atta Mills commissioned a task force to review and make recommendations on how best to deploy Ghana's oil and gas resources for national development.[15] The task force recommended an evacuation and treatment of associated gas from the Jubilee Field production. This led to the creation of the Ghana Gas Company that was assigned the responsibility 'to build, own and operate infrastructure required for the gathering, processing, transporting and marketing of natural gas resources.'[16] Ghana Gas also recommended the development of gas processing infrastructure projects in Atuabo, Domunli and Esiama in the Ellembelle and the Jomoro districts in Ghana's Western Region.

The Atuabo Gas project located on the coast of Western Ghana is part of the Western Corridor Gas Infrastructure Project of the Government of Ghana. In 2010, Ghana's former President Mills led a business delegation to China to finalize negotiation for a US$3 billion loan facility to Ghana. This loan facility is dedicated to the Western Corridor Gas Infrastructure Development Project for the construction or rehabilitation of roads, ports, and oil and gas processing. Out of that amount, US$1 billion was allocated for the gas processing infrastructure projects at Atuabo, Domunli and Esiama. The facility was secured from the Chinese Development Bank (CDB) on a non-concessional basis through Ghana's Ministry of Finance and Economic Planning. The Government of Ghana raised 15 per cent of the total amount while the CDB funds the remaining 85 per cent.[17] The loan is to be paid at LIBOR (London Interbank Offered Rate) plus 2.95 per cent with an upfront fee of 0.2 per cent and commitment fees of 1 per cent per year.

The whole US$850 million (part of the US$3 billion loan) investment programme of Ghana Gas is collateralized against Ghana's share of crude oil from the Jubilee Field.[18] Ghana National Petroleum Company and UNIPEC, a subsidiary of Sinopec and China's largest international trading company, signed a commercial agreement that committed Ghana to supply crude oil to China to repay the US$3 billion loan. Under the agreement, UNIPEC has secured an off-taker contract to lift Ghana's share of crude from the Jubilee Field, in which Ghana is committed to supply about 13,000 barrels of oil daily for 15.5 years to pay the US$3 billion loan. The Ghanaian Parliament gave its assent to the agreement in February 2012 following a long and heated debate between the majority (National Democratic Congress), which was in support of the deal, and the minority (led by the New Patriotic Party), which felt that the commercial agreement was exploitive and not in Ghana's best long-term interests.

The controversies surround Ghana's government failing to meet its part of the bargain.[19] This failure is compounded by the fact that the agreement anticipates that 60 per cent of the value of contracts involved in the gas project will go to Chinese vendors. Many observers, including from civil society organizations such as the Danquah Institute, which believed that the Chinese deal was not value for money, noted this one-sided allocation of future value.[20] Others also suggest the prices of the individual projects were forecast in deceptively broad terms so that when the deals are finalized, the ordinary Ghanaian will not be able to determine whether the arrangements are value for money or even where the budgeted money actually goes (Mohan 2015). There are also issues concerning the country's level of national debt, which has increased exponentially from US$8 billion to around US$20 billion under the National Democratic Congress government since it took power in 2008 (Mohan 2015).

The Atuabo Plant: benefits for Ghana and China

The Ghana government has pursued this project against all the criticisms highlighted above because of the perceived strategic importance of the project to the national energy independence. The biggest expectation of the plant is that the gas facility will help to close the gap between electricity supply and demand in Ghana. Gas from Atuabo will feed the Volta River Authority's Aboadze thermal plant, offering a more stable and lower-cost source of supply. Also, the reduced oil import burden is important to the Ghanaian government, given its rising debt load and heavy budget deficit.[21] In addition to supplying gas to the Aboadze thermal plant, the plant will also produce liquefied petroleum gas (LPG) for domestic use.[22] Currently, all of Ghana's LPG is produced at the Tema Oil Refinery, whose capacity is around 1,500 barrels per day but output is significantly lower.[23] Besides power generation, the plant will create employment opportunities for Ghanaian nationals, especially those training in the oil and gas sector (Darkwah 2013). Other benefits include the creation of new infrastructure to support a vibrant petroleum and petrochemical industry and provide a new economic growth sector for Ghana, starting with the Western Region.[24]

For China, this project presents a win-win situation: China can ensure that the commercial loan is repaid, obtains the much-needed oil and establishes contracts for its construction and procurement firms. The US$3 billion CDB loan to Ghana for the gas infrastructure made it possible for at least three Chinese firms to be involved in Ghana's nascent oil and gas sector. As part of the Master Facility Agreement, Sinopec, the lead contractor, secured the contract to construct the gas plant under a US$850 million subsidiary agreement. Second, SAF Petroleum Investments, a subsidiary of Sinopec, procures items required for the gas project and resells them to Sinopec. Third, UNIPEC is another subsidiary of Sinopec and secured an off-taker contract to extract Ghana's share of crude from the Jubilee Field.

China's investment in Ghana's gas project allows Beijing to secure entry into Ghana's new oil industry and bolster its energy repertoire in Ghana. Yet, there are several curious and perhaps attractive aspects about China's involvement in the Ghana oil and gas sector: the nature of the approach, terms of commitment and the tools China used to develop and leverage its relations. While Ghana's connection and ties with traditional European and American partners are intact, Chinese assistance is on the increase partly because China offers loans and development assistance in sectors that need revamping. Increasing cooperation between Ghana and China, and more generally between China and African nations under the framework of SSC, comes at the back of a mixed record of involvement of traditional partners in Africa's economy. After decades of Western aid and investment provided under conditions that are often viewed by policy-makers as paternalistic, many Ghanaian leaders are attracted to China's approach to economic development, although Chinese assistance is not without economic conditionalities. Specifically, what are the implications of the new and complex development landscape for African governments? What does China's approach to development cooperation mean for Africa's development and the achievement of the SDGs?

Implications of China's approach to infrastructure development

As seen in the case of the Atuabo Gas project, China's approach to development financing in Africa differs from those of traditional bilateral and multilateral donors. First, China increasingly favours a deal structure now called the Angola Mode or 'resources for infrastructure' system in which the borrowing country repays the infrastructure development loan through natural resources. With this arrangement, the funds for the infrastructure are not directly transferred to the government (as the case of the Atuabo Gas plant project shows). Instead, China signs a framework agreement with the government covering a specific programme of infrastructure investment (Brautigam 2009; Foster *et al.* 2009). The government of the beneficiary country awards a Chinese contractor to undertake infrastructure works (determined by the receiving government), supported by a credit from China Exim Bank. Repayment of the loan is in the form of commodity provided to China.

This commodity-backed loan has a long history on the African continent (Azarya and Chazan 1987: 117, 127). However, it seems China has found a common economic language with African states in their negotiation over resource-backed loans. Evidently, while Western countries and companies will normally expect hard currency in return for their investments or loans (SieberGasser 2011; Teunissen 2005), this deal structure shows that China is happy to accept 'innovative' ways of payment from their African counterparts. The Angola Mode relates to China's interest in natural resource supply from Africa, and at the same time meets African interests in access to finance and infrastructure development. This exchange method allows countries with resources but limited credit worthiness to use their natural resources for the development of infrastructure assets.

While commodity-backed loans may be convenient for resource-rich African countries, any global fall in commodity prices would show that such arrangements come with a high-degree of volatility and social cost. Considering the huge energy and infrastructure gap in most African countries, Chinese finance in areas such as hydropower and coal are very welcome. However, such investments are also exposed to climate and social risks. Indeed, 'the vast majority of the energy finance provided by Chinese development banks is in the fossil fuel sector – both in terms of extraction/refining and in power generation'.[25] Additionally, 'Chinese financial commitments in renewable energy are the smallest when compared to the MDBs [Multilateral Development Banks]' in the developing world, providing 'just one per cent of its power generation portfolio towards renewable energy sources outside of the hydropower sector' whereas 'the MDBs invest 27 per cent on non-hydro renewable energy'.[26] Whereas China's modest investment in wind power projects in countries such as Ethiopia and solar power in the Sudan are commendable, there is enormous potential for China's development banks to diversify into these types of renewable energy investments across Africa. Without such diversification, the commitment under the SDG framework to steer public finance towards energy and infrastructure in a manner that is environmentally sustainable and socially inclusive will not be realized in Africa.

Second, China's joint state-business approach to project funding in Africa has implications for the ability of the receiving country to determine how to utilize the funding. Since the Chinese government has close relationships with many Chinese companies, Beijing provides aid and then requires the funds to be spent on specified Chinese contractors. This arrangement results in the receiving government often being side-lined or forced to deal with new partners, which results in lack of local control. In the case of Ghana, the sole source negotiation aspect of the loan arrangement circumvents the 2003 Public Procurement Act. Additionally, despite a Local Content Bill being debated in Ghana's Parliament targeting 90 per cent local content in the petroleum industry by year 2020, the Ghanaian negotiators accepted 60 per cent of contracts going to Chinese vendors in the Master Facility Agreement regarding the gas project. Also, cheap credits from the Chinese government allow Chinese companies to underbid their competitors and engage in possible collusion. This criticism unfolds against the political backdrop that the donor community has raised concerns about the lack of transparency on the loans China has provided and also missing provisions for addressing aid effectiveness. Also, some charge that China is only focused on building African infrastructure with little attention to the institutional and operational considerations; and it has refused to adopt the environmental and social safeguard standards adopted by others, such as the World Bank.[27]

Concerns about Chinese development assistance and the Angola Mode financing structure reveal that China's intervention in Africa present real challenges. However, China's approach suggests that it is charting a different path in relation to development cooperation and assistance to African countries. Influenced mainly by its own experience of development, its needs and those of recipient African countries, the Chinese government shows innovative understanding and practices of development. The mixed-package financing mode of commercial and concessional loans, and the so-called no-strings policy regarding political and economic governance are all in sharp contrast to the practice of the countries of the traditional development partners in the global North (Davies 2008; Grimm *et al.* 2011; Hensengerth 2013; Rotberg 2008).

The contribution of infrastructural development to broader economic and social development, particularly in Africa, is now widely acknowledged (Amoah 2014; Foster *et al.* 2009). China's focus on infrastructural development in Africa, which includes the construction of hydroelectric dams, roads, bridges, schools, hospitals and health centres, contributes to improving the well-being of some people in Africa.[28] Also, the involvement of Chinese multinational companies in Africa means that there is the potential for more job creation and access to cheaper goods and services as well as the possibility of technology transfer.

However, there are several challenges that need to be resolved in order for the aforementioned benefits to be fully realized in Africa. The developmental benefits of Chinese engagement in Africa will require responsible African agency. African governments need to, as a matter of urgency, establish and enforce adequate regulatory frameworks to ensure transparency in decision-making and the implementation of environmental and social safeguard policies, to encourage the transfer of skills and technology, and to require foreign actors to use local labour and materials. These broad regulations should be applied to all investors, whether from China or any other development partner. Ghana, like many other African countries, has many development partners. China's increased involvement in Ghana is encouraging other nations to step up their role in Ghana (Harrison 2009). This may bode well for Ghana's development and it seems to welcome this 'competition' between external partners that could result in more development assistance.[29]

Yet, because of the infrastructure challenge in Ghana and China's assistance in that sector, Ghana seems desperate to take anything from China.[30] Just because China is assisting with badly needed infrastructure does not mean Ghana and for that matter any African country should slide into the danger of allowing China to have too much power and control in the national economy. Ghana and African states should not be the pawn of any external world power.

While the 'China option' and China's development intervention may not necessarily be only positive, it certainly may reduce the developmental dominance of Western actors in Africa and bolster the negotiating position held by African governments. Yet Ghana and African countries in general need to be clear about the fact that as they continue to be raw material producing countries, changing the destination of the export of those raw materials does not necessarily change the basic fact about the structure of their economies, which rely on non-renewable natural resources and are driven by raw material production. China becoming the 'new' partner in town, or the destination of preference for the exports of African raw materials or the source of development financing, does not change the reality about the African economy.

The fundamental nature of the African economy requires strategic realignment and diversification if African countries are to bring prosperity to the masses of their people and achieve the SDG targets. That involves moving away from raw material producing economies to industrializing value adding economies and diversifying economies beyond a narrow reliance on natural resources so as to reduce the extent of Africa's dependence on external powers. If Ghana and all African countries commit to an independent path to development, Chinese, American, French, Japanese, British and other investments and cooperation must be welcomed only when they align with or are consistent with the fundamental goals of their economic transformation strategies. Any investment or engagement that digresses from this economic goal should be resisted. In this vein, the question that needs to be asked should no longer be about what the intentions or practices of the Chinese or any other foreign actors are in Africa. The question should be about what Africans are doing in their engagement with external actors.

Conclusion

This chapter examined the potential of SSC cooperation mechanisms for the achievement of the SDGs on the African continent. It focused on China's infrastructure development practices in Ghana to show how recent Chinese investment in Ghana has targeted Ghana's underdeveloped sector, the energy infrastructure, making China an important partner in Ghana's infrastructure development effort.

The chapter also probed into the modalities through which China offers its development assistance to Ghana. Similar to its engagement across Africa,

Chinese development assistance to Ghana is based on an integrated system that bundles aid, trade and investment fuelled by infrastructure financing through commodity-backed loans. I argued that this mode of financing infrastructure development was used to build the Atuabo Gas project in Ghana and is appealing to Ghanaian policy-makers partly because it helps to bridge its energy infrastructure gap, but has some adverse implications on Ghana's development, particularly on the management of its new oil and gas industry and debt sustainability.

China's recent engagement in Ghana and across Africa presents both opportunities and threats. While Chinese assistance is not without conditionalities, its investment in the economic infrastructure is very attractive to African countries not least because investment in infrastructure is an important enabler for achieving a number of the SDGs. However, the concern is that the 'age of choice' where African countries have 'new' options for financing development besides the traditional Development Assistance Committee (DAC) donor may actually lead to diversified dependency (Greenhill *et al.* 2013). Diversified dependency or 'dependency redux' is a situation where reliance on the new emerging powers such as China is simply reproducing anew a state of underdevelopment in Africa (Taylor 2014). While the jury may still be out on this as Africa–China relations are fluid and ever changing, however, judging from ongoing dynamics, the outcome of China's developmental impact in Africa may lead to some form of dependency (or interdependency) in some countries and sectors depending on the host country's capacity and willingness to engage the Chinese on their terms. This potential differential outcome suggests that China's contribution to the achievement of the SDGs and its impact in any African state will be a reflection of the African country in question: where there is the capacity, commitment and willingness to engage the Chinese for mutual benefits, the results will be more or less beneficial to the host African country. Hence, the agency of African actors is very critical for the realization of any positive benefits from Chinese intervention across Africa. The call, therefore, is for African countries to ensure that they engage China strategically and require Beijing to provide financing within a framework consistent with each country's long-term strategic development plans, including the SDGs.

Notes

1 The US$200 million African Union (AU) new headquarters in Addis Ababa inaugurated in 2012, was fully financed and built by China as a gift to the AU and is symbolic of China's new interest and engagement in Africa's infrastructure.
2 This chapter draws on a broader study on the role of African agency in Africa–China relations (see Odoom 2016).
3 The term 'South' here is a political term, not to be understood geographically. Undoubtedly, China is part of the northern hemisphere; however, it shares some features of a developing country, such as still considerable levels of absolute poverty and substantial structural shortcomings in its economy.

4 The Bandung conference was attended by 29 states. The African nations attending were Egypt, Ethiopia, Gold Coast (Ghana), Liberia, Libya and Sudan.

5 'The West' or 'Western' is a somewhat elusive term, including European and North American, but also some Asian (Japan, South Korea) and Pacific states (Australia, New Zealand). For the purposes of this study and with regard to development cooperation, it is defined here to mean those states organized in the Organisation for Economic Co-operation and Development (OECD), and specifically those in the OECD's Development Assistance Committee (DAC).

6 This section borrows substantially from Isaac Odoom (2015) 'Dam in, Cocoa out; Pipes in, Oil out: China's engagement in Ghana's Energy sector', *Journal of Asian and African Studies*, pp. 1–23.

7 This is a term that is gaining currency among China–African scholars. It loosely describe a situation where African countries use oil or other natural resources as collateral to receive large-scale infrastructure projects from China or Chinese companies. It is also commonly referred to as the 'Angola Model' or 'Angola Mode' to signify its supposed emergence with Angola and China Exim Bank loan arrangements (see Corkin 2013).

8 Interview with Chinese academic, Peking University, Beijing 28 March 2014.

9 See World Bank Report, 'Agriculture for Development' (2008). Available at: siteresources.worldbank.org/INTWDR2008/Resources/WDR_00_book.pdf (accessed 26 April 2017).

10 See Hussein, Kanguru, Astin and Munjanja (2012) *PLoS Medicine*. Available at www.journals.plos.org/plosmedicine/article/file?id=10.1371/journal.pmed.1001264&type=printable (accessed 26 April 2017).

11 See Saving Mothers: Giving Life (2013). Available at: www.savingmothersgivinglife.org/docs/SMGL_Annual_Report_2013.pdf (accessed 26 April 2017).

12 According to Ghana's former President Mahama (during his 2015 State of the Nation Address to Parliament) access to electricity in Ghana is 76 per cent and ranked 2nd only to South Africa in sub-Saharan Africa. See 'Ghana News – Full audio: State of the Nation Address'. Available at www.myjoyonline.com/news/2015/February-26th/full-audio-state-of-the-nation-address.php (accessed 26 February 2015). For details about the National Electrification programme see 'Guide to Electric Power in Ghana' 2005.

13 See Myjoyonline: Ghana News – Full audio: State of the Nation Address. Available at www.myjoyonline.com/news/2015/February-26th/full-audio-state-of-the-nation-address.php (accessed 26 February 2015).

14 This case study draws on: Isaac Odoom (2015).

15 Interview with Ghana Gas official in Accra, Ghana, September, 2012.

16 See, 'Project Background' Ghana Gas Company website. Available at ghanagas.com.gh/the-project/background/ (accessed 24 February 2015).

17 See, 'Finance plan' Ghana Gas Company. Available at www.ghanagas.com.gh/the-project/financing-plan/ (accessed 25 February 2015).

18 In July 2014, in a rather surprising twist to the saga of the US$3 billion CDB loan, Ghana government announced a proposal to take only $1.5 billion instead of the $3 billion as originally signed.

19 Interview with Franklin Cudjoe, CEO IMANI (Policy Think Tank). Accra, August 2012.

20 Interview with Gabby Otchere-Darko, Director of Danquah Institute Accra, August 2012.

21 *Ibid.*

22 See 'Benefits' Ghana Gas Company. Available at ghanagas.com.gh/the-project/benefits/ (accessed 10 March 2015).

23 See 'Atuabo Gas project start-up will boost Ghana's energy sector', BMI Research (18 November 2014). Available at www.businessmonitor.com/news-and-views/atuabo-gas-project-start-up-will-boost-ghanas-energy-sector#sthash.iFYxPaIT.dpuf (accessed March 10, 2015).
24 See 'Benefits' Ghana Gas Company. Available at www.ghanagas.com.gh/the-project/benefits/ (accessed 10 March 2015).
25 See Gallagher *et al.* (2016: 21). Available at www.bu.edu/pardeeschool/files/2016/05/Fueling-Growth.FINAL_.version.pdf
26 *Ibid.*, p 16.
27 See Bosshard (2008) for a critique of Chinese investments in Africa.
28 Interview with Ghana government official Accra, August 2012.
29 Interview with Ghana government official Accra, August 2012.
30 Interview with Ghanaian academic, Accra, September 2012.

References

Aidoo, R. (2010) China-Ghana Engagement: An Alternative Economic Liberalization in Sub-Saharan Africa. Unpublished PhD Dissertation: Miami University, USA.

Alden, C. (2005) China in Africa, *Survival*, 47 (3): 147–64.

Alden, C. and Large, D. (2010) China's Exceptionalism in Africa: from Rhetorical to Substantive Difference? South African Institute of International Affairs: University of the Witwatersrand, Johannesburg.

Alden, C., Morphet, S. and Vieira, M. A. (2010) *The South in World Politics*. New York: Palgrave Macmillan

Amanor, K. and Chichava, S. (2016) South–South cooperation, agribusiness, and African agricultural development: Brazil and China in Ghana and Mozambique, *World Development*, 81, 13–23.

Amoah, L. G. A. (2014) China, architecture and Ghana's spaces: concrete signs of a soft Chinese imperium? *Journal of Asian and African Studies*, 49 (4): 1–18.

Andrews, N., Khalema, N. E. and Assié-Lumumba, N. T. (2015) (eds.) *Millennium Development Goals (MDGs) in Retrospect: Africa's Development Beyond 2015*. Cham: Springer.

Aurégan, X. (2016) The Millennium Development Goals and Chinese involvement in French-speaking West Africa: which contributions for which issues? *African Geographical Review*, doi: 10.1080/19376812.2016.1171155.

Azarya, V. and Chazan, N. (1987) Disengagement from the state in Africa: reflections on the experience of Ghana and Guinea, *Comparative Studies in Society and History*, 29 (1): 106–131.

Bhabha, H. (1994) *The Location of Culture*. London: Routledge.

Bosshard, P. (2007) China's role in financing African infrastructure, *International Rivers Network*. Available at: www.internationalrivers.org/sites/default/files/attached-files/chinaeximbankafrica.pdf (accessed 3 May 2017)

———. (2008) *China's Environmental Footprint in China*. SAIIA China in Africa Policy Briefing 508, April. Available at www.internationalrivers.org/files/attached-files/saiia_policy_briefing_508.pdf (accessed 26 April 2017).

Brautigam, D. (2009) *The Dragon's Gift: The Real Story of China in Africa*. Oxford: Oxford University Press.

———. (2011) China in Africa: What Western Donors Can Learn, Norfund. Available at www.norfund.no/getfile.php/Documents/Homepage/Reports%20and%20presentations/Studies%20for%20Norfund/Norfund_China_in_Africa.pdf (accessed 26 April 2017).

Breslin, S. (2005) China and the political economy of global engagement. In R. Stubbs and G. R. D. Underhill (eds) *Political Economy and the Changing Global Order.* Oxford: Oxford University Press.

———. (2007) *China in the Global Political Economy.* London: Palgrave Macmillan.

Chaturvedi, S., Fues, T. and Sidiropoulos, E. (eds) (2012) *Development Co-operation and Emerging Powers – New Partners or Old Patterns?* London: Zed Books.

Chen, (2010) *Chinese Participation in Infrastructure Development in Africa: Roles and Impacts.* The Foundation for Growth and Poverty Reduction, China-DAC Study Group, International Poverty Reduction Centre in China (IPRCC) and OECD DAC, EU-China policy dialogues support facility, Working Paper, pp. 8–19.

China Africa Policy (2006) Ministry of Foreign Affairs of the People's Republic of China. Available at www.focac.org/eng/zt/zgdfzzcwj/t230479.htm (accessed 3 May 2017).

Chun, Z. (2015) Shaping China-Africa Co-operation on Post-2015 Agenda. *The China Monitor* Special edition: FOCAC VI: African initiatives toward a sustainable Chinese relationship, Centre for Chinese Studies, Stellenbosch, South Africa.

Cohn, T. H. (2012) *Global Political Economy: Theory and Practice.* Toronto: Pearson Education Inc.

Corkin, M. L. (2013) *Uncovering African Agency: Angola's Management of China's credit Lines.* Farnham: Ashgate.

D'Alessandro, C. and Zulu, L. E. (2016) From the Millennium Development Goals (MDGs) to the Sustainable Development Goals (SDGs): Africa in the post-2015 development agenda. A geographical perspective, *African Geographical Review*, doi: 10.1080/19376812.2016.1253490

Darkwah, A. (2013) Keeping hope alive: an analysis of training opportunities for Ghanaian youth in the emerging oil and gas industry, *International Development Planning Review*, 35, 120–34.

Davies, M. (2008) How China Delivers Development Assistant to Africa. Centre for Chinese Studies, University of Stellenbosch, February 2008.

DeHart, M. (2012) Remodelling the global development landscape: the China model and South–South cooperation in Latin America, *Third World Quarterly*, 33 (7), 1359–75.

Foster, V. and Pushak, N. (2011) *Ghana's infrastructure: a continental perspective.* World Bank Policy Research Working Paper Series. Washington, DC: World Bank.

Foster, V., Butterfield, W., Chen, C. and Pushak, N. (2009) *Building Bridges: China's Growing Role as Infrastructure Financier for sub-Saharan Africa.* World Bank/PPIAF, Trends and Policy Options No. 5, Washington, DC: World Bank. Available at www.openknowledge.worldbank.org/bitstream/handle/10986/2614/480910PUB0Buil101OFFICIAL0USE0ONLY1.pdf (accessed 26 April 2017).

French, H. W. (2014) *China's second continent: How a million migrants are building a new empire in Africa.* New York: Vintage.

GOV (2010) China-Africa Economic and Trade Cooperation. Information Office, State Council of the People's Republic of China. Available at english.gov.cn/official/2010–12/23/content_1771603.htm (accessed 1 November 2013).

Greenhill, R., Prizzon, A. and Rogerson, A. (2013) The Age of Choice: Developing Countries in the New Aid Landscape. Synthesis Report. London: ODI.

Grimm, S. (2015) Placing FOCAC in its South-South Co-operation narrative. *The China Monitor*, Special edition: FOCAC VI: African initiatives toward a sustainable Chinese relationship. Centre for Chinese Studies: University of Stellenbosch.

Grimm, S., Rank, R., McDonald, M. and Schickerling, E. (2011) *Transparency of Chinese Aid: An analysis of the published information on Chinese external financial flows*. Publish What You Fund and Centre for Chinese Studies. Stellenbosch: Stellenbosch University.

Grimm, S. and Zhang, C. (2013) South-South Cooperation and the MDGs: Preparing for a post-2015 setting. Background paper to the European Report on Development, Brussels: EU.

Habiyaremye, A. (2013) 'Angola mode' trade deals and the awakening of African lion economies, *African Development Review*, 25 (4): 636–47.

Harrison J. E. K. (2009) Toward sustainable development in Ghana: the China factor. In S. T. Freeman (ed.) *China, Africa and the African Diaspora: Perspectives.* Washington, DC: Aasbea, pp. 212–16.

He, W. (2007) The balancing act of China's Africa policy, *China Security*, 3 (3).

Hensengerth, O. (2013) Chinese hydropower companies and environmental norms in countries of the global South: the involvement of Sinohydro in Ghana's Bui Dam. *Environment, Development and Sustainability*, 15 (2): 285–300.

Jiang. W. (2009) Fueling the dragon: China's rise and its energy and resources extraction in Africa, *The China Quarterly*, 199 (September): 585–609.

Manji, F. and Marks, S. (eds) (2007) *African Perspectives on China in Africa.* Cape Town: Fahamu and Pambzuka.

Mawdsley, E. (2007) China and Africa: Emerging Challenges to the Geographies of Power, *Geography Compass*, 1 (3): 405–21.

Melville, C. and Owen, O. (2005) China and Africa: A New Era of 'South-South' Cooperation, *Open Democracy*, 8 July.

Mohan, G. (2015) Queuing up for Africa: the geoeconomics of Africa's growth and the politics of African agency, *International Development Planning Review*, 37 (1): 45–52.

Mohan, G, and Power, M. (2011) China and the geo-political imagination of African 'development'. In C. Dent (ed.) *China-Africa Development Relations.* New York: Routledge.

Moyo, D. (2009) *Dead aid: why aid is not working and how there is a better way for Africa.* New York: Farrar, Straus & Giroux.

Odoom, I. (2015) Dam in, cocoa out; pipes in, oil out: China's engagement in Ghana's energy sector, *Journal of Asian and African Studies*, First Published October 26, 2015 10.1177/0021909615599419.

———. (2016) *Beyond Fuelling the Dragon: Locating African Agency in Africa-China Relations*. Unpublished Doctoral Dissertation. Edmonton, Canada: University of Alberta.

Pérez, J. Chaturvedi, S., Sidoropoulos, E., and Fues, T. (2014) (eds) *Institutional Architecture and Development: Responses from Emerging Powers*. Johannesburg: Jacana Media.

Power, M., Mohan, G. and Tan-Mullins, M. (2012) *China's Resource Diplomacy in Africa: Powering Development?* London: Palgrave Macmillan.

Reisen, H. (2007) Is China Actually Helping Improve Debt Sustainability in Africa? Paper presented at Emerging Powers in Global Governance Conference, Paris.

Rotberg, R. (ed.) (2008) *China into Africa: Trade, Aid, and Influence.* Washington, DC: Brookings.

Rupp, S. (2013) Ghana, China, and the Politics of Energy, *African Studies Review*, 56 (1): 103–30.

Sautman, B. V. (2006) *Friends and Interests: China's Distinctive Links with Africa.* Center on China's Transnational Relation Working Paper No. 12 Hong Kong: The Hong Kong University of Science and Technology.

Shaw, T. M. (1979) The semi-periphery in Africa and Latin America: Sub-imperialism and semi-industrialism, *Review of Black Political Economy*, 9 (4): 341–58.

Shaw, T. M. (2010) Can the BRICs become a bloc? The emerging politics of the emerging powers: The BRICs and the global South, *China Monitor* 52, 4–6.

SieberGasser, C. (2011) *The Legal Character of Sino-African Tied Aid: Cunning Fox or Wise Dragon?* Working Paper No 2011/47, May. NCCR Trade Regulation.

Six, C. (2009) The rise of postcolonial states as donors: a challenge to the development paradigm? *Third World Quarterly*, 30 (6): 1103–21.

Taylor, I. (2009) *China's New Role in Africa.* Boulder, CO: Lynne Rienner.

———. (2010) *The International Relations of Sub-Saharan Africa.* London: Continuum.

———. (2014) *Africa Rising? BRICS – Diversifying Dependency*. Oxford: James Currey.

Tejasvi, A. (2007) *South-South Capacity Development: The Way to Grow?* Washington, DC.: World Bank.

Teunissen, J. J. (2005) Clichés, realities and policy challenges of Africa: by way of introduction. In J. J. Teunissen and A. Akkerman (eds) *Africa in the World Economy: The National, Regional and International Challenges*. The Hague: Fondad, pp. 1-22.

Tull, D. M. (2009) China's engagement in Africa: scope, significance, and consequences. In J. W. Harbeson and D. Rothchild (eds) *Africa in World Politics: Reforming Political Order*. Boulder, CO: Westview Press.

United Nations (UN) General Assembly (2009) Promotion of South-South Cooperation for Development: A Thirty-Year Perspective. Report of the Secretary-General, 27 October 2009 (A/64/504).

UNCTAD (2009) *Economic Development in Africa: Strengthening Regional Economic Integration in Africa's Development*. Geneva: United Nations Conference on Trade and Development.

———. (2010) *Economic Development in Africa Report 2010: South-South Cooperation: Africa and the New Forms of Development Partnership*. Geneva: United Nations Conference on Trade and Development.

United Nations Development Programme (UNDP) (2015) The Millennium Development Goals Report 2015. New York: UNDP.

Vickers, B. (2012) Towards a new aid paradigm: South Africa as an African development partner, *Cambridge Review of International Affairs*, 25 (4): 535–56.

Wallerstein, I. (1974) *Semi-Peripheral Countries and The Contemporary World Crisis.* New York: Academic Press.

Wallerstein, I. (1976) *The Modern World-System: Capitalist Agriculture and the Origins of the European World-Economy in the Sixteenth Century*. New York: Academic Press

Wallerstein, I. (1997) *The Capitalist World Economy*. New York: Cambridge University Press.

6 Natural resource governance and sustainable development in Africa

Are we there yet?

Korbla P. Puplampu and Kobena T. Hanson

Introduction and problem

There is an increasing recognition of the role of natural resources in Africa's development possibilities. From the global, continental, to regional and national levels, there has been a consistent effort to shore up the policy and institutional framework required for natural resource governance and sustainable development in the sub-region (ACBF 2013; Hanson *et al.* 2014; NEPAD 2001, 2003; UNDP 2003). The UNDP (2003), within the framework of the UN-sponsored Millennium Development Goals (MDGs), serves as a useful point of departure. Of the eight main goals, MDG 7 focused on environmental sustainability. Environmental sustainability, particularly the sustainable management of natural resources undergird MDG 1 which seeks to alleviate poverty and childhood mortality – the focus of MDG 4 (IFPRI 2016; Ochola *et al.* 2010; UNEP 2007). Revenue from natural resources would support public health initiatives like nutrition campaigns, immunization and vaccination centres that would eventually decrease the likelihood of childhood diseases and mortality. The African Union, the continental political body, launched the NEPAD (2003) *Action Plan for the Environment Initiative* and *Africa's Capacity Development Strategic Framework* (AU and NEPAD 2010) and both documents aimed at a better understanding of the role of natural resources in environmental stewardship and the region's development agenda.

The global and continental initiatives notwithstanding, historicizing the role of natural resources, specifically oil and gas, in the development process reveals an ambiguous relationship. This ambiguity is best captured by Karl's (1997) influential study, *The Paradox of Plenty*, leading to the resource 'curse' debate (Arthur 2012; Dietz *et al.* 2007; Nwonwu 2016; Okpanachi and Andrews 2012; Omojola 2012; Ross 2008, Shaxson 2008; Stevens and Dietsche 2008; Stiglitz 2012). One key aspect of the debate is the impact of natural resources on the larger economy, particularly the negative consequences for democratic governance and elite capture of the economic and political institutions. The role of natural resources in African development has been the focus of several studies (Alao 2007; Collier and Hoeffler 2004, 2005; Humphreys 2005; Onuoha 2016). The literature has clearly showed that oil wealth in countries such as Angola, Nigeria and Equatorial Guinea have not dramatically improved the living conditions of the citizens. While one cannot discount the value of the debate, it is also important to place it in a broader context of the complexities in the relationship between the African state and international capital mobility (Onuoha 2016).

Such a consideration is critical to better contextualize the extent to which the Sustainable Development Goals (SDGs), the new global initiative that transcends the MDGs and related continental policies and institutions, will live up to expectation (UNDP 2015). Several components of the SDGs have implications for charting a path towards a future based on principles like equality and calls for partnership. For example, SDGs 1 (end poverty), 2 (no hunger) 3 (good health and well-being), 6 (clean water and sanitation), 7 (renewable energy), 8 (good jobs and economic growth), 9 (industry, innovation and infrastructure), 13 (climate action) and 17 (partnership for global development) are contingent on natural resource governance and sustainable development Africa (Besada *et al.* 2016; Mugagga and Nabaasa 2016; Africa Progress Panel 2015).

This chapter, against the backdrop of the MDGs and SDGs, examines the relationship between natural resource governance and sustainable development in Africa. The chapter will interrogate the extent to which relevant aspects of the MDGs and SDGs align with the discourse of natural resource governance and sustainable development. Given that natural resources are often considered as public goods, but their exploration involves private capital, mostly from foreign entities, including multinational corporations, the role of natural resources in development revolve around the state. Meanwhile, the African state and its role in development, like its counterparts in a global era, has been the site of significant contestations due to or in response to forces of globalization (Onuoha 2016). The dominant neoliberal paradigm of contemporary globalization calls for a minimal state in both the economic and political spheres. As a result, the extent to which the African state can create the conducive environment for private capital investment in natural resource governance and sustainable development is a legitimate area of inquiry.

The chapter proceeds through three main sections. The first section reviews conceptual and theoretical questions on the state, natural resource governance and sustainable development. The second section will focus on selected case studies on natural resources in Africa. The final section will analyse the relationship between natural resource governance and sustainable development within the context of the MDGs and SDGs before providing some concluding remarks and policy suggestions.

The state, natural resources, governance and sustainable development: an overview

Whether the African state is conceptualized on the Marxian-inspired argument of an instrument of capital that exploits labour or the Weberian focus on bureaucratic or institutional apparatus, both the historical and contemporary African state relied on private sector involvement in the extractive natural resource industry (Elbra 2017). For example, gold was an essential part of the colonial adventure in Ghana to the extent that the British named the colony as Gold Coast until the country attained political independence and changed the name in 1957. Colonial development models in countries as diverse as Congo, Gabon, South Africa, Zambia and Zimbabwe were all sustained by mineral wealth. In the contemporary age, the Gulf of Guinea, stretching from Nigeria to Angola, has become a haven for the discovery of proven oil and gas deposits (AfDB and AU 2009; World Bank 2012: 16). Bauxite, copper, gold, tin and zinc are other minerals with significant deposits on the African continent (World Bank 2012: 15).

The colonial past nonetheless, many contemporary African countries have not been able to harness their mineral wealth for national development (Barma *et al.* 2012; UNDP 2011; World Bank 2012). Sierra Leone, Liberia and Zimbabwe have been tied to the notion of 'blood diamonds', while the oil wealth in countries such as Angola, Equatorial Guinea, Nigeria and Sudan have demonstrated how oil revenue does not necessarily translate to national development for all citizens. The result is the abysmal performance of African countries on several indicators of human development (Davis 2016; UNDP 2015). Therefore, there are no guarantees that the recent discoveries of oil in Ghana and Uganda, for example, would provide any predetermined transformation in both countries (Gelb and Majerowicz 2011; Okpanachi and Andrews 2012).

Beyond oil and gas, water, particularly in the transboundary form, is another important natural resource in Africa's development prospects (Chikozho 2014; Mugagga and Nabaasa, 2016; Muller and Wright 2016; Paisley and Henshaw 2013). There are 263 transboundary water basins worldwide which account for about 60 per cent of freshwater flow and provide support to nearly two billion people in approximately 145 nations (Paisley and Henshaw 2013: 1). Africa has 9 per cent of freshwater and 55 transboundary river basins (Chikozho 2014; Mugagga and Nabaasa 2016) and water resources in 63 river basins are shared among several countries, with countries such as Benin, Botswana, Chad, Congo, Egypt, Eritrea and Gambia depending on flow from neighbouring countries for 40 per cent to 60 per cent of their water needs (Muller and Wright 2016: 2–13). Major transboundary commissions and agreements in Africa include the Abidjan Convention, Nile River Basin, Niger River Basin, Okavango River Basin and the Senegal River Basin (International Waters Governance 2016a; Muller and Wright 2016; Paisley and Henshaw 2013; Saruchera and Lautze 2016).

Consistent with the continental initiatives in the oil and gas sector, the African Union (AU), in 2008, asked member countries to 'ensure the equitable and sustainable use, as well as promote integrated management and development, of national and shared water resources' (cited in Muller and Wright 2016: 1). As appropriately argued by the Africa Progress Panel (2015), Africa has tremendous needs for water but also has great potential in terms of underground water resources. Thus, the AU charged the African Ministers' Council on Water to deepen the potential of water resources in the region's development, liaise with regional economic communities under the auspices of the African Network of Basin Organizations (Muller and Wright 2016).

The question in the case of both oil and water, the two natural resources at the centre of this chapter, remains the capacity imperatives of the state and its institutional apparatus for harnessing natural resources for development (ACBF 2013; NEPAD 2003). For oil, the investment framework requires a climate that international capital might find attractive, but at the same time ensures that oil revenue can be maximized and utilized for the national development agenda. For water, the transboundary implications call for 'successful technical cooperation and capacity interventions' (ACBF 2013: 243). Indeed, natural resource exploration and the development process have to be sensitive to key tenets of governance and sustainability.

Governance revolves around the use of power, particularly state power, in the decision-making machinery. It is about authority, the performance of institutions, accountability, transparency and equity in the attainment of development goals. Natural resource governance seeks to examine how principles of governance are brought to bear on the exploration and utilization of natural resources for sustainable development. While the state has been the traditional site of power and vital in the discourse on governance, the contemporary world is littered with various networks on natural resources from the African Union-inspired African Mining Vision to global initiatives like Extractive Industries Transparency Initiative, and Publish What You Pay that have direct and indirect impact on governance. Consequently, the 'emerging shape of governance means that we need to stop thinking of state power as something that is indivisible and territorially exclusive' (Held *et al.* 2001: 146). The foregoing is akin to the idea of capacity building and performance as enunciated by the African Capacity Building Foundation (ACBF) which is 'the ability of people, organizations, and society as a whole to manage their affairs successfully; and that is the process by which people, organizations, and society as a whole unleash, strengthen, create, adapt, and maintain capacity over time' (ACBF 2011: 30–1). Governance is essential for any measure of sustainable development.

Sustainable development, as a concept, springs from several sources. From a governance perspective, sustainable development requires, again, a focus on the state's role in the development process. Both modernization and dependency theories on development required the state's institutional presence in exploring natural resources for the development, sometimes aided by financial assistance from multilateral institutions such as the World Bank and the International Monetary Fund (Wood 1986). This approach to harnessing the environment for national development was based on the Post-Second World War approach to development policies and the environment (Sick 2012). In this orientation, policy-makers had a blasé attitude to the impact of the environment on development, an attitude that over time changed to a more concerted effort at mitigating the role of environmental issues, at both the national and global levels, and with consideration to sustainable development.

The genesis of sustainable development can be attributed to several policy declarations, beginning with Meadows *et al.* (1972), *The Limits to Growth*. An important aspect of the study was how the relationship between population change and economic growth could impact the environment, specifically natural resources, since such resources are finite in nature. The implication is that economic collapse and environmental disaster are moving in tandem, except if society engage with and address challenges in the two areas. The second major initiative was the World Conference on Environment and Development (WCED) (1987) document *Our Common Future* which defined sustainable development as the development that 'meets the needs of the present without compromising the ability of future generations to meet their own needs' (WCED 1987: 3). Sustainable development reiterates the call for a better understanding, for instance, of the relationship between natural resources and the environment. The momentum from the above found a tangible expression in the 1992 Rio Earth Summit with its Agenda 21 (UNCED 1993) and the Rio + 20 *The Future We Want*. While most of these global environmental initiatives have not commanded or attained the expected consensus, the attempts to, at least, discuss or propose the initiatives demonstrate an awareness of the need for a policy framework to guide and inform the delicate business of harnessing the environment and natural resources for human development (Beckers 2012; Ishwaran 2012).

One essential ingredient in the ongoing policy framework is the ability of African leaders to mobilize resources for their national development and environmental action plans. This is because with the emergence of non-state actors, including both for-profit and non-profit institutions at the national and global levels, national development has become a contested site (Beaudet 2012; World Bank 2004). The contestation suggests that policy outcomes are not predetermined, but rather contingent on the complexities in the relationship between state and non-state actors and institutions. Hence, we cannot overemphasize the centrality of political leadership in creating the space for choices and decision-making, and for this study, with respect to natural resource governance in Africa (Puplampu 2014; Swatuk 2005).

Given that African countries are not the only ones with natural resources, the crucial issue is how African countries, particularly their political leaders, manage the natural resources relative to the development of their citizens. In other words, if African leaders are committed to national development via natural resources, they have to factor in the conceptual and theoretical implications of governance and sustainable development. The African state is at the anchor of both concepts, even though the state has also been the site of contestations in an era of globalization, especially in terms of its relationship to multilateral and national development institutions, multinational corporations and civil society organizations. Natural resource governance and sustainable development coalesce around how to utilize resources for national development in a sustainable manner. With transparency and accountability as the central planks in natural resource governance, sustainable development ties natural resources to national development in terms of current and future resource availability and in a manner that is long lasting and impactful.

The natural resources terrain in Africa: selected case studies

In addition to major resources in the extractive sector including oil, gas and diamonds, the natural resources regime in Africa also include water resources, fisheries and forestry. In surveying the landscape of African countries and their interaction with natural resources, the following cases and the subsequent analysis are revealing on the grounds of transboundary natural resource governance and sustainable development: Chad–Cameroon Oil Pipeline Project and Sudan Oil Project as well as the Niger River Basin Authority (NBA) and the Okavango River Basin (ORB) (ACBF 2013; Mugagga and Nabaasa 2016). Oil, a hydrocarbon, has a prominent role in any society. From politics, to economy and social relations, oil is an indispensable natural resource and that accounts for the significance of oil prices to producers, distributors and consumers worldwide.

The Chad–Cameroon Oil Pipeline and Sudan Oil projects provide valuable insights into the role of the state and the range of actors in the political economy of Africa's oil industry. The Chad–Cameroon oil pipeline project commenced following the discovery of oil in Chad, and as a landlocked country, it required an access point, such as a seaport, to transport the oil to world market. After considering several options, the project sponsors (World Bank, the Governments of Chad and Cameroon and a Consortium of USA-based ExxonMobil and Chevron; and Malaysia-based Petronas) selected a route to the Cameroon coast with the genesis of the Chad–Cameroon pipeline project in 2000 (Arbogast 2009; Gérin and Houdin 2010; Pegg 2009; Winters and Gould 2011).

The three significant actors are the Governments of Chad and Cameroon, particularly the former, the World Bank and the Consortium. With Chad under the leadership of Idriss Déby and Cameroon under its long-time leader, Paul Biya, the World Bank got involved in the financing arrangements because of the Consortium's demands. The Consortium was concerned about the investment climate in Chad, and that the World Bank's involvement would enable it to use its 'leverage to create specific policies and institutions' (Winters and Gould 2011: 233) and showcase it as a model for 'doing development' in the global South, particularly in terms of good governance and sustainable development. The agreement the Government of Chad signed with the World Bank had provisions on how much oil revenue would be available to the government and the use of such revenue, the role of civil society organizations in a watchdog capacity, and the zeal to create, nurture and develop institutional capacity. There is considerable agreement in the literature that the World

Bank's role in the project was a failure, an outcome that raises vital questions that are addressed in a subsequent section.

President Omar al-Bashir has ruled Sudan for more than two decades and was the President when the country began exporting crude oil in 1999 (Obi 2007; Idahosa 2002). While Sudan has split into North and South following the 2011 plebiscite, the analysis here precedes the break-up. However, since the oil wealth is predominantly located in South Sudan, Juma (the capital of South Sudan) and Khartoum (capital of Sudan), the two governments now have to negotiate the terms of transfer of oil to ports in Sudan, with South Sudan being landlocked like Chad. Similar to Chad, the production of oil in Sudan was made possible by several multinational companies. First, beginning with Arakis Energy, a Canadian company, that sold its shares to Talisman Energy, another Canadian mining company. Second, Talisman Energy in 2003 also sold its shares to Oil Natural Gas Corporation (ONGC) Videsh Ltd, a subsidiary of India's national oil company, in what has by then become a controversial oil project (BBC 2003; Idahosa 2002). The controversy of Talisman's investment in Sudan underscores the complex relationship among the Sudanese state, multinational corporations and civil society in both national and global levels (Axworthy 2001; Idahosa 2002; Kobrin 2004; McBride 2005).

Beyond oil, the other natural resource at the focus of this study is water. Water is the source of life, providing for the sustenance of all living organisms, from human, to plants and animals. Thus, water is 'a universal component of every living thing but more importantly of life human' (Mugagga and Nabaasa 2016: 216). In view of its significance and transboundary dimensions, discussions on water management and sustainable development loom large in the African development discourse. Two major river basins here are the Niger River Basin Authority and the Okavango River Basin. The NBA consists of seven West African countries (Benin, Burkina Faso, Côte d'Ivoire, Guinea, Mali, Niger and Nigeria) and two Central African countries (Cameroon and Chad) (Muller and Wright 2016; Andersen *et al.* 2005). In terms of geographical scope, the Niger River is the third longest in Africa, and its two main branches are reinforced by tributaries from Guinea, Côte d'Ivoire, Burkina Faso and Benin (International Waters Governance 2016b).

Most of the countries in the NBA are in the low human development category of the UNDP (2015), human development index. Thus, the river basin provides a unique opportunity for both national and regional development. Formally ratified in 1980, the NBA, with the ultimate goal of coordinating water polices of its members, seeks to gather the data for infrastructure development, transportation and any other activity that would have implications for water pollution in the region and agricultural related industries (International Waters Governance 2016b; Muller and Wright 2016). With an eye on the continental 2008 water initiative and a 'Water Charter', the NBA has been working not only with the African Union but also with external global partners and donors, including the Islamic Development Bank, the European Union, the World Bank and the UN-sponsored Global Environment Facility

(International Waters Governance 2016b). The overwhelming concern is developing the necessary capacity to collect the required data and the subsequent analysis to ensure the economic development of member states, a goal that can only be attained within a framework of regional integration that is infused with principles of environmental sustainability and mutual interests.

The Okavango River Basin includes Angola, Namibia and Botswana and the Permanent Okavango Water Basin Commission and was formally established in 1994 (International Waters Governance 2016c; Marcantonio 2016). The Okavango River has its source in the Cuito and Cubango Rivers in Angola and flows through Namibia to Botswana (International Waters Governance 2016c). The Commission, like other transboundary water initiatives, is in the business of how to advise member states on water usage with an eye on 'equitable allocation, conservation, and sustainable operation and maintenance of any waterworks in the basin; and controls [on] water pollution and aquatic weeds in the basin' (Chikozho 2014: 124).

The Commission, to better inform its decision-making process, has been working with member states, external stakeholders to deal with emerging problems like upstream-downstream challenges of water usage. Some of the main external partners include the Swedish International Development Agency (SIDA) and the UN-sponsored Global Environment Facility and the United States Agency for International Development (USAID) (International Waters Governance 2016c). The Global Environment Facility, for example, has been instrumental in the preparation of a transboundary diagnostic analysis of hydro-environment threats and the development of an action plan to 'facilitate the joint management of the Basin's water resources and to protect its aquatic ecosystems and biological diversity' (International Waters Governance 2016c). These initiatives call for high levels of cooperation and mutual trust among member states. Botswana, for example, has over 60 per cent dependency on the Okavango River and is vulnerable to upstream activities. It therefore requires transboundary cooperation to continue to benefit from the downstream activities of the river system (Muller and Wright 2016: 5).

The above overview reveals issues such as institutional capacity of both public and private actors, the role of the state and its relationship with civil society and global partnerships including international capital in a context of transparency, accountability and democracy and environmental stewardship. These themes, against the backdrop of the MDGs and SDGs with respect to governance and sustainable development in Africa, are analysed in the next section.

Natural resource governance and sustainable development: an analysis

The natural resources at the focus of this analysis, oil and water, literally cannot mix. However, they occupy a pivotal role in the African development discourse because natural resource governance and sustainable development have significant implications for addressing relevant aspects of both MDGs and SDGs. Oil revenue and harnessing the potential of transboundary water basins can make a big contribution to alleviating poverty and hunger (MDG 1 and SDG 1 and 2); provide for environmental sustainability (MDG 7), partnership for development (MDG 8 and SDG 17), good health and well-being (SDG 3), decent work and economic growth (SDG 8), industry, innovation and infrastructure (SDG 9) and climate action (SDG 13). These goals can best be attained on the basis of governance and sustainability.

The first theme for analysis is environmental sustainability and forging partnership for global development. In terms of environmental sustainability, the utilization of oil, as a finite resource, has to focus on how the seeds of oil revenue for development are sowed today with an eye on tomorrow. This main principle of sustainability was evident in the World Bank's role in the Chad–Cameroon pipeline project when Chad passed the Petroleum Resource Management Law 001 (PRML). Key aspects of the law was an escrow account in which 10 per cent of revenue would be posted to a Future Generations Fund for a post-oil Chad development regime, 80 per cent for direct development and poverty reduction expenditures, 5 per cent on the oil-producing region, with the remaining 5 per cent for discretionary spending (Gérin and Houdin 2010: 16–17; Moss and Young 2009: 10; Winters and Gould 2011: 233–4).

To shore up the governance dimension of oil revenue utilization, the PRML also called for the creation of a watchdog group (Collège de Contrôle et de Surveillance des Ressources Pétrolières [Collège]), made of up representatives of non-governmental organizations and some prominent and independent public officials, to monitor revenues and spending. It is a maxim in policy analysis to focus on what governments actually do, rather than what they intend to do. While the PRML was consistent with a natural resource governance regime and sustainable development, the Government of Chad did not live up its obligations. First, President Déby moved, for example, to exert influence over the Collège with the selection of his close associates and eventually 'had direct influence over at least six of the nine members of the Collège' (Winters and Gould 2011: 235). While the group performed creditably, it did not have any power of enforcement, depended on government for funds and was underfunded and toothless.

The second issue was the utilization of oil revenue for development, specifically the regional distribution of development projects and adherence to the letter and spirit of the escrow account (Gérin and Houdin 2010; Winters and Gould 2011). Operating in a climate of deep patronage, the distribution of development projects were pursued with a keen eye on regional identities and thus some regions did not fare well. For eastern Chad, the war situation complicated any concerted attempt at development. President Déby, in the view of the conflict situation and the desire to assume a greater control over oil revenue, initiated demands on the World Bank and, by default, the

Consortium, to renegotiate the terms of the PRML. In a series of moves, the eventual result was that the Chadian Parliament abolished the legislation on the Future Generations Fund, and did not support the Collège, which stopped its mandated work by 2007. The World Bank, unable to

> enforce the spirit or even the letter of the original agreement … quietly decided to remove itself from the oil pipeline project. In early 2008, the Bank requested that Chad repay the remaining amount due on the pipeline loan. Chad quickly complied.
>
> (Winters and Gould 2011: 239; see also Barma *et al.* 2012: 7)

To analyse the World Bank's role in Chad, one has to consider Myrdal's (1968: 896) classical concept of the 'soft' state as unable to enforce its policies and the contemporary neoliberal argument for a minimal state presence in the political and economic spheres. While it is generally assumed that the African state is weak and further weakened by globalizing imperatives, it is revealing how the Government of Chad pursued policy options directly opposed to that of the World Bank and multinational corporations. President Idriss Déby of Chad orchestrated the move for Parliament to abolish the provisions relating to the escrow account and the Future Generations Fund because the government faced a new and immediate threat of armed insurrection and other security concerns (Gérin and Houdin 2010; Winters and Gould 2011). Without discounting the role of the Chadian government in preserving social order, the basis of the unrest lay in the unfair distribution of the national development largesse in view of the oil wealth and other aspects of identity politics the President initiated in the first place. In other words following the tenets of the arrangements for the oil wealth and a deep commitment to governance even before the oil wealth would have prevented the arms insurrection in the first place, thus making it all the more critical the role of political leadership in any programme on governance and sustainable development (Puplampu 2014).

The use of oil revenue to address security concerns was also at play in the case of President Omar al-Bashir in Sudan. Talisman, a Canadian company, was implicated in providing revenue to the Sudanese state to purchase arms that sustained the war between northern and southern Sudan (McBride 2005; Matthews 2005). The question then was how to reconcile questions of human rights violations and governance with Canada's human security agenda and the behaviour of Canadian companies abroad (Axworthy 2001; Idahosa 2002; Matthews 2005). The human security agenda seeks to put 'people first and recognizes that their safety is integral to the promotion and maintenance of international peace and security' (Axworthy 2001: 20). Not surprising, civil society groups put the Canadian government's human rights credentials under intense scrutiny in terms of Talisman's activities in the Sudan. Even though the Harker Report (2000), the Canadian government-commissioned study, documented the extent to which Talisman's revenue to the Sudanese government financed the conflict between the North and the South in Sudan, the Canadian government was virtually powerless in this context. Although Talisman, similar to the World Bank in Chad, eventually left Sudan, the case lays bare the complexities of natural resource governance in terms of the relationship between African states and private foreign capital. Certainly, the state in both Chad and Sudan undermined sustainable development by scuttling provisions of natural resource governance and devoted oil revenue to the purchase of arms. Canada's democratic and human rights credentials were of no use in the Talisman case, because global capital mobility, especially in an era of globalization, does not have any allegiance to any entity beside the profit motive.

Both the NBA and the ORB demonstrate different aspects of governance and sustainable development and their significance can be better situated in a framework of regionalism, the second analytical theme (Mugagga and Nabaasa 2016; Muller and Wright 2016). This is because the 'inherent complexity of water resources management is intensified where water is shared in transboundary rivers, while approaches to regional integration must be adapted to the different dynamics of each region and each shared river' (Muller and Wright 2016: 1). Furthermore, water, as part of the commons, in a context of national and regional development and transboundary environment becomes a public good and requires appropriate levels of partnership (Hanson 2015). For example, partnership and a high level of cooperation among the riparian states is required when in view of upstream and downstream flow, one country's use of water could impact another (Chikozho 2014; Muller and Wright 2016). The problems of Egypt and other members of the Nile River Basin are a clear example and a cautionary tale of how member countries interact with the upstream and downstream of the Nile River (Paisley and Henshaw 2013). In the particular case studies under review, Botswana, as part of the ORB, has to contend with upstream problems and its water availability calls for cooperation not just with the two other ORB members, but a host of other countries who are also members of the larger Southern Africa Development Conference (Puplampu 2015).

A regional approach is even more relevant in the case of NBA, since its members straddle two regional economic communities (RECs), the Economic Community of West African States (ECOWAS) and the Community of Sahel-Saharan States (CEN-SAD) and both commissions have to cooperate at a deeper level, especially since double and multiple memberships in RECs are not problem free (Puplampu 2015). Countries with membership in two or more regional organizations are over-stretched financially and thus their contributions to the activities of RECs are unpredictable. Consequently, RECs do not have sufficient funds to support water basin commissions, which require financial resources to carry out impact studies on upstream and downstream activities; a situation that is further worsened by the fact that RECs experience organizational inertia largely because of the failure of political leadership (Puplampu 2015). Both ECOWAS and CEN-SAD had to contend with conflicts and other forms of political instability in member states (Mugagga and Nabaasa 2016: 220): Côte d'Ivoire in the case of the former and Chad in the latter. Addressing the above issues will enable the transboundary water commissions to contribute to SDGs, particularly 1 (no poverty); 2 (no hunger); 3 (good health), 14 (life below water) and 15 (life on land) (Mugagga and Nabaasa 2016).

The third theme in the analysis is the MDG 8 and SDG 17 call for a global partnership in development. In the cases under review, multinational corporations were major players, especially in the case of the mining sectors. The role of Talisman Energy in Sudan and the Consortium in the Chad–Cameroon project reinforce the view that the interests of shareholders were their main concern and the nature of global partnership is not likely to change that calculation. At stake is the institutional capability of the state in crafting legal agreements that will protect the interests of citizens. As the Chad–Cameroon case clearly shows, even though the World Bank insisted and got the Government of Chad to agree to the watchdog role of civil society groups, the Government of Chad conveniently reneged on that provision of the general agreement. The significant lesson is that the supposedly weak African state of Chad was able to flex its muscles with the World Bank and the Consortium of multinational corporations, a situation that contradicts the notion of the vanishing, minimal role of the state in the economy and society an era of neoliberal globalization (Onuoha 2016). Perhaps, the strategic political leadership of Chad's President Idriss Déby was of consequence. He was able to persuade Parliament – one key, if not the most venerable, institution of democratic governance – to abolish the legislation that committed the Government of Chad to the Future Generations Fund (Barma *et al.* 2012: 7). That highlights the disjuncture between the theory and practice of democratic governance, especially when principles of identity politics are at stake, as was the case in Chad, rather than a deep commitment to democratic principles and practices.

Political leadership, as Puplampu (2014) notes, not only sets the tone for the state's role, but also its role in setting the policy agenda when it comes to natural resources, which are subject to cyclical changes in production and price levels and national choices are conditioned by state ideology. While it was definitely in Chad's national interest to use oil revenue to defend its territorial sovereignty and promote the development process, Idriss Déby's identity-based governance also created the conditions for the emergence of the armed group contesting his power in the first place (Winters and Gould 2011). Put another way, pursuing a broad-based national development agenda, devoid of identity politics would have minimized the armed conflict. The implicit result is that the relationship between the national government and the interests of foreign investors do not necessarily give rise to improvements in the living conditions of the citizens. The Chad example reminds us of the need to focus on the necessary and sufficient factors for better outcomes in global partnerships as well as the democratic trajectory of African countries.

The idea of partnership entails several assumptions. First, it is assumed or expected that parties in the partnership consider each other as equal. Second, the partnership is expected to produce equal outcomes. These assumptions often break down in the global relations between the global North and South. When it comes to natural resource, the capital investment requirements are enormous and beyond the capability of the African state, an inadequacy that opens the window for Northern-based private sector participation, specifically multinational corporations. Thus, in the case of the Chad–Cameroon pipeline project, the private consortium was able to influence the orientation of the World Bank towards the project. In an era of neoliberal globalization where capital is relatively footloose relative to labour, it is not surprising that Talisman pulled out of Sudan when there was a general perception that their activities were contributing to the Sudan government's ability to wage war against its citizens. In both the Chad–Cameroon and the Sudan oil projects, the value of the resource was key in attracting private capital, a situation that was different in the case of the river basin case studies. The nature of the partnership in these cases followed the traditional patterns of international development assistance. Perhaps, the nature of that support is a reflection of the nature of the resource. There is a concerted effort at partnership in the case of the water basin projects, perhaps because of the transboundary implications of water.

A far-reaching concern in the dynamics of global financial assistance, with significant implications for democratic governance, is the emergence of and arrival of China in Africa (Kopiński and Sun 2014). The World Bank, the traditional source of development assistance to Africa countries, has to rethink its practices in a competitive environment provided by China's foreign development institutions, the Export-Import Bank of China and the China Development Bank. While both the World Bank and China development institutions operate on the basis of tying in the aid package, two noticeable differences are the latter taking less time in making a decision to finance a development project and providing the assistance without a sustained interest in or focus on the internal domestic politics or governance of African countries (Odoom in this volume, Kopiński and Sun 2014; Gérin and Houdin 2010). The World Bank, operating under the larger notion of the so-called Western canon, has therefore presented China's benign neglect of governance and other issues like human rights as an attempt to undo their work in Africa on those issues. While that perception might be justified, it is naive, ethnocentric and hypocritical when considered against the development trajectory of countries such as South Korea and Singapore; a trajectory that ignored labour rights and had the implicit endorsement of the West (Codjoe 2003).

The issue as Booth and Cammack (2013) and Booth (2011) have argued is to be sensitive to what works. That means not to completely discard local institutions instead of innovating them; not to discard local culture, instead of exploring what aspects of the culture can be beneficial; and maintaining a specific and deliberate focus on enabling local problem-solving at the centre of global governance initiatives (Booth 2011). The focus should not be on 'good governance' per se, but the 'governance that works'. Governance that works as Booth and Cammack (2013) remind us pays the required attention to institutional and policy practices that constitute a 'good fit'. That means to be attuned to context and not an obsession with the general idea of 'best practices'. Unfortunately, the broader discourse on development, including both the MDGs and SDGs tend to stress 'best practices'. However, the case studies examined in this study lend some credibility to 'good fit' and not a strict adherence to 'best practices'. The issue is not the irrelevance of 'best practices', since such practices will require context and a focus on the capacity of institutions and policies. The lack of capacity at the institutional and policy levels continues to be the missing link in the development possibilities in several African countries.

Conclusion and policy options

Sustainable development is about the present and the future, and governance is essential in that relationship, especially when it comes to the role of natural resources in African development. The ability to harness the development opportunities calls for capable internal (national) and external (regional and global) institutions and policies. In a world of significant forms of inequality, democratic governance and the development puzzle relative to natural resource governance and sustainable development can be both enabling and constraining. The enabling possibilities range from improving the financing options for the African state, synergies from RECs to the role of multinational corporations, while the constraining issues raise questions about the outcomes of partnership, for example, whether they are equal and equitable.

The following policy considerations warrant renewed emphasis. First, stable and old democracies, for example, Canada and the USA, are not necessarily the only exemplar for African countries. The Canadian government was at pains to reconcile the human security aspects of its foreign policy in the late 1990s and early 2000s with the role of Talisman, a Canadian-based company. In the case of the USA, access to natural resources, especially oil, is a national security imperative, and tends to pursue policy measures that will ensure an impeded flow of natural resources. Analysts have therefore noted significant policy-shifts in how the USA interacts with oil-rich African countries, for example, Angola and Equatorial Guinea, perhaps as a pre-emptive attempt to the increasing relevance of China in the African political economy (Gua *et al.* 2016; Manyok 2016; Novati and Montanini 2016).

It is evident that older or established democracies will be oblivious to the democratic credentials of African countries, especially those with oil resource endowments, if they create a policy platform for their multinational companies to work in those countries. It is no secret that multilateral institutions like the World Bank, and many of the multinational corporations active in Africa's political economy, have biases and strong roots in the global North.

Although their activities are geared towards the profit motive, since that is an overriding aspect of their mandate, African countries have to be aware of that reality and explore other options wrought by the possibilities of the current global imaginary. The emergence of China, while not problem free in the international aid arena, offers another option besides the World Bank and other traditional sources for development financing.

Second, natural resource governance, like any aspect of the development process, requires an optimum mix of institutions and policies, while focusing on the complexities of the state's relations with internal and external forces. In the African context, such an attention is warranted and essential. On one hand, the state of the African state, as reflected in many African countries, is one of consistent paralysis especially with the democratic impulses stifled by leaders who continue to find ingenious ways to entrench themselves in power. On the other hand, the possibilities of communication engendered by the internet point to novel ways of holding governments accountable. This latter pathway, if properly harnessed, will serve as an effective bulwark on the whims and caprices of African leaders who perceive the state in such personal terms and are not prepared or inclined to give up the reins of power. Understanding the relationship between the governance and the development agenda will be vital in and concretizing natural resource governance and sustainable development in Africa towards and beyond the 2030 mandate of the SDGs.

References

AfDB and AU (2009) *Oil and Gas in Africa*. Oxford: Oxford University Press for the African Development Bank and the African Union.

African Capacity Building Foundation (ACBF) (2011) *African Capacity Indicators 2011 – Capacity Development in Fragile States*. Harare: ACBF.

———. (2013) *Africa Capacity Indicators 2013 – Capacity Development for Natural Resource Management*. Harare: Africa Capacity Building Foundation.

Africa Progress Panel (2015) *Power People Planet: Seizing Africa's energy and climate opportunities*. Geneva: Africa Progress Panel.

Alao, A. (2007) *Natural Resources and Conflict in Africa: The Tragedy of Endowment*. Rochester: University of Rochester Press.

Andersen, I., Dione, O., Jarosewich-Holder, M. and Olivry, J-C. (2005) *The Niger River Basin: A Vision for Sustainable Management*. Washington, DC.: World Bank.

Arbogast, S. V. (2009) Project financing and political risk mitigation: the singular case of the Chad-Cameroon pipeline, *Texas Journal of Oil, Gas, and Energy Law*, 4 (2): 269–98.

Arthur, P. (2012) Averting the resource curse in Ghana: assessing the option. In L. Swatuk and M. Schnurr (eds) *Natural Resources and Social Conflict: Towards Critical Environment Security*. London: Palgrave Macmillan, pp. 108–27.

Axworthy, L. (2001). Human security and global governance: putting people first, *Global Governance*, 7 (1): 19–23.

AU and NEPAD (2010) *Africa's Capacity Development Strategic Framework*. Midrand: NEPAD Planning and Coordinating Agency.

Barma, N. H., Kaiser, K., Le, T. M. and Viñuela, L. (2012) *Rents to Riches: The Political Economy of Natural Resource-Led Development*. Washington, DC: World Bank.

BBC News (2003) Talisman Pulls Out of Sudan. Available at news.bbc.co.uk/2/hi/business/2835713.stm (accessed 28 April 2017).

Beaudet, P. (2012) Globalization and development. In P. A. Haslam, J. Schafer and P. Beaudet (eds) *Introduction to International Development: Approaches, Actors, and Issues*, 2nd Edition. Don Mills, ON: Oxford University Press, pp. 107–24.

Beckers, T. (2012) After Rio+20: from patchy achievements to sustained reform, *Environmental Development*, 3, 1–4.

Booth, D. (2011) *Governance for Development in Africa: Building on What Works*. Africa Power and Politics Policy Brief No. 1, April 2011.

Booth, D. and Cammack, R. R. (2013) *Governance for Development in Africa: Solving Collective Action Problems*. London: Zed Books.

Chikozho, C. (2014) Strategic capacity-building imperatives vital for transboundary water cooperation in Africa. In K. T. Hanson, C. D'Alessandro and F. Owusu (eds) *Managing Africa's Natural Resources: Capacities for Development*. New York: Palgrave Macmillan, 118–39.

Collier, P. and Hoeffler, A. (2002) On the incidence of civil war in Africa, *Journal of Conflict Resolution*, 46 (1): 13–28.

———. (2004) Greed and grievance in civil war, *Oxford Economic Papers*, 56 (4): 563–95.

———. (2005) Resource rents, governance and conflict, *Journal of Conflict Resolution*, 49 (4): 625–33.

Codjoe, H. M. (2003) Is culture the obstacle to development in Ghana? A critique of the culture-development thesis as it applies to Ghana and South Korea. In W. J. Tettey, K. P. Puplampu and B. J. Berman (eds) *Critical Perspectives on Politics and Socio-Economic Development in Ghana*. Leiden: Brill, pp. 335–63.

Davis, T. J. (2016) Good governance as a foundation for sustainable human development in sub-Saharan Africa, *Third World Quarterly* (July), pp.1–19. dx.doi.org/10.1080/01436597.2016.1191340.

Dietz, S., Neumayer, E. and de Soysa, I. (2007) Corruption, the resource curse and genuine saving, *Environment and Development Economics*, 12 (1): 33–53.

Elbra, A. (2017) *Governing African Gold Mining: Private Governance and the Resource Curse*. London: Palgrave Macmillan.

Gelb, A. and S. Majerowicz (2011) *Oil for Uganda – or Ugandans? Can Cash Transfers Prevent the Resource Curse*? CGD Working Paper No. 261. Washington, DC: Center for Global Development.

Gérin, J. and Houdin, C. (2010) *Chad, the Challenge of Development: Policy Implications of the Chad-Cameroon Petroleum Project*. Ottawa: The North-South Institute.

Gua, J., Chuanhong, Z., Alcides, V. and Langton, M. (2016) Chinese state capitalism? Rethinking the role of the state and business in Chinese development cooperation in Africa, *World Development*, 81, 24–34.

Hanson, K. T. (2015) (ed.) *Contemporary Regional Development in Africa*. Farnham: Ashgate.

Hanson, K. T., D'Alessandro, C. and Owusu, F. (2014) (eds) *Managing Africa's Natural Resources: Capacities for Development*. New York: Palgrave Macmillan.

Harker, P. (2000) *Human Security in Sudan: The Report of a Canadian Assessment Mission – January*. Ottawa: Department of Foreign Affairs and International Trade.

Held, D., McGrew, A., Goldblatt, D. and Perraton, J. (2001) Managing the challenge of globalization and institutionalization cooperation through global governance. In C. W. Kegley Jr and E. R. Wittkopf (eds) *The Global Agenda: Issues and Perspectives*, 6th Edition. Boston, MA: McGraw Hill, pp. 134–46.

Humphreys, M. (2005) Natural resources, conflict, and conflict resolution: uncovering the mechanisms, *Journal of Conflict Resolution*, 49 (4): 508–37.

Idahosa, P. (2002) Business ethics and development in conflict (zones): the case of Talisman, *Journal of Business Ethics*, 39 (2): 227–46.

International Food Policy Research Institute (IFPRI) (2016) *Global Nutrition Report 2016: From Promise to Impact: Ending Malnutrition by 2030*. Washington, DC: IFPRI.

International Waters Governance (2016a) All Frameworks. Available at www.internationalwatersgovernance.com/ (accessed 31 December 2016).

———. (2016b) Resources – Niger Basin. Available at www.internationalwatersgovernance.com/ (accessed 31 December 2016).

———. (2016c) Resources – Okavango River Basin. Available at www.internationalwatersgovernance.com/ (accessed 31 December 2016).

Ishwaran, N. (2012) After Rio+20: translating words in action, *Environmental Development*, 4, 184–5.

Karl, T. (1997) *The Paradox of Plenty: Oil Booms and Petro-States*. Berkeley, CA: University of California Press.

Kobrin, S. J. (2004) Oil and politics: Talisman energy and Sudan, *International Law and Politics*, 36, 425–56.

Kopiński, D. and Sun, Q. (2014) New friends, old friends? The World Bank and Africa when the Chinese are coming, *Global Governance*, 20, 601–23.

McBride, S. (2005) *Paradigm Shift: Globalization and the Canadian State*, 2nd Edition. Halifax: Fernwood.

Manyok, P. (2016) Oil and Darfur's blood: China's thirst for Sudan's Oil, *Journal of Political Sciences & Public Affairs*, 4: 189. doi:10.4172/2332-0761.1000189.

Marcantonio, R. A. (2016) The Okavango River Basin Agreement: An Analysis, *African Geographical Review*, 35 (3): 227–46.

Matthews, R. O. (2005) Sudan's Humanitarian Disaster: Will Canada live up to its responsibility to protect? *International Journal*, 60 (4): 1049–64.

Meadows, D., Randers, J. and Behrens, W. (1972) *The Limits to Growth*. New York: Universe.

Moss, T. and Young, L. (2009) *Saving Ghana from Its Oil: The Case for Direct Cash Distribution', Center for Global Development*. CGD Working Paper No. 186. Washington, DC: Center for Global Development.

Mugagga, F. and Nabaasa, B. B. (2016) The centrality of water resources to the realization of sustainable development goals: a review of potential and constraints on the African continent, *International Soil and Water Conservation Research*, 4, 215–23.

Muller, M. and Wright, A. (2016) *Unlocking Africa's Transboundary Water Potential*. Abidjan: African Development Bank.

Myrdal, G. (1968) *Asian Drama: An Inquiry into the Poverty of Nations*. New York: Twentieth Century Fund.

New Partnership for African Development (NEPAD) (2001) *NEPAD Policy Document*, English Version. Available at www.nepad.org

———. (2003) *New Partnership for Africa's Development – Action Plan for the Environment Initiative*. Midrand: NEPAD.

Novati, G., Calchi, P. C. and Montanini, M. (2016) Energy and the regional players: the odd rivalry between the EU and China in Africa. In J. M. Godzimirski (ed) *EU Leadership in Energy and Environmental Governance: Global and Local Challenges and Responses*. New York: Palgrave Macmillan, pp. 135–55.

Nwonwu, F. O. C. (2016) The paradox of natural resource abundance and widespread underdevelopment in Africa, *International Journal Of African Renaissance Studies – Multi-, Inter- And Transdisciplinarity*, 11 (2): 52–69. dx.doi.org/10.1080/18186874.2016.1246512

Obi, C. I. (2007) *Oil and Development in Africa: Some Lessons from the Oil Factor in Nigeria for the Sudan*. DIIS Report No. 7.

Ochola, W., Sanginga, P. and Bekalo, I. (2010) (eds) *Managing Natural Resources for Development in Africa: A Resource Book*. Nairobi: University of Nairobi Press.

Okpanachi, E. and Andrews, N. (2012) Preventing the oil 'resource curse' in Ghana: lessons from Nigeria, *World Futures*, 68 (6): 430–50.

Omojola, B. (2012) Africa oil and gas today – the more, the merrier, *Africa Today*, 29 September. Available at www.africatoday.com (accessed 28 April 2017).

Onuoha, G. (2016) A 'rising Africa' in a resource-rich context: change, continuity and implications for development, *Current Sociology*, 64 (2): 277–92.

Ross, M. L. (2008) Blood barrels: why oil wealth fuels conflict, *Foreign Affairs*, 87 (3): 2–8.

Paisley, R. K. and Henshaw, T. W. (2013) Transboundary governance of the Nile River Basin: past, present and future, *Environmental Development*, 7, 59–71.

Pegg, S. (2009) Chronicle of a death foretold: the collapse of the Chad-Cameroon Pipeline Project *African Affairs*, 108 (431): 311–20.

Puplampu, K. P. (2014) The capacity question, leadership and strategic choices: environmental sustainability and natural resources management in Africa. In K. T. Hanson, C. D'Alessandro and F. Owusu (eds) *Managing Africa's Natural Resources: Capacities for Development*. New York: Palgrave Macmillan, pp. 162–84.

———. (2015) Regionalism, globalization and economic integration in Africa. In Hanson, K. T. (ed.) *Contemporary Regional Development in Africa*. Farnham: Ashgate, pp. 27–45.

Saruchera, D. and Lautze, J. (2016) Transboundary river basin organizations in Africa, *Water Policy*, 8 (5): 1053–69.

Shaxson, N. (2008) *Poisoned Wells: The Dirty Politics of African Oil*. New York: Palgrave Macmillan.

Sick, D. (2012) Environment and development. In P. A. Haslam, J. Schafer and P. Beaudet (eds) *Introduction to International Development: Approaches, Actors, and Issues*, 2nd Edition. Don Mills: Oxford University Press.

Stevens, P. and Dietsche, E. (2008) Resource curse: an analysis of causes, experiences and possible ways forward, *Energy Policy*, 38, 56–65.

Stiglitz, J. (2012) Resource rich, cash poor – why new discoveries of natural resources probably won't help Ghana, Uganda, Tanzania or Mozambique, *Slate Magazine*, 12 August. Available at www.slate.com (accessed 28 April 2017).

Swatuk, L. A (2005) From 'project' to 'context': community based natural resource management in Botswana, *Global Environmental Politics*, 5 (3): 95–124.

United Nations Conference on the Environment and Development (UNCED) (1993) *Agenda 21, Programme of Action on Sustainable Development – Rio Declaration on Environment and Development*. New York: United Nations Department of Public Information.

United Nations Development Programme (UNDP) (2003) *Human Development Report 2003 Millennium Development Goals: A Compact Among Nations to end Human Poverty*. New York: Oxford University Press for UNDP.

———. (2011) *Managing Natural Resources for Human Development in Low-Income Countries*. Washington, DC: UNDP – Regional Bureau for Africa.

———. (2015) *Human Development Report, 2015*. New York: Oxford University Press for UNDP.

United Nations Environment Programme (UNEP) (2007) *Global Environment Outlook (GEO4) Environment for Development*. Nairobi: UNEP.

Winters, M. S. and Gould J. A. (2011) Betting on oil: The World Bank's attempt to promote accountability in Chad, *Global Governance*, 17, 229–45.

Wood, R. E. (1986) *From Marshall Plan to Debt Crisis: Foreign Aid and Development Choices in the World Economy*. Berkeley, CA: University of California Press.

World Bank (2012) *Africa's Pulse: An Analysis of Issues Shaping Africa's Economic Future*, October, Vol. 6. Washington, DC: World Bank (Office of the Chief Economist for the Africa Region).

World Commission on Environment and Development (WCED) (1987) *Our Common Future*. Oxford: Oxford University Press.

———. (2004) *Global Development Prospects: Realizing the Development Promise of the Doha Agenda*. Washington, DC: World Bank.

7 Does the sophistication of exports matter in sustaining growth in middle-income African countries?

Vanessa T. Tang

Introduction

Economists and policy-makers alike seek to understand the ways in which countries successfully nurture and grow their domestic economies. This is particularly relevant with respect to export markets. In this increasingly competitive global economy, while preferential trade partnerships and liberalization schemes are viewed as critically important for nations to build economic relations and to prosper, it is arguably even more important for the least developed and developing nations to find innovative ways to promote long-run economic growth in gross domestic product (GDP). The need for GDP growth is compelling and vital as the World Bank establishes that economic growth has been the powerful instrument in the reduction of poverty observed in the last 25 years (World Bank 2014). Also, even more compelling as the world makes the transition from the Millennium Development Goals (MDGs) to Sustainable Development Goals (SDGs), an inclusive sustainable economic growth is a prerequisite in the SDGs.

In considering the link between exports and economic growth, economists and policy-makers tend to examine the overall pattern of trade indicators, especially the export volume of trade or the contribution of exports to GDP. However, these indicators simply reflect the 'quantity' of trade. A primary shortcoming of this approach is that the 'quality' or 'sophistication' of exports receives little attention. There is a paucity of research on this subject, in particular for African countries.

At the turn of the century, a small but growing literature has emerged that argues that, in examining the growth and development of nations, the most important consideration is not how much a country exports, but the nature of its exports (Anand *et al.* 2012; Jarreau and Poncet 2012; Jouini *et al.* 2016; Lall *et al.* 2006; Hausmann *et al.* 2007; Hidalgo and Hausmann 2009; Minondo 2010; Mishra *et al.* 2011; Poncet and Waldemar 2013; Santos-Paulino 2011). However, the majority of the existing studies that aim to examine this crucial consideration tend to focus on the impact of trade on developed and emerging nations. The nuances of how the least developed and developing African nations enter the trade game and distinguish themselves have received little attention.

While Africa has witnessed unprecedented economic growth in the first decade of this century with the capacity to transcend fragility (Shaw and Fanta 2013), there are still few African countries that have achieved high, sustained economic growth. Mauritius as an outlier of Africa is, however, one of the exceptions. Over time, the country has managed to achieve superior, sustained growth performance, which is founded on sound institutions and policies (Frankel 2010; Sacerdoti *et al.* 2005). Since 1980, Mauritius' real GDP growth has averaged more than 5 per cent, and its per capita GDP is above US$16,000, based on purchasing power parity (Tang 2015) in comparison to sub-Saharan African (SSA) regional average estimates of per capita GDP of just over US$3,000 (World Bank 2015). Also, the country is, today, ranked well ahead of its SSA counterparts in human development.

In addition, as illustrated in figure 7.1, relative to other middle-income African countries, Mauritius stands out in superior and sustained growth performance. The country has also successfully achieved the fundamental MDGs relating to poverty eradication, universal primary education, health improvement, gender equality and global partnership for development (World Bank 2016). With regard to the MDG target of halving absolute poverty, Mauritius has outperformed global and regional middle-income estimates; poverty is negligible in Mauritius with less than 1 per cent of the population living on US$1.90 (in purchasing power parity terms) as illustrated in figure 7.2.

In addition, unlike many African countries that remain relatively undiversified in production and exports (Hanson and Tang 2015), the structure of the Mauritian economy has changed dramatically, and modern-day Mauritius boasts a diversified economy from a once monocrop agricultural economy into manufacturing and services.

It is well established that structural change matters if a country is to achieve superior performance. However, more importantly, structural change should involve the country adopting new activities with higher-productivity levels (Hausmann *et al.* 2007; Hidalgo and Hausmann 2009; Kali *et al.* 2013; Poncet and Waldemar 2013; Saadi 2012). The capacity of a country to outperform others therefore resides in the actual nature of production or, more specifically, the sophistication of exports in production.

This chapter thus investigates the effect of export sophistication on economic performance. To examine this idea, an emerging body of studies (Hausmann *et al.* 2007; Jarreau and Poncet 2012; Jouini *et al.* 2016; Minondo 2010; Poncet and Waldemar 2013; Rodrik 2006; Santos-Paulino 2011; Xu 2010) have focused on the sophistication of exports in merchandise trade. More recently, recognizing the changing structure of trade, in that services are becoming increasingly tradable, Mishra *et al.* (2011) and Anand *et al.* (2012) have investigated the impact of service export sophistication on growth.

Given the rising importance of the quality of trade as a potential driver of economic growth, this chapter considers the role of export sophistication in the growth of a set of middle-income African economies. It is reasonable to assume that in Africa, the growth of the 'richer', and by extension the

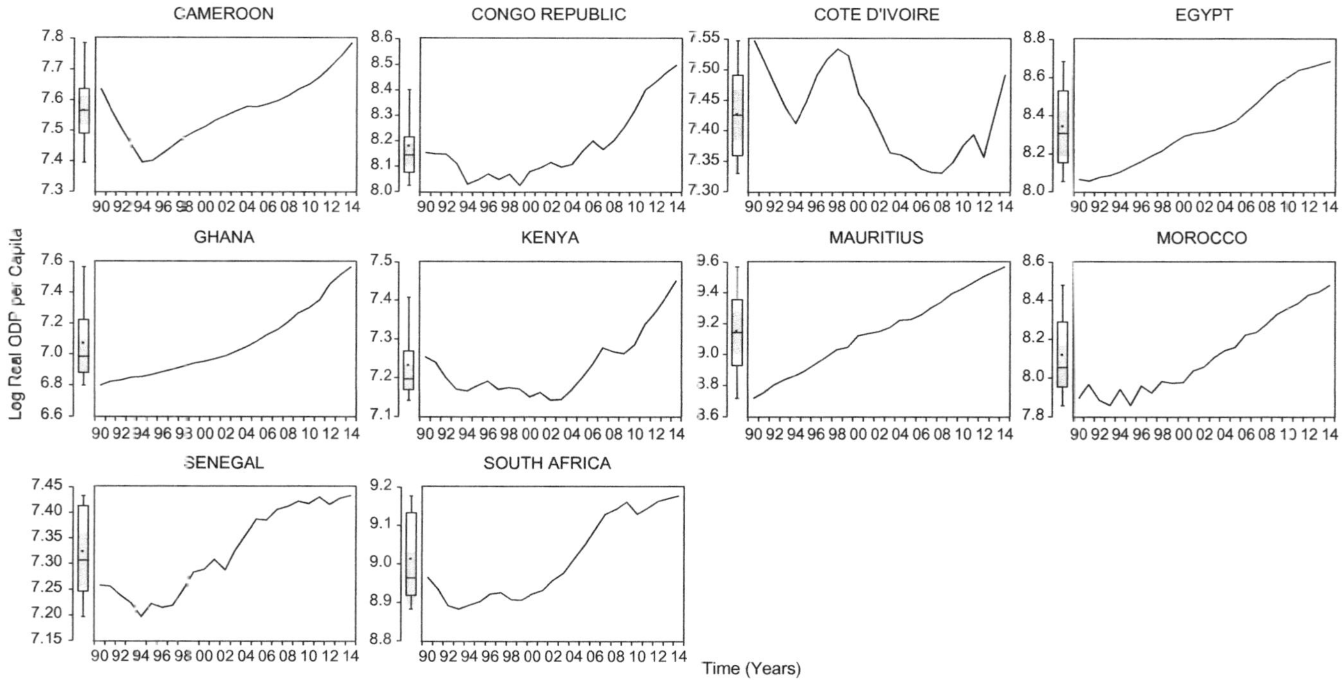

Figure 7.1 Middle-income African countries' real GDP per capita

Source: Authors' compilation based on the World Development Indicators, World Bank Database, 2015.

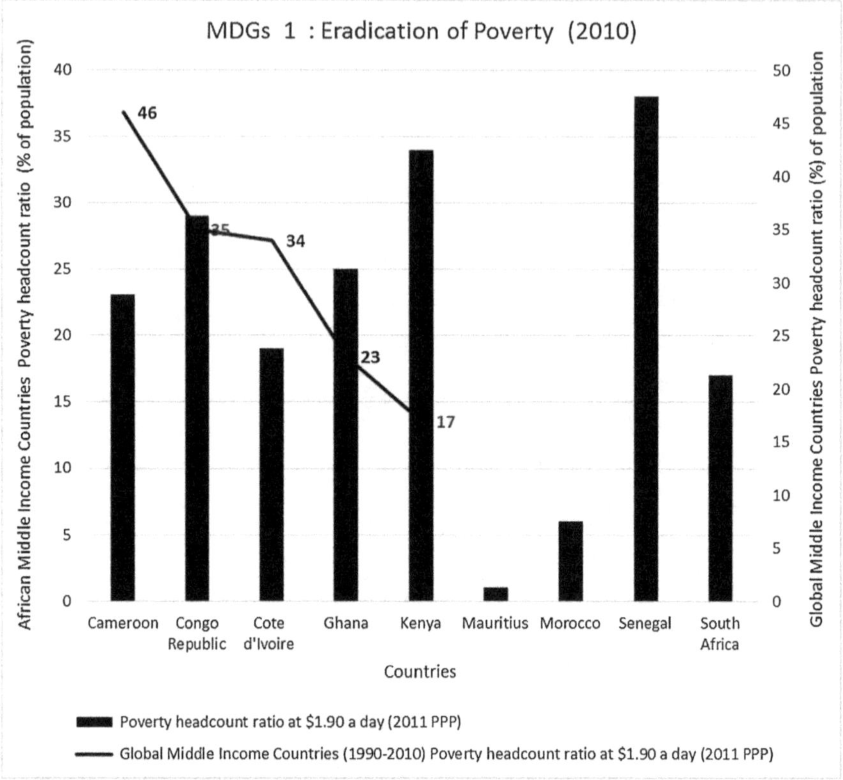

Figure 7.2 MDGs: eradication of poverty

Source: Authors' compilation based on the World Development Indicators, World Bank Database, 2016.

middle-income, African countries may be associated with increased sophistication and innovations in trade. In fact, the African service industry is gradually growing and becoming more productive and tradable. This is notably reflected in the spread and success of Nigerian Nollywood films and Ivorian *Coupé Décalé* music (Shaw and Fanta 2013) as well as Kenya's call centres. In this chapter, therefore, we will consider the effects of both goods and service exports' sophistication on growth.

In terms of methodology, the chapter follows the recent seminal works of Mishra *et al.* (2011) and Anand *et al.* (2012) that addressed the effect of export sophistication on growth through service exports, and in constructing an index of service export sophistication. In view of limited country-specific data and very few high-income African countries, we construct a panel data set of export sophistication in goods and services from 1990 to 2014 linking ten middle-income economies. More specifically, we include two upper-income countries: Mauritius and South Africa; and eight lower-middle-income African economies: Cameroon, Congo Republic, Côte d'Ivoire, Egypt, Ghana, Kenya, Morocco and Senegal. The data set is then used in panel growth regressions to determine whether there is evidence of an empirical relationship between export sophistication and real income per capita growth for middle-income African countries (MIACs).

The chapter is structured as follows. The following section reviews the literature on export sophistication, as well as the conceptual framework. This is followed by a discussion of the empirical measures that flow from the conceptual framework and the presentation and discussion of the empirical results. Conclusions are drawn in the last section.

Export sophistication: conceptual framework and review

The conceptual framework for export sophistication has a different meaning for different scholars and for different contexts. However, the general description is based on the notion that all economies do not behave in the same manner or, for that matter, prosper equally. Spence and Karingi (2011: 9) note that 'No country is uniformly competitive or uncompetitive: in each case there is a range of positive and negative residuals across products and partners'. Competitiveness with respect to export markets is fluid.

In modern theories, the degree to which countries compete depends on the nature of the export economy, the production structure, what they produce and what they export (Hausmann *et al.* 2007). In short, it is not sufficient for a country to simply produce a good and then export it. As important, if not more important, than merely increasing the volume of production and exports is what is being produced and exported. Thus, the role and value of the sophistication of exports have been increasingly supported in the recent literature (Hausmann *et al.* 2007; Hidalgo and Hausmann 2009; Lall *et al.* 2006).

Also arguably, the degree to which export markets are diversified certainly matters as well as a means of self-insurance, especially since global trade is often characterized by major downswings in demand; driven by factors such as changes in consumer preferences and their purchasing power. Furthermore, to successfully diversify into new activities, knowledge of foreign consumer preferences is important to reduce entrepreneurial costs and uncertainties (Hausmann and Rodrik 2003; Vettas 2000).

Apart from consumer demands and preferences, the fragmentation of global production and trade has transformed the nature and composition of global trade (Dean *et al.* 2011; Lall *et al.* 2006). The subdivision of production processes across countries in order to exploit differences in wages, logistics and other costs (Lall *et al.* 2006: 222) is largely undertaken by foreign firms (Dean *et al.* 2011) and multinationals (Poncet and Waldemar 2013). The fragmentation of global production and trade that involves market manipulation to benefit the host economy (sometimes to the detriment of more vulnerable competitive rivals) may explain the differences and growth in global trade and is thus a useful conceptual framework to understand the sophistication of production and trade.

As with trade fragmentation, export sophistication is an exploitative act predicated on the notion that, in order to prosper economically, a country should improve its exports, in part by specializing and diversifying them, as well as exploit the vulnerabilities of other countries to gain greater standing. In this possibly zero-sum global trade game, developing countries must still engage in development-'friendly' competition and work 'cooperatively' in order to conduct trade (Lall *et al.* 2006). The paradox lies in the fact that both zero-sum and positive-sum games co-exist.

In their study, Lall *et al.* (2006) also assert that assuming the presence of free markets – or at least, realistically, limited intervention with respect to trade – exporting countries will have a greater chance of competing with existing prosperous nations if they diversify their exports and remain open to trade. Much of the research on the subject of diversification has involved the assessment of parent industry-specific markers or indicators to determine the health of export markets and trade. Such empirical analysis, however, as noted by Lall *et al.* (2006) relies on product classification with the assumption that production occurs in an environment of similar development and technology.

In response to this dilemma, the study of export sophistication by Lall *et al.* (2006) creates a sophistication index that aims to differentiate between products and to reflect the specialization and competitive advantage of exported goods on the basis that the advanced or wealthier economies produce the more sophisticated goods. Therefore, in their construction at the product level, the measure of sophistication considers the weighted average per capita incomes of exporting countries with the weights taken as the share in world exports, which they referred to as 'PRODY' following the original notation of Rodrik (2006). PRODY is thus a measure of the product's (PROD) content of per capita income (Y) and implies that the product that a nation produces and exports has an intrinsic level of productivity and sophistication.

However, a limitation in Lall *et al.*'s (2006) measure of sophistication is that using the country's share in world exports would lead to an overestimation of large country's size effects (Hausmann *et al.* 2007). Subsequently therefore, Hausmann *et al.* (2007) developed a similar measure of sophistication but use a different weighting by considering instead a weighted index of revealed comparative advantage. PRODY is therefore constructed to reflect the weighted average of the income levels of exporters' goods where the weights are simply the Balassa revealed comparative advantage, which they referred as EXPY, following Rodrik's measure of Export Sophistication (EXPY).

In aiming to explain the important role of sophistication in the success of exporting countries, the case of China, a major global and regional player in trade, is instructive for many African countries where industrialization has stagnated. China's changing export structure and rapid growth in global trade is intriguing. Its production and exports now include a wide range of products and the country is also moving into the production of a number of relatively 'dynamic' goods that are seen to be more closely associated with those of developed economies (Weiss 2010).

Rodrik (2006) uses the EXPY measure to examine China's exports and has noted the remarkable diversification of China's trade, and argued that the changes in the country's export structure towards higher-productivity goods, such as high-tech electronics, is indeed an important factor in its economic performance. While Lall *et al.* (2006) agree that the nature of exports matters for performance, in their study, however, China's exports do not appear 'special'; in terms of overall sophistication, the country ranks 20th out of 30 countries.

Nonetheless, over the past few years, China has been particularly competitive in comparison to other East Asian (Adams *et al.* 2006) and Latin America (Jenkins *et al.* 2008) countries, as well as African countries. Adams *et al.* (2006) have argued that competitiveness with respect to exports can be ascertained by examining a country's share of exports in relation to global trade. In this framework, China has out-exported virtually every other country, especially those in East Asian markets. Adams *et al.* (2006) and a number of other studies (Hausmann *et al.* 2007; Hidalgo and Hausmann 2009; Jarreau and Poncet 2012; Schott 2008; Xu 2010) stress that in the quality spectrum of exports, diversification into the export of higher-tech products, as opposed to raw materials and low-tech goods, is vital. Weiss (2010: 1269) buttresses the fact that for more technologically sophisticated manufacturers, the prospects for demand growth are more favourable, and the terms of trade shifts will be less unfavourable than for simple manufacturers.

China has, in large part, been successful because, as Lall *et al.* (2006) note, it has focused on diversification, producing higher-tech exports, as well as fragmentation, while still incorporating its comparative trading advantage in the export of low-level products and manipulating labour and exchange rates. This course of action has benefited China due to (1) its domestic markets or size, (2) the fact that it now has a reputation of being a major global trading partner, and (3) it captures a high share of foreign direct investment (FDI). In short, China's export sophistication has been multi-variable. A similar argument can be made for India, which, like China, has operated partly on the basis of its size (Adams *et al.* 2006). However, while China's growth experience has been leveraged by total factor productivity growth in goods, India's has been leveraged by its comparative advantage in the service industry.

While clearly not the only determinant of competitiveness and export sophistication, exports from both China and India are sophisticated in part because they opted for more pronounced trade liberalization policies that have thus strengthened trade relations and increased FDI (a mutually beneficial relationship), which is the norm rather than an exception. In short, competitiveness, and implicitly export sophistication, in China rests on the following factors: favourable exchange rate; low wages and ample supplies of labour; reduced cost of communication and transportation; flow of FDI and foreign management and its implications for productive abilities; large-scale size of domestic market; openness to trade and access to world markets; and the facilitation and encouragement of foreign trade policy (Adams *et al.* 2006).

On the other hand, Spence and Karingi (2011) contend that while export sophistication relies on export diversification, in parallel it is crucial to bolster trade relations and facilitate trade. They assert that a central component in facilitating trade with industrialized and developing trade partners is ensuring that trade-related costs are either reduced or remain low. Nevertheless, while trade-related costs cannot be completely eliminated, such costs can be reduced by liberalizing trade and removing tariffs and non-tariff barriers to trade.

Additionally, policy implementations as well as labour market absorption are critical, as observed by Palma (2009) in a study on export sophistication examining varying economic performance in Latin America and Asia. Palma argues that Latin America and East Asia have different trade and industrial policies. In the mid-twentieth century, East Asian policies resulted in an increase in exports and GDP. Conversely, Latin America lost nearly half of its export share – a distinct setback considering that, during the first half of the twentieth century, Latin America had a greater share of exports in GDP. Palma suggests that this reversal of fortunes can be attributed to a number of factors including 'a weakened demand for primary commodities in OECD markets since the Korean War and trade and industrial policies characterized by strong anti-export bias' (Palma 2009: 206). Also according to Palma, exports can only effectively increase economic growth if growth and labour absorption occur via both export markets and the overall economy.

In the case of Latin America, leadership did not play this two-pronged game well, likely because of systemic geopolitical problems that undermined political as well as market stability in the final decades of the twentieth century. These political liabilities prevented Latin American countries from properly and expeditiously diversifying their exports, keeping them in economic limbo and remaining static in a fluid and dynamic global marketplace. In contrast, the East Asian countries heeded the call, and adjusted their policies accordingly, not only opening themselves up to outside markets and potential trade partners, but strategically liberalizing trade relations in a direct about-face to the closed, Marxist-Communist economics that had permeated the region during the Korean and Vietnam War eras. Given its anti-liberalization politics during that time, this was accordingly difficult for Latin American countries to achieve.

At the turn of this century, attention is now increasingly on the large influential emerging Southern nations. Santos-Paulino (2011) asserts that in the case of the Southern emerging economic powers (Brazil, China, India and South Africa) export sophistication rests heavily on the specialization of products as a means to increase export value in the aggregate. The recent literature has indicated that specialization is a key indicator of export sophistication, and that specialization is dependent on the spill-overs argument, that is, positive externalities stemming from the transmission of knowledge or technology that can benefit internal and external markets (Amable 2000; Guariglia and Santos-Paulino 2008; Hausmann *et al.* 2007; Lall *et al.* 2006; Puga and Trefler 2010; Santos-Paulino 2010). Ultimately, as Santos-Paulino (2011) found, specialization, and likely by extension, export sophistication, can vary even among similar large emerging countries such as Brazil, China, India and South Africa.

However, while growth and development adequately requires a smooth transition from the production and export of raw, low-tech products to the production and export of high-tech products, it also requires more advanced and stable political and legal frameworks that can assist in creating dynamic export economies. Arguably, the differences among these countries can be attributed to their varying regional dilemmas and geopolitical conflicts as much as their traditionally economic issues (Santos-Paulino 2011).

Furthermore, instructive for many African economies that remain undiversified, according to Minondo (2010), countries that specialize in manufactured goods and hi-tech products should grow faster than countries specializing in primary commodities. But also in the long run, it is not just specialization in more productive goods that causes faster growth, but specialization in goods whose quality can be improved (Minondo 2010: 285). Similarly, Seyoum (2005) argues that sophistication can be achieved in the high technology industry and that improved technological infrastructure, the ability to attract FDI and improved human capital, by extension a skilled workforce, accompanied by home demand conditions are the main drivers of high performance of nations' hi-tech industries (Seyoum 2005: 76). Ancharaz's (2009) study confirms Seyoum's (2005) findings and maintains that the rise of fast growing countries, as in the Chinese economy, will see mostly resource-rich extractive industries in the sub-continent gaining, while those that compete with China in the manufacturing sector, such as Mauritius and South Africa, may invariably lose out in the export markets.

Schott (2008) found that China was increasingly producing a wide range of products and penetrating markets in competition with the United States and OECD countries. However, Schott (2008: 24) argues that this does not necessarily point to the quality of China's exports, but is simply due to China's size relative to the United States and OECD countries. Schott thus concludes that developed nations like the United States and those in the EU have little to fear from Chinese competition; rather, they might expect many gains from the emergence of this country.

In contrast, Liang (2008) found that Chinese exports were fuelled by sophisticated technologies resulting from its policies that encouraged FDI. This finding is plausible as the 'attraction of FDI inflows has often been contemplated as one powerful tool to promote quality upgrades to the country product structure' (Poncet and Waldemar 2013: 104).

Contrary to the findings discussed above, Raju and Fitzpatrick (2010), in Peru, found that while there is a lack of support for an export sophistication-led growth argument, investments in infrastructure, human capital and a supportive macro- and micro-economic environment are critical for growth. Weiss (2010: 1278) using data on China with a focus on the electronics industry that is perceived to be the country's best industry, and labour intensive industries such as clothing, accepted the thrust of arguments put forward by Rodrik (2006) and Hausmann *et al.* (2007) that the structure of export matters for growth. However, Weiss (2010) argues that China's export sophistication may be overstated and less 'special', and states, among others, that this may partly be due to the different time periods of study and China's rapidly shifting export structure.

In a world of freer trade, many developing as well as developed countries are feeling threatened by lower-wage trading partners. For example, China has displaced the textiles and apparel manufacturing industries in many countries (Ancharaz 2009). On a related topic, in noting the Japanese manufacturing industries' reduced competitive edge (especially against South Korea and China), Mitsuyama (2013) observes that the future of these industries rests on their willingness and ability to improve their export products, mainly by manufacturing the kind of products whose individual units are not capable of mutual substitution. The same argument can be advanced for countries that are lagging behind. As Lall *et al.* (2006) further contend, to successfully integrate themselves into production networks and increase exports, countries should aim to improve what they already export, by adding to their export arsenal, diversifying their exports, or fragmenting them, or adopting a strategy that combines all of these strategies.

To this end, the conceptual framework for export sophistication is not straightforward in finding a relationship between productivity and economic performance of nations. The ideas, derivations and findings that have been put forward rely on a multi-dimensional phenomenon and multi-variable framework.

Empirical approach

There is strong and growing evidence in the literature that specializing and exporting goods that are more sophisticated or of higher income content can enhance growth more than specializing in others. The notion of export sophistication, which dates back to the seminal contributions of Lall *et al.* (2006) and Hausmann *et al.* (2007), continues to be a subject of debate. These seminal studies have provided useful insights that suggest that the 'quality' of traded commodities or the sophistication of exports matters for economic growth.

In measuring a country's export sophistication, most studies, including Mishra *et al.* (2011) and Anand *et al.* (2012), have followed the Hausmann *et al.* (2007) measure of sophistication, thereafter referred as HHR. More specifically, the Hausmann *et al.* (2007) study argues that it is not merely the quantity of exports that matters for growth but the 'productivity' or sophistication of a country's exports. Their study shows that countries that export goods associated with higher-productivity levels seem to grow more rapidly, even after controlling for initial income per head, human capital levels, and time-invariant country characteristics. Hence, Hausmann *et al.* (2007: 14) conclude that what potentially causes growth is the resulting act of transferring resources from lower-productivity activities to higher-productivity goods. This implies an acknowledgement of the important role for diversification.

The HHR export sophistication index captures the sophistication level of a good *j* which refers to the income or productivity level of exporters on growth. $PRODY_j$ is then constructed to reflect the weighted average of the income levels of good *j* exporters where the weight is simply the revealed comparative of each country *i* in good *j*:

$$PRODY_j = \sum i\left\{\left[(x_{ij} / X_i) / \sum i(x_{ij} / X_i)\right] * Y_i\right\} \quad (1)$$

Similarly, in the case of services, Mishra *et al.* (2011) and Anand *et al.* (2012) constructed measure $PRODY_j$ to reflect the income or productivity level associated with service *j*, and this was constructed using the service export (*x*) share of country *i* in the world export of service *j*, divided by the total share of *j* in the world exports of *j* and the ratio multiplied by the per capita income (Y) of country *i*. The measure PRODY is thus the weighted average of per capita GDP, and the weights the revealed comparative advantage in service *j*.

$$EXPY_i = \Sigma j\left[\left(x_{ij} / X_i\right) * PRODY_j\right] \quad (2)$$

The service export sophistication measure EXPY is then the weighted income value of service exports, computed as the sum of PRODY using as weights the share of service in total service exports.

The model, data and methodology

We follow Mishra *et al* (2011) and Anand *et al* (2012), sophistication measure, which follows the well-established HHR framework; however, the novel research of the effect of service export sophistication on growth has been overlooked. Their studies attempt to assess the effects of service export sophistication on economic growth and in constructing a static service sophistication index. We also follow the static EXPY measure in both goods and services. This means that an increase in EXPY measures a nation's rise from a low PRODY to a high PRODY. This study therefore contributes to the literature by investigating the significance of service exports as well as the export sophistication of goods on economic growth. We use panel data and analysis and consider the investigation of a set of ten middle-income African countries (Cameroon, Congo Republic, Côte d'Ivoire, Egypt, Ghana, Kenya, Mauritius, Morocco, Senegal and South Africa) for the period 1990 to 2014. (The data description and sources are presented in table 7.2.)

We thus estimate the following growth model in our panel of countries:

$$y_{i,t} - y_{i,t-1} = \alpha' Y_{i,t-1} + \beta' E_{i,t} + \varphi' CD_{i,t} + \varepsilon_{i,t} \tag{1}$$

Where y_t stands for the output in each country i; we use the growth rate of real GDP per capita as dependent variable; $Y_{i,t-1}$ is the level of GDP per capita in the previous period and it is used to control for convergence; E is the measure of export sophistication for each country *i*; CD is a set of control variables in each country *i*, and include the role of financial development (for which we use the ratio of M2 share in GDP as a monetary proxy); human capital (for which we use the enrolment ratio in secondary school as a proxy); openness to trade (for which we use export and import as a share of GDP); diversification of exports (for which we use the Herfindahl-Hirschmann Index (HHI) as a measure – however, because data is only available post 1995, we use the 1995 index value for the years prior); as well as the level of institution (for which we use a political score in political regime from autocratic to democratic). Following Mishra *et al.* (2011) and Anand *et al.* (2012), we use a static service sophistication measure and we also consider the importance of goods export sophistication.

The data is annual and ranges from 1990 to 2014. Our dataset contains 25 observations for each country. We also include a possible candidate for a dummy variable and we finally settled for a binary dummy that performed the best, namely a dummy for small economies (DSMALL) defined as countries with a population of less than five million.

The association between trade and growth is likely to be bi-directional. A key econometric concern is the endogenous nature of the link between the sophistication of exports and growth. Hence, it is not always clear whether the coefficient in our growth regressions robustly reflects the effect of the sophistication of exports on growth. To address this dilemma in controlling for the endogeneity issue, we adopt an instrumental variable approach in the use of a two-stage least squares (2SLS) estimation method and lagged values of our regressors as instruments since we found the explanatory export sophistication variables to be endogenous. Also, the 2SLS method is appropriate and can circumvent potential sources of bias.

In addition, prior to estimating the regressions, we tested for multicollinearity. Overall multicollinearity is not a problem. A test for multicollinearity is the pair-wise correlations among the regressors. The results of the correlations are presented in table 7.3. Also, a summary of the descriptive statistics are presented in table 7.4 and the results indicate that the variables used in this study are evenly distributed across sample. Furthermore, as common in growth models, heteroscedasticity is a potential problem and we use the White test to correct for the heteroscedasticity problem.

Empirical results

This section presents and analyses the results of our panel regressions. We follow the strategy used in Mishra *et al.* (2011) and perform the regressions with both fixed effects (FE) and dynamic panel general method of moments (GMM). It is worth noting that the Hausmann test rejects the use of the random effects (RE) method in favour of the FE model.

The primary aim and interest of this study is to investigate whether export sophistication can indeed provide an additional channel of growth for middle-income African economies. Turning to the panel regression results, the table 7.1 below presents the estimated results for both the FE and the dynamic panel GMM approach.

Table 7.1 Fixed effects and general method of moments results of export sophistication

Dependent variable: real GDP per capita growth (PPP 2005)				
Method: Panel method				
LN Variable	*FE*		*GMM*	
	Coefficient	*t-Statistic*	*Coefficient*	*t-Statistic*
LAG initial RGDP per capita	–0.003389	–0.422517	–0.0003401	–1.227263
Trade openness	0.057221	4.002462***	0.044400	3.832233***
Polity score	0.001408	3.34413***	–0.000375	–0.764332
Human capital	0.007543	0.285108	0.022077	1.702772*
Financial development	–0.031843	–1.188272	0.003591	0.742642
DSMALL			–0.053372	–3.713208***
DISLAND			0.036166	2.558501**
HHI-diversification	0.007477	0.430202	0.007789	0.864534
EXPY-GDS	0.031843	1.919057**	0.028359	2.763744***
EXPY-SVS	0.063912	1.262874	0.025544	1.346016
Adjusted R-squared	0.29		0.22	
F-statistic	9.14		4.3	
DW statistic	1.7		1.8	
No of observations (Instrument)	250		250 (12)	

*Significant at 10 per cent **Significant at 5 per cent ***Significant at 1 per cent

What is striking from the estimated significant results of this study is that, with respect to both measures of export sophistication and using different panel estimations, only the sophistication of goods export (EXPY-GDS) is statistically significant and hence matters for GDP per capita growth. What is, however, insignificant and does not influence growth in per capita GDP is the sophistication of service exports (EXPY-SVS).

Our results support Anand *et al.* (2012) findings with regard to their estimates of the whole of SSA. Eventually, it is only the sophistication of goods that is significant. It is remarkable to uncover that in contrasting their SSA estimates, their EXPY results are also relatively low with an estimated coefficient of ranges around 0.11 at 10 per cent significance compared to our estimated significant results of around 0.03. This is plausible as the sample size is different and also this study focuses on a set of 'richer' middle-income African economies. Also, as Anand at *et al.* (2012: 20) stressed 'SSA sophistication was roughly as expected given its stage of development and size'. It is worth noting the recent study by Jouini *et al.* (2016) in addressing seven North African countries' export product sophistication that follows the HHR EXPY measure. In addition, Jouini *et al.*'s study shows that the impact of EXPY on growth is also positive and significant at 10 per cent level, but produces very low impact with an estimated value of 0.0002 which, therefore, can hardly be viewed as a key channel of growth in North African countries.

Regarding the importance of investment in human capital, as expected, our study shows that human capital in the form of investment in education is positive and significant at 10 per cent level. The contribution of human wealth is undoubtedly important for middle-income African countries (MIACs) and in this study the estimated coefficient ranges around 0.02. Our results support very closely those of Mishra *et al.* (2011) for their sample of countries with an income below US$10,000. Their estimated results of human capital as measured by the years of schooling, although insignificant, has a 0.03 impact on growth.

Additionally, what has a highly significant result is the importance of political framework and trade integration. Regarding the former variable impact, our estimated results show a positive and negative impact on growth, and which ranges around 0.001. In contrast, Mishra *et al.* (2011) also show a positive and negative effect on growth with a higher estimate of around 0.01. Regarding the degree of a country's integration through the openness to trade measure, it is noted that the estimated coefficient of trade shares in the GMM model is robustly consistent in sign, values and significance. The openness to trade has a positive effect of around 0.05 in MIACs' growth. The estimated coefficient of trade shares is around 0.05 and is statistically significant at 1 per cent level. Our results thus support the openness-led growth hypothesis for MIACs through the traditional trade shares ratio channel. The results are also consistent with empirical African studies, such as Anand *et al.* (2012)

Table 7.2 Annual data description and sources

Variables	*Descriptions*	*Sources*
RGDP	Real per capita GDP (constant 2005 US dollar)	World Bank World Development Indicators 2015
TOPEN	Trade as a share of GDP	World Bank World Development Indicators 2015
Human capital	Secondary school enrolment	UNESCO statistics and World Bank World Development Indicators 2015
Finance	M2 share of GDP	IMF International Financial Statistics 2015
HHI	Herfindahl-Hirschmann Index of diversification. HHI ranges between 0 and 1. Index value closer to 1 indicates low diversification	UNCTAD 2015 available at www.unctadstat.unctad.org
Institutional political score	Value between +10 and –10. The polity score is computed by subtracting the autocratic score from the democratic score; the resulting unified polity scale ranges from +10 (strongly democratic) to –10 (strongly autocratic)	Democracy armed conflict and intervention datasets, available at www.systemicpeace.org/polityproject.html
GEXPY	Goods export sophistication	Mishra *et al*. data and UN Comtrade database 2015 and IMF International Financial Statistics 2015
SEXPY	Service export sophistication	Mishra *et al*. data and UN Comtrade database 2015 and IMF International Financial Statistics 2015
DSMALL	A dummy value of 1 for countries population less than five millions else 0	
DISLAND	A dummy value of 1 for island state else 0	

Table 7.3 Correlation matrix: export sophistication-led growth model

Statistics	*LNY*	*LNLAGY*	*LNGEXPY*	*LNHHI*	*LNTOPEN*	*POLS*	*LNHK*	*LNFIN*	*LNSEXPY*	*DSMALL*	*DISLAND*
LNY	1	0.1553	0.1980	0.0903	0.2098	0.1006	0.3097	0.1776	0.1112	0.19942	0.163003
LNLAGY	0.1553	1	0.5376	–0.3711	0.2062	0.3266	0.1898	0.6708	0.3316	0.3767	0.52972
LNGEXPY	0.1980	0.5376	1	–0.2208	–0.0467	0.1927	0.4286	0.4047	0.3083	0.2295	0.04483
LNHHI	0.0903	–0.3711	–0.2208	1	0.4650	–0.2382	0.1247	–0.6283	0.2610	0.5052	–0.00349
LNTOPEN	0.2098	0.2062	–0.0467	0.4650	1	0.2688	0.3009	0.0297	0.2706	0.7415	0.49746
POLS	0.1006	0.3266	0.1927	–0.2382	0.2688	1	0.4564	0.2339	0.0118	0.2227	0.47337
LNHK	0.3097	0.1898	0.4286	0.1247	0.3009	0.4564	1	0.2628	0.2939	0.3613	0.42078
LNFIN	0.1776	0.6708	0.4047	–0.6283	0.0297	0.2339	0.2628	1	0.0453	0.0121	0.40954
LNSEXPY	0.1112	0.3316	0.3083	0.2610	0.2706	0.0118	0.2939	0.0453	1	0.3189	0.16382
DSMALL	0.1994	0.3767	0.2295	0.5052	0.7415	0.2227	0.3613	0.0121	0.3189	1	0.6667
DISLAND	0.1630	0.5297	0.0448	–0.0034	0.4974	0.4733	0.4207	0.4095	0.1638	0.6667	1

Table 7.4 Summary of descriptive statistics: export sophistication-led growth model

Statistics	*LNY*	*LNLAGY*	*LNGEXPY*	*LNHHI*	*LNTOPEN*	*POLS*	*LNHK*	*LNFIN*	*LNSEXPY*	*DSMALL*
Mean	0.01672	7.53155	9.10128	–1.28210	4.23240	0.61600	1.68846	3.61738	9.15579	0.20000
Median	0.01866	7.30572	9.12042	–1.35797	4.16345	–2.00000	1.72633	3.58551	9.18789	0.00000
Maximum	0.36830	9.34242	9.74000	–0.16846	5.05536	10.0000	2.27109	4.72359	9.56512	1.00000
Minimum	–0.08349	6.21509	8.29825	–2.18655	3.45774	–8.00000	0.98954	2.44643	8.79273	0.00000
Std. dev.	0.03832	0.88919	0.37707	0.49229	0.38632	6.62208	0.25635	0.62376	0.12922	0.40080
Jarque-Bera	2.73528	19.451	11.659	6.248	13.028	31.087	3.220	15.192	4.451	94.401
Probability	0.000000	0.000060	0.002939	0.04397	0.00148	0.00000	0.19987	0.00050	0.10800	0.00000
Sum	4.17994	1882.888	2275.322	–320.526	1058.101	154.000	422.116	904.345	2288.949	50.000
Sum sq. dev.	0.36557	196.87	35.40	60.34	37.16	10919.1	16.36	96.88	4.158	40.00
No of obs	250	250	250	250	250	250	250	250	250	250

and Jouini *et al.* (2016), in supporting the hypothesis that African economies tend to be more open to trade and growth when trade openness is measured by the share of trade in GDP. This may also be suggestive of the benefits of free trade arrangements.

Conclusion

This chapter contributes to the small but growing body of evidence on export sophistication-led growth focusing on middle-income African economies. Overall, the pattern that emerges from our study is that what MIACs produce and export matters since the measure of the effect of export sophistication of goods on growth clearly support a positive and significant association. However, unlike Mishra *et al.*'s (2011) findings regarding the significance of service export sophistication, this study does not show the influence of this variable. Furthermore, based on the results of this study, it is not unreasonable to infer that the growth effect of an upgrade in exports or sophistication in exports is, while weak and severely lacking, not negligible. What is also not negligible is the openness to trade and investment in human capital. While being a small economy can be a disadvantage, being a small island economy, however, in line with expectations as in the case of Mauritius, is not a disadvantage.

To this end, considering the need for policy-makers to work towards SDGs, the findings of this study provide an alternative channel through the sophistication of exports in igniting economic growth in African countries. Policies aimed at increasing economic performance could be more effective if policy measures promote openness to trade and facilitate the production and sophistication of exports. This calls for a combined effort from both public and private sectors to invest and create an environment conducive to the promotion of exports; a key requirement as set out under SDG 17 and associated target 12 in the 2030 Agenda for sustainable development.

References

Adams, F. G., Gangnes, B. and Shachmurove, Y. (2006) *Why Is China So Competitive? Measuring and Explaining China's Competitiveness*. Oxford: Blackwell, pp. 95–126.

Amable, B. (2000) International specialization and growth, *Structural Change and Economic Dynamics*, 11 (4): 413–31.

Anand, R., Mishra, S. and Spatafora, N. (2012) *Structural Transformation and the Sophistication of Production*. IMF Working Paper 12/59.

Ancharaz, V. (2009) David v. Goliath: Mauritius facing up to China, *European Journal of Development Research*, 21 (2): 622–43.

Dean, J. M., Fung, K. C. and Wang, Z. (2011) Measuring vertical specialization: The case of China, *Review of International Economics*, 19 (4): 609–625.

Frankel, J. (2010) Mauritius: African Success Story. Available at www.nber.org/papers/w16569 (accessed 3 July 2016).

Guariglia, A. and Santos-Paulino, A. U. (2008) *Export Productivity, Finance and Economic Growth: Are the Southern engines of growth different?* Research Paper, United Nations University (UNU).

Hanson, K. T. and Tang, V. T. (2015) Contemporary regional development in africa: reflections and implications. In K. T. Hanson (ed.) *Contemporary Regional Development in Africa*. Farnham: Ashgate, 1–27.

Hausmann, R. and Rodrik, D. (2003) Economic development as self-discovery, *Journal of Development Economics*, 72 (2): 603–33.

Hausmann, R. Hwang, J. and Rodrik, D. (2007) What you export matters, *Journal of Economic Growth*, 12 (1): 1–25.

Hidalgo, C. A. and Hausmann, R. (2009) The building blocks of economic complexity. *Proceedings of the National Academy of Sciences*, 106 (26): 10570–5.

International Monetary Fund (IMF) (2015) International Financial Statistics. CD-ROM.

Jarreau, J. and Poncet, S. (2012) Export sophistication and economic growth: evidence from China, *Journal of development Economics*, 97 (2): 281–92.

Jenkins, R., Peters, E. D. and Moreira, M. M. (2008) The impact of China on Latin America and the Caribbean, *World Development*, 36 (2): 235–53.

Jouini, N., Oulmane, N. and Peridy, N. (2016) North African countries' production and export structure: towards a diversification and export sophistication strategy, *Canadian Journal of Development Studies*, 37 (2): 217–38.

Lall, S., Weiss, J. and Zhang, J. (2006) The sophistication of exports: a new trade measure, *World Development*, 34 (2): 222–37.

Liang, Y. (2008) Why are China's exports special: the role of FDI, regional trade, and government policies, *Chinese Economy*, 41 (6): 99–118.

Minondo, A. (2010) Exports' quality-adjusted productivity and economic growth, *The Journal of International Trade and Economic Development*, 19 (2): 257–87.

Mishra, S., Lundström, S. and Anand, R. (2011) *Service Export Sophistication and Economic Growth*. World Bank Working Paper 5606.

Mitsuyama, H., Iijima, M. and Uchimoto, Y. (2013) Consideration of the technological brands and price premium strategies for SPM in Japan, *International Journal of Business Performance Management*, 14 (4): 356–67.

Palma, J. G. (2009) Flying-geese and waddling-ducks: the different capabilities of East Asia and Latin America to 'demand-adapt' and 'supply-upgrade' their export productive capacity. In G. Dosi, M. Cimoli and J. E. Stiglitz (eds) *Industrial Policy and Development: the Political Economy of Capabilities Accumulation*. Oxford: Oxford University Press, pp. 203–38.

Polity IV (2015) Polity IV Project: Political Regime Characteristics and Transitions, 1800–2015. Available at www.systemicpeace.org/inscr/inscr.htm (accessed 5 December 2015).

Poncet, S. and de Waldemar, F. S. (2013) Export upgrading and growth: the prerequisite of domestic embeddedness, *World Development*, 51, November, 104–18.

Puga, D. and Trefler, D. (2010) Wake up and smell the ginseng: International trade and the rise of incremental innovation in low-wage countries, *Journal of Development Economics*, 91 (1): 64–76.

Raju, S. and Fitzpatrick, B. (2010) Financial market development, economic development and growth diagnostics: An application to Peru, *International Business and Economics Research Journal*, 9 (9): 24–66.

Rodrik, D. (2006) What's so special about China's exports? *China and World Economy*, 14 (5): 1–19.

Saadi, M. (2012) Export sophistication and the terms of trade of the developing and emerging countries, *International Review of Applied Economics*, 26 (5): 623–42.

Sacerdoti, E. El-Masry, G. Khandelwal, P and Yao, Y. (2005) *Mauritius Challenges of Sustained Growth*. Washington, DC: International Monetary Fund.

Santos-Paulino, A. U. (2010) Export productivity and specialization: A disaggregated analysis, *The World Economy*, 33 (9):1095–116.

———. (2011) Trade specialization, export productivity and growth in Brazil, China, India, South Africa, and a cross-section of countries, *Economic Change and Restructuring*, 44 (1): 75–97.

Schott, P. K. (2008) The relative sophistication of Chinese exports, *Economic Policy and Review*, 23 (53): 5–49.

Seyoum, B. (2005) Determinants of levels of high technology exports: an empirical investigation, *Advances in Competitiveness Research*, 13 (1): 64–79.

Spence, D. M. and Karingi, N. S. (2011) The impact of trade facilitation mechanisms on international trade and poverty reduction, *Trade and Investment for Development*, 67 (1): 1–37.

Shaw, T. M. and Fanta, E. (2013) Introduction: comparative regionalisms for development in the 21st century: Insights from the global South. In E. Fanta, T. M. Shaw and V. T. Tang (eds) *Comparative Regionalisms for Development in the 21st century: Insights from the Global South*. Farnham: Ashgate, 1–17.

Tang, V. T. (2015) Does learning by importing, self-selection of markets and financial innovation matter for exporting firms in the special economic zones? *Investment Management and Financial Innovations*, 12 (1): 198–206.

United Nations Commodity Trade Statistics (UNCOMTRADE) (2015) Available at http://comtrade.un.org (accessed 5 December 2015).

United Nations Conference on Trade and Development (UNCTAD) (2015) Available at http://unctadstat.unctad.org/TableViewer (accessed 25 August 2015).

Vettas, N. (2000) Investment dynamics in markets with endogenous demand. *The Journal of Industrial Economics*, 48 (2): 189–203.

Weiss, J. (2010) Changing trade structure and its implications for growth. *The World Economy*, 33 (10): 1269–79.

World Bank (2014) *Growth*. Washington, DC: World Bank. Available at www.worldbank.org/en/topic/macroeconomics/brief/growth (accessed 25 August 2016).

———. (2015) *World Development Indicators 2016*. Washington, DC: World Bank. Available at databank.worldbank.org/data/Views/Reports/ReportWidgetCustom.aspx?Report_Name=MDG-Table&Id=c658ae98&inf=n (accessed 24 June 2015).

———. (2016) *World Development Indicators 2016*. Washington, DC: World Bank. Available at databank.worldbank.org/data/Views/Reports/ReportWidgetCustom.aspx?Report_Name=MDG-Table&Id=c658ae98&inf=n (accessed 25 August 2016)

Xing, Y. (2012) Processing trade, exchange rates and China's bilateral trade balances, *Journal of Asian Economics*, 23 (5): 540–7.

Xu, B. (2010) The sophistication of exports: Is China special? *China Economic Review*, 21 (3): 482–93.

Xu, B. and Lu, J. Y. (2009) Foreign direct investment, processing trade, and the sophistication of China's export, *China Economic Review*, 20 (3): 425–39.

8 The Internet of Things and the sharing economy

Harnessing the possibilities for Africa's sustainable development goals

Kobena T. Hanson and Korbla P. Puplampu

Introduction

When global leaders and development practitioners gathered in 2015 to adopt the Sustainable Development Goals (SDGs), progress had been made across the board, from fighting poverty to improving education and health, and reducing hunger, but there still was more to be done. In the 15 years preceding the adoption of the SDGs (i.e. between the Millennium Development Goals (MDGs) and SDGs), improvements in the knowledge economy and enhancements in the area of information and communication technologies (ICTs), particularly the internet, 'have catalyzed major shifts in the global economy and ICTs are playing a transformative role in improving economic and social outcomes for low income and marginalized populations' (Garrity 2015: 1).

While the SDGs are undoubtedly an ambitious undertaking, and nowhere is this task more daunting as on the African continent, it is also increasingly recognized that Africa's future and ability to deliver on the SDGs, will be determined by the strategic choices, particularly the capacity, leadership and policy abilities that Africans individually and collectively demonstrate. A key area where Africa needs to strategically map out and harness its opportunities is an area vibrant in the emerging technology, the vast potential of the Internet of Things[1] (IoT) and the associated sharing economy.[2] These areas offer promising solutions to transform the operation and role of many existing systems such as transportation, health, tourism and manufacturing.

In the global North, there are already well-established companies in many domains of the IoT/sharing economy. However, in the global South, and sub-Saharan Africa (SSA) in particular, IoT/sharing economy businesses are still in their infancy but growing fast. Across much of SSA, the spread of mobile devices has heralded a digital revolution to serve as a catalyst of growth. The emerging IoT/sharing economy has spurred 'micro entrepreneurs' and facilitated the creation of new markets and economic opportunities. Granted, the IoT/sharing economy services in most sectors in Africa are in their formative stages compared to the experiences in the global North, where the growth and adoption of such platforms (local and foreign) and associated services have been impressive, from M-Pesa, M-Kopa, 2go, BBOXX, eBird, Airbnb, Uber to eBay. Enterprising citizens can now generate income by renting assets as varied as mobile phones, vacant rooms (Airbnb), engaging in mobile money transfers (M-Pesa), and more. These resourceful individuals possessing desirable assets are becoming 'micro-entrepreneurs'. It is for this and other reasons that Agyeman *et al.* (2013) note that today, the IoT/sharing economy is gaining prominence across Africa and presents an attractive opportunity to redistribute goods, services or experiences.

This chapter contends that these embryonic developments have the potential to drive Africa in its quest to meet its SDG targets while spurring on socio-economic development. Specifically, IoT/sharing economy companies and peer-to-peer networks are poised to become a significant segment of Africa's future economic activity, stimulating new consumption, raising productivity, catalysing entrepreneurship, and generating new tax revenue and invariably transforming the lives and livelihoods of many. This view is also espoused by International Telecommunication Union (ITU) and Cisco (2016) who, in their recently published report titled *Harnessing the Internet of Things for Global Development*, note that the sharing economy will have a major impact in areas such as grassroots delivery of health care and education – two areas key to the SDGs – by positively transforming communities; a prospect that would have been unimaginable just a few years ago.

Following the introduction, the chapter highlights the dynamics accounting for the meteoric rise of the IoT and sharing economy broadly, and across sub-Saharan Africa in particular. Next, the chapter focuses on the opportunities and possibilities of the emerging development, while also addressing the challenges that it presents, notably consumer protection, labour regulation, property rights, taxation, and discriminatory practices. The chapter then looks at how sub-Saharan Africa can, and should, ride on the wave of the sharing economy and IoT to deliver on the SDGs, tapping into their vast potential to advance the central tenets of the SDGs. In concluding, the chapter submits that Africa can seize the twenty-first century among others by leveraging the emerging technologically driven and revised landscape, in the process unlocking previously unused, or underutilized skills and assets, while creating wealth for individuals, albeit in a very flexible manner (Wosskow 2014).

Drivers and trends of the IoT/sharing economy: the global and African contexts

The IoT/sharing economy broadly refer to the phenomenon of using the plethora of mobile technologies to turn unused or underutilized assets, skills or services owned by individuals into productive resources. Its ingenuity lies in its uncanny ability to harness new technologies to reduce transaction costs and connect people offering assets or services to consumers. In so doing, the IoT/sharing economy generates value by matching these assets with consumers in need of, and willing to pay for, the services those assets could provide.

According to PwC (2014a), as of 2013, the sharing economy alone comprised a market of approximately US$15 billion globally. This figure is expected to grow to US$335 billion by 2025, more than 20 times the current size (PwC 2014b). While the rising sharing economy is driven by three separate market drivers – societal, economic, and technological (Owyang 2013) – there is no denying that at the core of its appeal and continued growth is one crucial factor: trust. Trust is the enabling factor inherent within all sharing-sector activities. As Wosskow (2014: 18) points out, trust is central to the sharing economy, and 'is critical for all peer-to-peer (p2p) businesses'.

Other associated elements driving the growth of the sharing economy include rising unemployment rates coupled with declining purchasing power of consumers, invariably motivating people to seek creative ways to earn or save money, which is why consumers are currently more receptive to peer-to-peer business models centred on consumer needs both as a potential supplier and buyer (Dervojeda *et al.* 2013: 2). Additionally, the needed technologies for hosting online p2p platforms, have in recent years, become available at more reasonable costs. In the case of sub-Saharan Africa, the experience of M-Pesa is a good case in point.

A couple of trends have been mapped out regarding the evolution of the IoT/sharing economy. First, technological advancements have allowed businesses to spread to diverse markets while staying convenient and flexible. A worthy example is 'Spotify', the music streaming service, which conveniently offers consumers access to millions of music tracks, via their phone, tablet or computer. Second, is the growth in p2p based businesses. Here, unlike in the conventional marketplace, entrepreneurs are facilitating access for consumer-to-consumer-owned property or skills and competencies. Using online platforms that connect consumers that own certain assets and skills with consumers in temporary need of these assets/skills, businesses are facilitating p2p markets for potentially all manner of products or services (Dervojeda *et al.* 2013).

Across SSA, the full potential of the IoT/sharing economy is only just starting to become clear, and more research is needed to show how local communities are engaging with this development. Transportation, health care, agriculture, hotel and tourist industry, and banking are all areas 'where IoT/sharing economy models are starting to transform communities and services, but we need to do more to understand these benefits' (Wosskow 2014: 17). The strong demand for mobile technologies across the sub-region has created a huge array of sharing economy platforms that are readily available, affordable and scalable. Many countries in SSA already have the basic infrastructure in place to support sharing economy businesses (Zhao 2016). Sharing practices have become a widespread phenomenon with the development and accessibility of information and communication social technology that easily connects strangers, supports peer-to-peer collaboration, incentivizes people to cooperate, acquires data about the past and present, and can predict future behaviour of participants involved in sharing practices. Apart from the creation of new jobs through the hiring of new staff, companies operating in the sharing economy also generate substantial amounts of indirect employment. Digital innovation, particularly the growth in mobile telephony, is creating entirely new ways of doing business.

In the absence of official, or even comprehensive, statistics it is difficult to determine precisely who is participating in Africa's sharing economy, and what the impacts and net effects are. However, as per figure 8.1, consumers across Africa are obviously open to sharing, even though many countries across SSA face challenges that can make doing business in the traditional sense unattractive. These challenges include unreliable or poor governance, access to credit or funding difficulties, weak or non-existent regulation and enforcement. At the same time, features of the IoT/sharing economy, flexibility, peer-to-peer review systems, can be utilized to negotiate these hurdles (van Welsum 2016), and help overcome governance and regulatory issues.

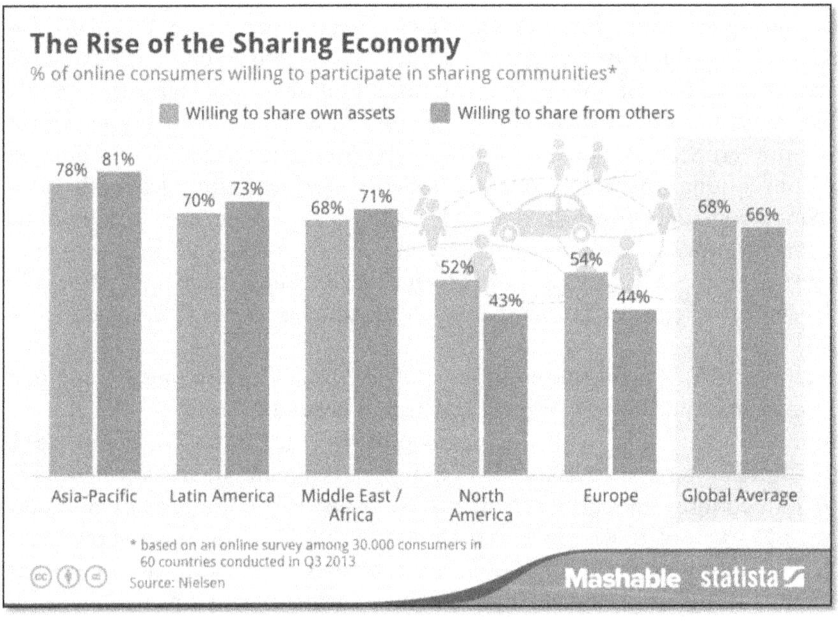

Figure 8.1 Percentage of consumers per region, willing to participate in sharing communities

Source: infographic.statista.com/normal/chartoftheday_2323_The_Rise_of_the_Sharing_Economy_n.jpg

Opportunities and possibilities

Micro-entrepreneurs are transforming many sectors of the African economy, including accommodation, skills and transport, and changing the way businesses work with each other. In the process, they have empowered a host of consumers to capitalize on their property and skills and reduce the cost of ownership. As Wagner *et al.* (2015) put it, IoT/sharing economy initiatives offer new possibilities to consumers by providing them an alternative approach to the prevalent consumer mindset and by disrupting the classical understanding of the producer–consumer relationship. Indeed, across Africa, with its long history of a thriving informal economy, the rise of the IoT and sharing economy is evolving as a seamless transition and an opportunity to generate income, either full time or part-time, and/or as a complement to other forms and types of employment, being a parent at home, or while pursuing education (Oppong 2015; van Welsum 2016).

The aforementioned are clear indications of the extent to which the breakthroughs in ICTs are contributing to Africa's development (Hanson *et al.* 2015; Oppong 2015). Studies also show that while the growth and uptake of ICTs vary across the continent and the trends generally are positive (Oppong 2015; Biteye 2013; Prensky 2001a, 2001b). Among the regional blocs, South African Development Commission (SADC) has made significant strides in ICTs by way of access, although prices are still quite high. ECOWAS is closely behind SADC in terms of the relative performance of ICTs. However, similar to SADC, it faces high prices for services, but boasts of better broadband prices compared to SADC (Oppong 2015). A noteworthy aspect of ICTs in ECOWAS is the high cost within member countries compared to calls to distant locales such as the United States of America (Hanson *et al.* 2015). ICT features in EAC mirror those of SADC and ECOWAS, but with different outcomes (Oppong 2015). First, the cost of services are high; penetration of internet services is low; coverage is not extensive in Tanzania; limited in Ethiopia; and mobile signal coverage high in Sudan. The NEPAD (2013) portfolio on ICT infrastructure is spearheading the East Africa Submarine Cable System (EASSy) to connect EAC member countries, eventually tapping into the optical fibre submarine networking running from South Africa to Sudan.

With over 200 million people aged between 15 and 24 years, a figure that is expected to double by 2045, Africa has the world's largest youth population (Ighobor 2013). The continent's growing youth population is well educated, highly energetic, creative and talented; critical ingredients for future prosperity (Ighobor 2013; Kararach *et al.* 2011). The youth are also digital natives, born into the digital age and growing up using information and communication technologies (ICTs) in their daily lives (Oppong 2015; Prensky 2001a, 2001b). Africa's burgeoning population of digital natives are also the entrepreneurs and innovators for societal transformation (Biteye 2013; Kalan 2013; Kyem 2012).

At present there are many IoT technologies and associated businesses across Africa, ranging from eHealth models that enable health care providers to track the health of outpatients and send reminders to patients to take their medication; to power companies using connected meters to check usage, find faults and pre-empt surges in demand (Green *et al*, 2014; Opoku-Mensah 2016). In 2013 for instance, Gauteng Province in South Africa introduced e-tolling. This electronic toll collection system identifies vehicles electronically without any physical cash transactions taking place on the road or highway using an e-tag or by recoding the vehicle's licence number via overhead cameras installed on gantries, and interpreted by computers (Opoku-Mensah 2016) resulted in a dramatic reduction in traffic jams and provided a novel way to manage revenue collection.

Another example of IoT in practice is from Kenya, where the Nairobi County Council and IBM (International Business Machines) have installed sensor-based devices on council garbage trucks to effectively monitor them for efficient use (Opoku-Mensah 2016). Similarly in 2010 the National Agency for Food and Drugs Administration and Control (NAFDAC) in Nigeria, in an effort to combat counterfeiting resorted to product verification initiative using radio-frequency identification (RFID). The initiative carried out in collaboration with Verification Technology Limited (VTL) used tags equipped with RFID to secure the integrity of the drugs throughout the supply chain starting from manufacturers, distributors, wholesalers, retailers and even consumers (Opoku-Mensah 2016).

The IoT regime in Africa has been bolstered by other significant events. In May 2015, MTN Business unveiled the first pan-African Internet of Things (IoT) platform (Opoku-Mensah 2016) to complement the changing landscape in Africa. Relatedly, other social platforms such as Twitter, Facebook, and Africa's home-grown MXit, are providing spaces for dialogue and informal learning in an environment of fun and experimentation. Already, there are numerous examples of young entrepreneurial Africans driving new initiatives and transforming lives within their communities, countries and in some cases regions. The recent proliferation of local ICT development clusters, such as iHub and NaiLab in Kenya, Hive CoLab and AppLab in Uganda, Activspaces in Cameroon, BantaLabs in Senegal, or infoDev's mLabs in Kenya and South Africa, are helping to create the context for collaboration, training, application and content development, and pre-incubation of firms (World Bank Group, African Development Bank, and African Union 2012). Technology giant, Intel, is investing in Kenya's iHub to build a thriving community of local developers by providing training and resources. It is also partnering with ten Kenyan universities to increase the number of local developers working on localized app contents (Nyirenda-Jere and Biru 2015). Others have combined their interests in communal projects, such as the creation of the Cape Town Internet exchange (Oppong 2015). These labs serve as an accessible platform for bringing together technologists, investors, tech companies and enthusiasts. The labs further provide an environment to share experiences, brainstorm and use digital technology to create tech communities that have no borders.

The Rockefeller Foundation's Digital Jobs for Africa Initiative is another significant example of the kinds of strategies that are emerging (Grady 2013). Led by the Nairobi office, with pilot projects in Kenya, South Africa, Ghana, Nigeria and Morocco, the programme seeks to use digital jobs to help young people build transferable skill sets that make them resilient in their economies, strengthens their future employment opportunities, and enhances their adaptability to the changing nature of the workplace. And since 2010, some African countries, such as Tunisia, Rwanda and Algeria, have proactively set aside resources to support the advent of IoT (Opoku-Mensah 2016) so as to better embrace and prepare for the revised landscape.

Challenges

In tapping into the vast potential of the IoT/sharing economy, Africa needs to be mindful of the fact that while innovation and technology can contribute to the central tenets of the SDGs, specifically development and inclusion (i.e. by networking people and offering access to information and knowledge; helping enhance access to goods and services; creating spaces for new voices to speak up; contributing in diverse ways to good governance and international agency accountability; creating jobs and wealth), it also can create spaces of exclusion by denying some access, use and benefit from tech and tech-enabled processes and advances (Raftree 2015). At issue is the fact that technology functions within a social context and its embodiment and broader impact on society is not neutral. Thus, like any social phenomenon, technology, and in this context the IoT/sharing economy, will produce winners and losers. The focus therefore needs to be placed on the social environment and the underlying social structure.

The IoT/sharing economy also presents substantial risks. Countries have invested time and money into building their regulatory regimes, however imperfect, to protect workers, consumers, and property owners. Embracing the IoT/sharing economy requires a rethink or revamp of the regulatory structure. Issues such as consumer protection, labour regulation, property rights, taxation and discriminatory practices will all need to be revised in this fluid sharing economy landscape. Accordingly, grasping how and when to regulate IoT/sharing economy companies is essential to keep consumers, operators and traditional companies satisfied, innovating and growing. As Cagle (2014) cautions, issues pertaining to unregulated labour or the general lack of regulation, can lead to exploitation, limited access to health care or social services including unemployment benefits. And given the increasing popularity of IoT/sharing economy businesses among younger people, calls for regulation should be taken seriously. Similarly, there is the concern of collection and payment of taxes by sharing economy firms. It is possible that internet-based providers may use this platform as a way to avoid the taxes imposed on their traditional competitors. Ranchordás (2015), therefore, calls for a new legal framework as extant legal frameworks do not suffice. IoT/sharing economy practices challenge regulations on a daily basis, evidence in the tension between the need to encourage innovation and the need to protect customers from fraud, liability and practices that might endanger public health or safety (Cohen and Zehngebot 2014; Ranchordás 2015).

Regulators are at a crossroads: on the one hand, innovation in the IoT/sharing economy should not be stifled by excessive and outdated regulation; on the other hand, there is a real need to protect the users of these services from fraud, liability and unskilled service providers (Ranchordás 2015: 1). Similarly, while the ongoing dialogue about regulation, privacy and trade 'generally focuses heavily on sharing services, the IoT, where devices as mundane as refrigerators and home fire alarms are connected to the Internet, further complicate such concerns' (Ashton-Hart 2016: 149). Consequently, the ability of existing infrastructure to handle multiple lines of connectivity become paramount and require further attention.

The IoT/sharing economy challenges also bring into focus the debate surrounding governance and regulations that have been ongoing for a while (Opoku-Mensah 2016); and how African countries should strategize individually and collectively to make the best of these emerging developments to achieve specific SDG targets and socioeconomic transformation while ensuring that creativity is not stifled. Responding to the challenges requires a rethink and a strategic realignment of the role of the African Union, the various regional economic organizations and other specialized bodies in the region (Hanson, 2015).

Aside from challenges of regulation, analysts have also observed that while IoT/sharing economy businesses create opportunities to generate income, they do not necessarily tend to share the wealth equally, because of the different levels of endowment at the individual level. The wealth creation continues against the background of significant variations in assets (van Welsum 2016). These trends confirm the contention by Frantzeskaki *et al.* (2012: 22) that 'sustainable development at local or regional levels does not necessarily relate to, and translate into, national or global sustainability and vice versa'. So, while sharing may trigger localized sustainable lifestyle choices, this does not necessarily mean that they have a large enough scale to have macro-level impact, especially in view of the unreliable and unenforceable tax regime in several African countries (Fjeldstad *et al.* 2014).

Bearing in mind the nature of the African state, with many fragile and/or in a post-conflict situation, the need for a stable policy environment cannot be overemphasized. State capacity is therefore a critical topic that has to be enhanced and advanced comprehensively. Doing so effectively will involve transformative leadership and capacity development of the regulators, regulatory and enforcement institutions, as well as for individuals and institutions tasked with playing an oversight role. In 2010, the African Union (AU) embarked on a process of defining a framework for cybersecurity, culminating in the endorsement at the AU Summit in June 2014 of the African Union Convention on Cybersecurity and the Personal Data Protection. The broad objective of the Convention was to harmonize legislation related to e-transactions, personal data protection, and combating cybercrime. While definitely a step in the right direction, the regulatory framework governing the revised landscape and associated wealth being created needs attention. Again, while many IoT/sharing economy businesses already undertake precautions similar to that of traditional businesses (e.g. background checks on suppliers; online feedback mechanisms that encourage buyers and sellers to rate one another; etc.) (Dellarocas 2003), the aforementioned warning signs still need significant consideration.

Africa, the IoT/sharing economy and the SDGs

The unparalleled rapid growth of mobile technology use across Africa over the past decade has revolutionized communications in Africa, and the much-improved connectivity is transforming business and trade transactions (Oppong 2015). In 2000, Africa had less than 20 million fixed-line phones. However, by 2012, Africa had more than 500 million mobile phone subscriptions, more than in the United States or the European Union, making Africa the fastest growing region in the world (Oppong 2015). Driven by falling costs, mobile technologies and platforms are transforming everything from banking and health care (with text messages used to transfer money and send health advice), to agriculture (farmers can receive guidance, weather forecasts and market reports) and politics (Ekine 2010; Oppong 2015). These early success stories are essential to specific aspects of the SDGs. The application of mobile platform capabilities to detecting and mapping disease outbreaks relate to SDG 3, which calls for healthy lives and to promote well-being for all ages. In addition, SDG 4 focus on inclusive and equitable quality education is being addressed by the proliferation of educational resources, and the platforms for economic empowerment such as e-commerce and mobile banking are consistent to several SDGs, including 1, 2, 8 and 9

Africa's economic growth is being positively influenced by the growth of the IoT/sharing economy. Although still nascent, especially when compared to developments in the global North, the changing technology landscape is already attracting the interest of global players such as Uber and Airbnb in a way that aligns with SDGs 8, 9 and 17. Uber, for instance, launched its service in the region in 2012, starting in South Africa and expanding into Nigeria in 2014. Today, services are available almost all African countries. Local taxi hailing start-ups such as AfriCAB in Côte d'Ivoire, Sasa cabs in Kenya and Tranzit in Nigeria, as well as the Brazilian cab service Easy Taxi, have also emerged as key players in the region (GSMA 2015; Nyirenda-Jere and Biru 2015). Indeed, across Africa, IoT/sharing economy are facilitating the creation of new markets and economic activities where none previously existed.

The unfolding dynamics has made it possible for some countries to emerge as niche destinations. Nairobi, Kenya has been central to the developments of IoT/sharing economy and has been leading innovations in areas such as mobile money (M-Pesa) and crowdsourcing (Ushahidi) (GSMA 2015). Mobile money penetration and payments by phone have helped drive rapid growth not only in Kenya but across East Africa (Rosen 2016). Across Kenya, mobile phones have enabled consumers to set up, manage and access their own bank accounts via their mobile operator through the M-Pesa system (Opoku-Mensah 2016). A number of incubators and accelerators have also sprung up across the region, as is a flourishing app economy (Nyirenda-Jere and Biru 2015). Having over 15 million customers, M-Pesa accounts for 12 per cent of Kenya's GDP, with a further 31 per cent of GDP now being transacted through the service (GSMA 2015; Nyirenda-Jere and Biru 2015). Nascent markets of particular interest include Nigeria and Ethiopia, Africa's two most populous nations.

Other mobile banking platforms exist across Africa. These services allow clients to send money directly through a mobile device without the need for a fixed bank account. In Rwanda for instance, htxt.Africa (2015) attests to the meaningful way in which SIM cards are being used to connect point of sale terminals in remote areas, enabling merchants to accept credit or debit card payments. Several popular local apps originating from South Africa and Nigeria are now in operation. These include social networking and messaging apps (Mxit, 2go and How Far), and entertainment apps (Simfy Africa, Spinlet, iRokoTV, SOLO and iROKING). 2go, for instance, has more than 50 million registered users across Africa while How Far, which launched in Nigeria in February 2015, recorded more than 10,000 downloads in the Google Play Store within its first few months. Beyond entertainment and social networking, IoT technologies are being employed in many other sectors – sensors to monitor soil conditions and moisture levels; RFID tags for personalized care for their livestock; mobile phone for monitoring elections and enhancing governance; off-grid solar systems bringing affordable electricity to lower-income families (GSMA 2015; ITU and Cisco 2016; Opoku-Mensah 2016).

In Nigeria, where start-ups such as Konga, Wakanow, Iroko and Paga are booming, analysts predict that venture capital funding in tech start-ups and across the African continent will exceed half a billion dollars by 2018 (GSMA 2015). Competition and inherent challenges in delivering education and health care are driving providers to turn to digital technologies.

Aside from the growth in, and widespread acceptance of, distance education/e-learning (Hanson and Léautier 2011), enhancements in digital technology are transforming educational experiences and allowing many, who otherwise could not do so, access education in a more affordable manner. In Uganda, for example, initiatives such as BBOXX, which employs machine to machine (M2M) connectivity, and innovative off-grid energy suppliers are supplying solar power generators to rural consumers (Vodafone 2016). They are subsequently helping to enhance outcomes as was the installation of 51 BBOXX solar systems in eight primary schools in 2014, which resulted in enrolment rates increasing by 63 per cent, and the number of students who felt unsafe at night dropping from 85 per cent to less than 1 per cent.

The growing uptake of IoT/sharing economy will accelerate in a number of African markets as the mobile payments ecosystem expands and governments realize the systems can drive electrification quickly and at a comparatively low cost (Rosen 2016). Already, a leading provider of off-grid solar services in sub-Saharan Africa, M-Kopa, has sold over 400,000 systems across East Africa, especially in Kenya, Tanzania and Uganda, since its launch in 2011 (Rosen 2016). The system includes an eight-watt solar panel, six-volt lithium-ion battery, two LED lightbulbs, mobile phone charging station, torch and radio costs approximately US$217. Furthermore it is a form of green energy, and costs just US$60 more than what an average off-grid Kenyan household will spend on kerosene, batteries, phone charging and candles. The M-Kopa system not only enables customers to use the M-Pesa or Airtel Money to effect payments, but can also 'remotely monitor the amount of electricity captured/stored and whether the device is working appropriately through the device's connectivity module' (ITU and Cisco 2016: 37).

Elsewhere on the continent, creative uses of mobile telephony include, but are not limited to, the following: mPedigree, a service that verifies whether drugs are genuine by simply sending a text message query (Yeebo 2015). This is a vital service in the fight against the proliferation of counterfeit drugs on the continent. Today, mPedigree has labels on more than 500 million drugs. Clients include the drug companies AstraZeneca, Roche, and Sanofi. It has offices in Egypt, Ghana, India, Kenya, Nigeria, and Tanzania, with pilots in Uganda, Tanzania, South Africa, and Bangladesh.

Following the post-election violence in Kenya in 2007, the mobile app ushahidi.com, was created in Kenya that employs crowdsourcing to generate local incident mapping and coordinate emergency response services (Tavaana.org 2017). The app has subsequently been used globally.

In India and Mexico, the platform has been used to monitor elections. The app also enabled relief efforts during floods in Thailand and Pakistan and after the devastating 2010 earthquake in Haiti (Tavaana.org 2017).

In Niger, Tech-Innov, a tele-irrigation system for fields controlled by mobile phones is transforming lives and communities. The initiative has garnered much global praise and recognition including a distinguished medal at the International exhibition of Inventions of Geneva in 2012. Recently a derivative of Tech-Innov, the drinking water kiosk, has been judged the winner of the Green Design Contest in Nice, France, and subsequently honoured by the World Water Forum in Korea (stisolutions4sdgs 2016). Another app, M-Farm, is transforming Africa's agricultural landscape by providing farmers real time access to information about the weather, current retail prices for their products, potential buyers, as well as places where they can buy seeds (Bleiberg and West 2015).

In Southern Africa, particularly in Madagascar and South Africa, IoT technology eBird is being used to monitor endemic bird areas (EBAs) for conservation and support for tourism (Dlodlo 2012). The eBird application allows scientists to gather and track via mobile devices, precise data on bird sighting 'counts of individual birds for each of the recorded species, areas of interest and the time span in which sighting was performed' (Dlodlo 2012: 49). South Africa, is also employing internet-connected smart meters to measure household utility consumption in urban localities such as Johannesburg (htxt.Africa 2015). In the mining sector, sensors are being used to detect methane and rock movement; and fuel pipelines have been fitted with sensors to monitor leaks. Elsewhere in the retail sector, South Africa is utilizing RFID technology to track, by way of intelligent bar codes, items in a retail environment (htxt.Africa 2015).

In the environmental conversation and tourism industry, endangered species such as the black rhino in eastern and central Africa are being fitted with ankle collars that are connected to the global IoT network and relay movement and exact geo-location data to anti-poaching teams. Elsewhere in the agricultural sector the Syngenta's Kilimo Salama ('Safe Farming') weather station monitors agricultural events and facilitates linkages with insurance firms to mitigate risks associated with adverse weather (ITU and Cisco 2016: 33). This initiative collaborates with the M-Pesa mobile banking system, making for easy and accessible payment for beneficiaries.

From a broader developmental perspective, the growing mobile industry is, and will for some time to come, remain a key driver of economic growth and employment across the region. In 2014, Africa's mobile ecosystem generated 5.7 per cent of the continent's GDP, a contribution of just over US$100 billion in economic value; and this figure is expected to grow to 8.2 per cent of GDP by 2020 (GSMA 2015: 2). It is because of this potential that much attention is now being focused on these developments (GSMA 2015; Opoku-Mensah 2016), and why others contend that connected sensors and M2M connectivity represent the next frontier in the ICT4D story (ITU and Cisco 2016). Table 8.1 highlights some of the emerging IoT/sharing economic developments across the continent, and how they relate to the SDGs.

The IoT / sharing economy initiatives are certainly contributing towards the attainment of the SDGs. The ITU/Cisco (2016) report, *Harnessing the Internet of Things for Global Development* highlights how IoT, particularly sensor deployments, are enhancing development activities in areas such as research, policy formulation, service delivery, and monitoring and evaluation across a range of different sectors including agriculture, sanitation, natural resource management, and energy. These developments, together with the growing number of tech start-ups across Africa, are key to the extent to which the IoT/sharing economy will impact Africa's attainment of the SDGs as well as wider socioeconomic transformation (Opoku-Mensah 2016). Many others speak to the role IoT applications/sharing economy businesses can play in environmental monitoring, conservation and tourism, education, health, agriculture (Dlodlo 2012; GSMA 2015; Oppong 2015).

Table 8.1 Examples of African IoT interventions and SDGs

Sector	*SDG*	*Intervention(s)*
Health, water and sanitation	**SDG 3**: Ensure healthy lives and promote well-being for all at all ages. **SDG 6**: Ensure availability and sustainable management of water and sanitation for all.	Sensor- and SMS-enabled village water pumps (Rwanda, Kenya); RFID – secure integrity of drugs (Nigeria); GSM-connected refrigeration for vaccine delivery in the 'cold chain' (global); Sensor- enabled 'band aid' to monitor Ebola patients' ECG, heart rate, oxygen saturation, body temperature, respiratory rate and position, all remotely (West Africa).
Agriculture and livelihoods	**SDG 1**: End poverty in all its forms everywhere. **SDG 8**: Promote sustained, inclusive and sustainable economic growth, full and productive employment and decent work for all. **SDG 2**: End hunger, achieve food security and improve nutrition, and promote sustainable agriculture.	Connected micro-weather stations improving localized weather data and provision of crop failure insurance (Kenya); Soil-monitoring sensors used to improve tea plantation production (Rwanda); RFID based livestock programmes for tracking, theft prevention and vaccination records (Botswana, Senegal and Namibia).
Education	**SDG 4**: Ensure inclusive and equitable quality education and promote lifelong learning opportunities for all.	Smart identity cards with biometric features for all public school students to improve service delivery (Nigeria); Biometric clocking device to improve teacher attendance in real-time (South Africa).
Environment and conservation	**SDG 12**: Ensure sustainable consumption and production patterns. **SDG 13**: Take urgent action to combat climate change and its impacts. **SDG 14**: Conserve and sustainably use the oceans, seas and marine resources for sustainable development. **SDG 15**: Protect, restore and promote sustainable use of terrestrial ecosystems, sustainably manage forests, combat desertification, halt and reverse land degradation, and halt biodiversity loss.	Air pollution sensors to monitor urban outdoor air pollution (Benin); Acoustic sensors to monitor sea bird populations (Africa); Sensors and connectivity to protect game park perimeters and track animals (Africa).

(*continued*)

Table 8.1 (*Cont.*)

Sector	*SDG*	*Intervention(s)*
Resiliency, infrastructure and energy	**SDG 7**: Ensure access to affordable, reliable, sustainable and modern energy for all. **SDG 9**: Build resilient infrastructure, promote inclusive and sustainable industrialization, and foster innovation. **SDG 11**: Make cities and human settlements inclusive, safe, resilient and sustainable.	Networked fire/smoke alarms in high-density urban slums/ informal settlements (Kenya, South Africa); Off-grid micro solar electricity systems for electricity for lower-income households (East Africa); Connected black carbon- and use sensors to monitor cook stoves (Sudan); Sensor-connected *matatus* (mini-buses) tracking velocity, acceleration, and braking to curb dangerous operation of public transportation (Kenya).

Source: Adapted from Dlodlo (2012); ITU and Cisco (2016: table 3); Opoku-Mensah (2016).

The potential is unquestioned; however, Africa's policy-makers need to strategically scan their environment to identify the risks, possibilities and associated capacities needed to embrace and thrive in this evolving landscape if IoT/sharing economy initiatives are to leapfrog development. Realizing the possibilities of the IoT/sharing economy in terms of social and economic progress of bringing the more than four billion people with no internet access into the online world, also calls for leveraging the power of public–private partnerships and the huge potential of small and medium enterprises (SMEs) (Zhao 2016). Today's ICT ecosystem is primarily being driven by grassroots entrepreneurship, delivering local solutions to tackle local challenges. Entrepreneurs and SMEs offer up to 70 per cent of global employment (Zhao 2016), and their expertise, innovation and investment would be central to any meaningful effort to achieve the common goals enshrined in the SDGs.

Conclusion

If Africa is to seize the twenty-first century, and make the 'Africa Rising' narrative a reality, then, it needs to leverage the opportunities and possibilities of the sharing economy/IoT – the new, disruptive business platforms/models and challenges of 'traditional' businesses that enhance competition and offer new products and experiences to consumers.

According to McKinsey Global Institute (2013) in their report entitled *Disruptive technologies: Advances that will transform life, business, and the global economy*, 12 key technologies (i.e. mobile internet, automation of knowledge work, Internet of Things, cloud technology, advanced robotics, autonomous and near-autonomous vehicles, next-generation genomics, energy storage, 3D printing, advanced materials, advanced oil and gas exploration and recovery, and renewable energy) will drive truly massive economic transformations and disruptions in the coming years. The report goes on to point out that

> [f]rom monitoring the flow of products through a factory to measuring the moisture in a field of crops to tracking the flow of water through utility pipes, the Internet of Things [for example] allows businesses and public-sector organizations to manage assets, optimize performance, and create new business models.
>
> (McKinsey Global Institute 2013: 6)

Accordingly, how African agency in the form of national and regional initiatives and capacities might be strengthened vis-à-vis the emerging landscape of disruptive technologies including IoT/sharing economy is key. After all, Africa's development frameworks place an emphasis on the promotion, utilization and optimization of science, technology and innovation for accelerating the transformation agenda. The continent clearly has the edge and momentum in mobile technology penetration, usage and innovation. The economic benefits in terms of revenue and much-needed employment, particularly for the teeming population of digital natives, await the countries that create the right environment with strategic investment and supportive legislation. Embracing the challenges and opportunities head on, while collaborating with other neighbouring countries (Hanson *et al.* 2015; Oppong 2015), is crucial because no one can go at it alone. As Valensisi and Karingi's (2016) also note, a regional approach can offer the scope to integrate more closely the social and environmental concerns of the SDGs into existing development plans.

The transformation narrative spelt out in 'the UN 2030 Agenda for Sustainable Development and Africa's own 2063 Agenda, together with the public entrepreneurship paradigm, provides a much more hopeful way forward for African development than the paradigms of the last 30 years' (Besada *et al.* 2016: 19). The dynamic possibilities inherent in the leapfrogging potential in mobile technologies (Besada *et al.* 2016; GSMA 2015) provide the basis for a new kind of twenty-first century development process in Africa. The potential of the IoT/sharing economy are clearly limitless; and open up a number of valuable opportunities across different economic activities and change the landscape for employment, job creation and wealth generation. They further represent a paradigm shift in the labour market as it enables individuals to generate wealth, invariably transforming lives and livelihoods. To this end, the IoT/sharing economy has emerged as a viable alternative to fulfilling a variety of consumer needs. As the size and scope of the sharing economy/IoT have grown, so has the magnitude of its economic impacts.

Africa's thought-leaders and decision-makers need to strategically 'think and look ahead'. To do this effectively, efficiently and sustainably, they will need a good grasp of how technology will transform the socioeconomic landscape in the second half of the twenty-first century. Africans are already breaking down barriers through their use of mobile technologies, developing innovations to solve African problems, and exporting those innovations beyond their immediate geographic borders. It is time Africa's policy-makers follow suit with the appropriate policy and programmatic frameworks, while eliminating bottlenecks (Kararach, Besada and Shaw 2016). Perhaps, the synergies of involving multi-actors will jolt lagging African countries into action with a new sense of mission.

Notes

1 Originally coined by Ashton in 1999 in a presentation to Proctor and Gamble (2009) the Internet of Things is today broadly defined as 'a global infrastructure for the information society, enabling advanced services by interconnecting (physical and virtual) things based on existing and evolving interoperable information and communication technologies' (ITU and Cisco 2016).

2 Rapidly evolving cloud-computing platforms functioning in tandem with growing uptake in ICTs by consumers and a change in consumer behaviour and preferences have given birth to the 'sharing economy' (van Welsum 2016).

References

Agyeman, J., Mclaren, D. and Schaefer-Borrego, A. (2013) *Briefing: Sharing Cities.* Friends of the Earth, September, pp. 1–32.

Ashton, K. (2009) That 'Internet of Things' Thing, *RFID Journal*, 22 June.

Ashton-Hart, N. (2016) What Is the 'networked economy'? In C. A. Primo Braga and B. Hoekman (eds) *Future of the Global Trade Order.* San Domenico di Fiesole/Lausanne: European University Institute (EUI)/IMD.

Besada, H., Xue, J., Mathers, A. and Carey, R. (2016) Advancing African agency in the new 2030 transformative development agenda, *African Geographical Review*, dx.doi.org/10.1080/19376812.2016.1138232, pp. 1–26

Biteye, M. (2013) *Announcing Digital Jobs Africa.* The Rockefeller Foundation. Available at www.rockefellerfoundation.org/blog/announcing-digital-jobs-africa (accessed 11 November 2016).

Bleiberg, J. and West, D.M. (2015) "Three ways mobile is helping farmers in Kenya." *Brookings Tech Tank* (April 23). Available at https://www.brookings.edu/blog/techtank/2015/04/23/three-ways-mobile-is-helping-farmers-in-kenya/ (accessed January 15, 2017).

Cagle, S. (2014) Imagining the Future of Sharing, *The Nib – Medium.* Available at medium.com/the-nib/imagining-the-future-of-sharing-3fc2a6564a08 (accessed 15 August 2016).

Cohen, M. and Zehngebot, C. (2014) "What's Old Becomes New: Regulating the Sharing Economy." Boston Bar Journal, Vol. 56 (2). April 1 (Spring 2014). Available at https://bostonbarjournal.com/2014/04/01/whats-old-becomes-new-regulating-the-sharing-economy/ (accessed December 21, 2015).

Dellarocas, C. (2003) The digitization of worth of mouth: promise and challenges of online feedback mechanisms, *Management Science*, 49 (10): 1407–24.

Dervojeda, K., Verzijl, D., Nagtegaal, F., Lengton, M., Rouwmaat, E., Monfardini, E. and Frideres, L. (2013) *The Sharing Economy: Accessibility Based Business Models for Peer-to-Peer Markets*. Case Study No. 12, September. European Union.

Dlodlo, N. (2012) Adopting the internet of things technologies in environmental management in South Africa, *International Conference on Environment Science and Engineering IPCBEE*, 3 (2): 45–55. Singapore: IACSIT.

Ekine, S. (2010) *SMS Uprising: Mobile Activism in Africa*. Cape Town: Pambazuka.

Frantzeskaki, N., Loorbach, D. and Meadowcroft, J. (2012) Governing societal transitions to sustainability, *International Journal of Sustainable Development*, 15 (1/2): 19–36.

Fjeldstad, O-H., Chambas, G. and Brun, J-F. (2014) *Local Government Taxation in sub-Saharan Africa*. CMI Working Paper 2014: 2. Bergen: Chr. Michelsen Institute.

Garrity, J. (2015) *Harnessing the Internet of Things for Global Development*, 26 March. Available at ssrn.com/abstract=2588129 or dx.doi.org/10.2139/ssrn.2588129 (accessed 14 November 2016).

Grady, H. (2013) *Global Youth Economic Opportunities*. Paper presented at Making Cents International's 2013 Global Youth Economic Opportunities Conference, Washington, DC, 10–12 September. Available at www.rockefellerfoundation.org/blog/global-youth-economic-opportunities (accessed 10 November 2016).

Green, K., Clement, F. N., Torgbenu, S. M. W., Damalin, G., Benefour, S. and Wambugu, S. (2014) Improving lives in through mobile phones: the case of Ghana. In R. Krohn and D. Metcalf (eds) *Health Innovation: Best Practices from the Mobile Frontier.* Chicago: HIMSS, 273–8.

GSMA (2015) *The Mobile Economy: Sub Saharan Africa 2015*. London: GSMA.

Hanson, K. T. and Léautier, F. A. (2011) Enhancing institutional leadership in African universities: lessons from ACBF's interventions, *World Journal of Entrepreneurship, Management and Sustainable Development*, 7 (2–4): 386–417.

Hanson, K. T., Puplampu, K. P. and Owusu, F. (2015) Infrastructure development as a catalyst for regionalism and economic integration in Africa. In K. T. Hanson (ed.) *Contemporary Regional Development in Africa*. Farnham: Ashgate, pp.139–58.

htxt.Africa (2015) How the Internet of Things is Having an Impact in Africa. Available at www.htxt.co.za/2015/08/13/how-the-internet-of-things-is-having-an-impact-in-africa/ (accessed 6 December 2016).

Ighobor, K. (2013) Africa's Youth: A 'Ticking Time Bomb' or an Opportunity? Available at www.un.org/africarenewal/magazine/may-2013/africa%E2%80%99s-youth-%E2%80%9Cticking-time-bomb%E2%80%9D-or-opportunity#sthash.mj2178ff.dpuf (accessed 5 December 2016).

ITU (International Telecommunication Union) and Cisco (2016) *Harnessing the Internet of Things for Global Development*, June. Geneva: ITU. Available at www.itu.int/en/action/broadband/Documents/Harnessing-IoT-Global-Development.pdf (accessed 11 November 2016).

Kalan, J. (2013) African youth hungry for connectivity, *Africa Renewal*, May. Available at www.un.org/africarenewal/magazine/may-2013/african-youth-hungry-connectivity#sthash.PhaSoLUg.JFLMvq6o.dpuf (accessed 4 December 2016).

Kararach, G., Besada, H. and Shaw, T. (2016) African development, political economy and the road to Agenda 2063. In G. Kararach, H. Baseda and T. Shaw (eds) *Development in Africa: Reframing the Lens after the MDGs*. Bristol: Policy, pp. 365–92.

Kararach, G. K., Hanson, K. T. and Léautier, F. A. (2011) Regional integration policies to support job creation for africa' burgeoning youth population, *World Journal of Entrepreneurship, Management and Sustainable Development*, 7 (2/3/4): 177–215.

Kyem, P. (2012) Is ICT the panacea to sub-Saharan Africa's development problems? Rethinking Africa's contentious engagement with the global information society, *Progress in Development Studies*, 12 (2–3): 231–44.

McKinsey Global Institute (2013) *Disruptive Technologies: Advances that will Transform Life, Business, and the Global Economy*, May. McKinsey & Co. Available at www.mckinsey.com/business-functions/digital-mckinsey/our-insights/disruptive-technologies (accessed 28 February 2017).

Nyirenda-Jere, T. and Biru, T. (2015) *Internet development and Internet Governance in Africa*, May. Geneva/Reston, VA: Internet Society.

Opoku-Mensah, A. (2016) The Internet of Things in Africa: What will it take? 28 April. Available at www.linkedin.com/pulse/internet-things-africa-what-take-aida-opoku-mensah (accessed 11 November 2016).

Oppong, J. R. (2015) Innovation, Science and Technology: Regional Networks for Research and Technology Development in Africa. In K. T. Hanson (ed.) *Contemporary Regional Development in Africa*. Farnham: Ashgate, pp. 139–58.

Owyang, J. (2013) The collaborative economy, *Altimeter Research* (June 4): 1–27.

Prensky, M. (2001a) Digital natives, digital immigrants Part 1, *On the Horizon*, 9 (5): 1–6.

——— (2001b) Digital natives, digital immigrants Part 2: do they really think differently? *On the Horizon*, 9 (6): 1–6.

PwC (PricewaterhouseCoopers) (2014a) Five key sharing-economy sectors could generate 9 billion of UK revenue by 2015. Blog. Available at pwc.blogs.com/press_room/2014/08/five-key-sharing-economy-sectors-could-generate-9-billion-of-ukrevenues-by-2025.html

———. (2014b) The Sharing Economy: How Will it Disrupt Your Business? Megatrends: The Collisions. Blog. Available at pwc.blogs.com/fi les/sharing-economy-fi nal_0814.pdf (accessed 21 November 2016).

Raftree, L. (2015) Innovation, technology and the SDGs, 21 October 2015. Available at lindaraftree.com/2015/10/21/innovation-technology-and-the-sdgs/ (accessed 10 November 2016).

Ranchordás, S. (2015) Does sharing mean caring? Regulating innovation in the sharing economy, *Minnesota Journal of Law, Science & Technology*, 16 (1): 414–75.

Rosen, J. (2016) Africa Finds Power off the Grid, 2 December. *MIT Technology Review*. Available at www.technologyreview.com/s/603009/africa-finds-power-off-the-grid/ (accessed 6 December 2016).

Stisolutions4sdgs (2016) "Tele-Irrigation." (Technology Facilitation Mechanism). Available at (http://stisolutions4sdgs.globalinnovationexchange.org/innovations/tele-irrigation (accessed January 15, 2017).

Tavaana.org (2017) "Ushahidi: From Crisis Mapping Kenya to Mapping the Globe." Available at https://tavaana.org/en/content/ushahidi-crisis-mapping-kenya-mapping-globe (accessed January 15, 2017).

Valensisi, G. and Karingi, S. (2016) From global goals to regional strategies: towards an African approach to SDGs, *African Geographical Review*, June, pp. 1–16. Available at dx.doi.org/10.1080/19376812.2016.1185738 (accessed 20 November 2016).

van Welsum, D. (2016) Sharing is caring? Not quite. Some observations about 'the sharing economy'. *World Development Report 2016 Digital Dividends*. Washington, DC: World Bank Group.

Vodafone (2016) Why Africa is Feeling the Power of IoT, 7 March. Available at www.vodafone.com/business/why-africa-is-feeling-the-power-of-iot-2016-03-07 (accessed 6 December 2016).

Wagner, T., Kuhndt, M., Lagomarsino, J. and Mattar, H. (2015) Listening to Sharing Economy Initiatives – Report on a Global Survey. Available at www.scp-centre.org/wp-content/uploads/2016/05/Listening_to_Sharing_Economy_Initiatives.pdf (accessed 27 April 2017).

World Bank (2014) *Crowdfunding's Potential for the Developing World*. Washington, DC: World Bank Databank.

World Bank, African Development Bank, and African Union (2012) The Transformational Use of Information and Communication Technologies in Africa. Available at http://siteresources.worldbank.org/EXTINFORMATIONANDCOMMUNICATIONANDTECHNOLOGIES/Resources/282822-1346223280837/MainReport.pdf (accessed 2 May 2017).

World Economic Forum (WEF) (2013) *Circular Economy, Innovation and New Business Models Dialogue*. Young Global Leaders Sharing Economy Dialogue Position Paper 2013.

Wosskow, D. (2014) Unlocking the Sharing Economy: An Independent Review, November. Available at www.gov.uk/bis (accessed 15 August 2016).

Yeebo, Y. (2015) "The African Startup Using Phones to Spot Counterfeit Drugs." *BloombergBusinessnews* (July 31). Available at https://www.bloomberg.com/news/features/2015-07-31/the-african-startup-using-phones-to-spot-counterfeit-drugs (accessed January 15, 2017).

Zhao, H. (2016) Creating an inclusive digital economy is vital to achieving the SDGs, *International Trade Forum*, 2: 18–19. Available at search.proquest.com/openview/58029814f925ae66b44a17fc60826e7e/1?pq-origsite=gscholar&cbl=47429 (accessed 14 November 2016).

9 Environment and climate change in Africa in an era of sustainable development goals

Abbi M. Kedir

Introduction

Development without inclusive green growth and sustainability is no longer the preferred route to improving welfare in the globe (World Bank 2012). This is demonstrated in various international development conferences since the watershed year of 2015. Therefore, environment and climate change issues are at the heart of economic development as reflected in the Third Financing for Development international conference in July 2015 which led to the endorsement of Addis Ababa Action Agenda; Sustainable Development Goals (SDGs) agreed in September 2015 culminating in 17 goals to develop Agenda 2030 that replace the Millennium Development Goals (MDGs) and the climate summit under the CoP21 in December 2015.

The urgency of development focus on climate change is justified because existing scientific evidence shows the real threat posed by climate change on our environment. From a macroeconomic point of view, various scenarios from forecasting models also show its detrimental effect on economic growth[1] based on historical trends and recent modelling attempts (Abidoye and Odusola 2015; Dell *et al.* 2012; Gallup and Sachs 2000; Gallup *et al.* 1999; IPCC 2007). Over decades, African countries have experienced the negative macroeconomic consequences of climate change in the form of drought, food insecurity and human development despite encouraging GDP growth in recent years (Schellnhuber *et al.* 2013).

In terms of global agreed goals, the continent showed commitment to MDGs and the associated ambitious targets and some improvements were registered in the achievement of some of the goals. Building on the past, it is true that some African countries showed renewed and stronger commitment to the aspirational and ambitious goals of the SDGs. In turn, this leads to some countries to outperform others in the achievement of the SDGs by the target date of 2030.

Structurally, Africa is still largely agrarian and the climate effect has been felt strongly via reduced agricultural value added and employment and this vulnerability will continue if a concerted commitment and implementation of the globally agreed goals under SDGs is not pursued. For instance, the

1973 Sahel droughts severely affected GDP in Niger and Senegal, which led to a growth drop by about 10 and 19 per cent respectively (Berg 1976). Recent negative correlation between GDP growth and climate change have also been well documented (Brown *et al.* 2013; Dell *et al.* 2012) or specifically focusing on African countries (Abidoye and Odusola 2015; Brown *et al.* 2010).

The issue of environment and climate change is more pressing in Africa than in other places mainly due to the continent's limited contribution to global climate damage, but suffers the most due to its disproportionate vulnerability and limited ability for the development of adaptation and mitigation measures (Turco *et al.* 2015). The detrimental effects of environmental damage and climate change affect both formal and informal economic activities by disrupting commercial and industrial activities, damaging capital stocks or reducing income-generation capacity. In a time-series study of the effects of precipitation on the macroeconomy, Barrios *et al.* (2010) demonstrate that rainfall has been a 'significant determinant of poor economic growth' in Africa during the period 1960–2000. A non-linear econometric modelling work captures the historical variation induced by the intensity of climate-related events and the subsequent negative outcomes in terms of reduced crop yields and increased mortality (Deschênes and Greenstone 2011; Schlenker and Roberts 2009).

The chapter is organized as follows. In the second section we will briefly discuss the overlap between MDGs and SDGs with regard to goals that explicitly or implicitly address environment and climate change concerns. This will be followed by discussion of some issues of capacity development and institutional effectiveness. In the third section we review the progress so far starting from the era of MDGs to address environmental degradation and challenges of climate change. This will include a review of existing initiatives that explicitly have been adopted by African countries to pursue green growth principles and a prospective look at how the environmental and climate change challenges can be confronted under the SDGs. This will be supplemented by the discussion on the recent drought sweeping across Southern and the Horn of Africa which leads to worsening of the existing food insecurity of the continent. This recent food crisis is triggered and reinforced by the missed and below normal levels of rainfall because of El Niño. The section also makes reference to the existing policy initiatives and frameworks developed by a selected number on countries with regard to environment and climate change. Before concluding the study in the final section, we will provide a specific country case study that can give insights about potential beneficial pathways in protecting the environment and promoting sustainable development while adapting to climate change.

Consistency between MDGs and SDGs and capacity development in climate change

When the eight MDGs were launched in 2000, it was only goal number 7 that contained the word 'sustainability'. However, in the newly agreed SDGs

(2015–2030) or Agenda 2030, sustainability runs through many of the 17 goals. The goal that directly speaks to the theme of this chapter of environment and climate change when it comes to the MDGs is MDG 7 which is about *ensuring environmental sustainability*.

With the aspirations being more ambitious under the SDGs, the aspect of environmental sustainability does not necessarily fall under a single goal but rather spread across many. For instance, under the SDGs, the goals that relate to environment and climate change are Goal 2: 'End hunger, achieve food security and improved nutrition, and promote sustainable agriculture'; Goal 6; 'Ensure availability and sustainable management of water and sanitation for all'; Goal 7: 'Ensure access to affordable, reliable, sustainable, and modern energy for all'; Goal 11: 'Make cities and human settlements inclusive, safe, resilient and sustainable'; Goal 13: 'Take urgent action to combat climate change and its impact'; Goal 14: 'Conserve and sustainably use the oceans, seas, and marine resources for sustainable development'; and Goal 15: 'Protect, restore and promote sustainable use of terrestrial ecosystems, sustainably manage forests, combat desertification, halt and reverse land degradation, and halt biodiversity loss'. Goal 2 is linked with climate-smart agriculture which can take, among others, the form of soil fertility management for long-term agricultural development and adaptation of agricultural techniques to climate change.

Therefore, we do not have a goal-to-goal correspondence when it comes to the issue of environment and climate change between MDGs and SDGs. But this does not mean there is no consistency across the globally agreed goals in relation to the environment. Rather there is a clear recognition of the importance of environmental sustainability and a stronger reinforcement of the need to address climate change challenges under SDGs than MDGs. Under the SDGs, sustainability of social and economic development, as well as the environment, are equally valued.

To develop capacity and enhance institutional effectiveness in climate change matters, the continent can tap into existing knowledge from global sources especially in the area of renewables which are yet to be developed at a relatively affordable cost for Africa as a late comer and could benefit from already developed technologies elsewhere. The continent can learn from the experiences of other regions while defining and designing its own pathway. However, this learning should take local realities and history of African countries into consideration in an attempt to leapfrog traditional, carbon-intensive methods of growth and chart a low-carbon development trajectory (ECA 2016).

There are clear manifestations of the inability to successfully transform African economies on a sustainable development trajectory. The technical, financial and institutional barriers are enormous (e.g. in developing renewables) and there is a need for a systematic long-term capacity development drive in the continent despite variations across nations (Painuly 2001; WEC 1993). The barriers are partly self-inflicted by the poor and often corrupt institutional set-up within the continent and exacerbated by the limited attention and progressive marginalization inflicted by institutions outside the continent.

However, with the growth turn-around in the last 15 years or so, Africa is being perceived differently and the enthusiasm of countries within the continent for a bold future with reinforced sustainable development. The need for capacity development in the area of environment and climate change is well understood. For instance, capacity development has taken place in the form of training by multilateral organizations such as the African Development Bank (AfDB) which runs training courses on 'Capacity Development in Climate Change' to its staff stationed in 30 AfDB country offices. Judging the success or failure of such training and human capital development in the area of environment and climate change is a complex process. Much depends on the specific implementation of desirable environmental and climate change protocols by in-country AfDB staff. One should also note that this assessment of success or failure is restricted only to the projects that are financed by the bank. Furthermore, country level support was given by AfDB via its Climate Change Action Plan 2011–2015 (AfDB 2011).

In Africa, environmental impact assessment is relatively new with limited capacity, legal and institutional framework on the ground. Principle 17 of Rio Declaration (1992) on Environment and Development calls for use of environmental impact assessments as national decision-making tools in assessing whether or not proposed economic activities are likely to have significant adverse impact on the environment (Ogala 2007). Africa needs to develop its human capital base for environment and climate change. This can take the form of training of environmental science and management experts and skill transfers from developed countries. There is an acute shortage of experts who can undertake environmental auditing and advice on climate change adaptation strategies. Overall, these and other capacity deficiencies can derail the existing optimism surrounding sustainable development at the policy level (Ebohona *et al.* 1997).

Africa, environment and climate change in the context of MDGs and SDGs

Opportunities in the form of institutional, regional and global commitments

As in many parts of the world, the realization of the damage done to the environment by economic policies and other human actions in Africa came later than desired. Hence there were no significant improvements in the environment after MDGs were agreed. However, as discussed earlier, the environment and climate agenda are elevated under the SDGs, running through many of them. Countries have realized that growth cannot continue with business-as-usual modes of operation and have signed up to global commitments to make progress in the realm of sustainable development that keeps the environment at its core. Policy uncertainty in the area of environment and climate change is less severe now relative to the period 2000–2015 (i.e. the era of MDGs). The role of public bodies is equally important as the role of the private sector which still has to be convinced about the cost-effectiveness of the globally agreed environmental goals under the SDGs.

Countries have attempted to take various measures to address the challenge of climate change and environmental degradation via afforestation, renewable energy development, water harvesting and other adaptation strategies. Continentally, there have been settings that stimulated discussions with an attempt to affect policy directions in Africa. For instance, the five series of Climate Change and Development in Africa (CCDA I to CCDA V) took place with participation drawn from all relevant stakeholders. These forums examined various opportunities in climate change that can enhance Africa's transformative and inclusive economic growth and development agenda. Particularly CCDA V was convened prior to the United Nations 21st Conference of the Parties (COP21) in Paris to iron out a clearer African position in the context of SDGs before the global climate summit took place in December 2015. This is one of the rare occasions that Africa demonstrated a commitment and a clear stand in global conferences. The last CCDA reviewed the particularities of the climate change dialogue that took place across the continent and reflected on the performance of the United Nations Framework Convention on Climate Change (UNFCCC) in achieving its stated objectives of emissions reduction and sustainable development. In line with a long-term developmental visions, the CCDA V focused on addressing climate change, sustainable development and equity issues provided for in Article 2 of the UNFCCC, against the backdrop of the broad theme on 'Prospects for Sustainable, Resilient and Creative Economies in Africa in the Context of a Changing Climate'. CCDA V brought together reflections on the African climate change experiences and informed the Paris framework on African perspectives. Such policy-focused meetings lay the foundation for developing climate sensitive development policies and processes in Africa in the post-Paris era and constitute key progress made in defending the position of African countries in global agreements with implications for the lives of millions of Africans.

The success in the area of environment and climate change in future depends on how successfully African countries handle two main issues: a global transition from the MDGS to Agenda 2030 (or SDGS) and a regional transition from New Partnership for Africa's Development (NEPAD) to Agenda 2063 with its ten-year implementation plan. For success in the next 15 years, access to finance is critical. For instance, many countries do not possess the required resources to transform their environmental and climate change agenda mainly because donors are still not delivering on their commitment. Specifically, many countries lack the institutional capacity that can deal with the complexity of the existing architecture of applying successfully to global climate change funds or finance. Infrastructure funding and financing of renewables are critical to operationalize the SDGs' environmental and climate change-related goals. The AfDB's financing of renewables (i.e. a third of the bank's energy portfolio) and clean energy projects (i.e. about half of its energy portfolio) are encouraging developments coupled with efforts by individual countries in the continent. Therefore, success under Agenda 2030 will be a challenge but there is a renewed hope after the December 2015 COP21 climate summit in Paris, where the concerns of developing nations were better received than in previous summits.

El Niño climatic condition, drought and food crisis in Africa

The consequences of climate change and sudden weather shocks are devastating in Africa. Although the macroeconomic growth figures have been encouraging since the early days of 2000, Africa is the only continent where the number of poor has actually increased, even if the head count ratio shows a slight decline when one compares the poverty figure of 1990 with that of 2015. Therefore, the poverty battle has not been won under the MDGs, and growth has failed to be inclusive. Now it is made worse by a food crisis affecting a number of countries, especially in Southern and Eastern Africa.

At the backdrop of all global climate change summits and sustainable agriculture initiatives, there is the continued challenge facing Africa – drought. From the later part of 2015 and much of 2016, the consequences of El Niño climatic conditions and its intensity continue to have a devastating impact on the region. The drought is strongly felt in the Southern, Eastern and Horn of Africa. However, by early 2017 a better rain scenario has been observed for Southern Africa although other parts of Africa are still faced with weather-related food insecurity. For instance, an estimated 10.2 million Ethiopians are in need of emergency food assistance with reserves running out quickly and the country is facing its worst drought of 30 years (Kedir 1995). This is unfortunate because Ethiopia has registered remarkable economic growth in the last 15 years, built relatively effective early warning systems and established Africa's largest safety net programme: the Productive Safety Net Programme (PSNP)[2] (UNDP 2016).

It is not just Ethiopia; other African countries are also in need of emergency food assistance. Excluding Ethiopia, there is an outstanding appeal by the World Food Programme (WFP) of the United Nations to support 18 million people from seven African countries (UN Foundation 2016). The countries affected by the global dimension of El Niño and in urgent need of assistance worth about US$200 million are Lesotho, Madagascar, Mozambique, Swaziland, Zambia, Zimbabwe and Malawi. It is expected that the undesirable climatic conditions might get worse with the risk of flooding looming towards the end of 2016[3] potentially increasing the number of individuals in the seven Southern African countries dramatically to about 33 millions. The prolonged drought, the missed harvests, the rising food prices and the overall food crisis present a huge challenge to the encouraging course of economic development and up-turn in growth in the continent since 2000. Food insecurity and hunger, as long-standing difficulties, might weaken the African rising narrative unless practical steps are taken to tackle the problems associated with environmental degradation and climate change. There cannot be inclusive growth which ensures empowerment that address underlying poverty at all levels in Africa by the due date of Agenda 2030, if the number of hungry people and those in chronic poverty increases in the face of relatively strong GDP growth figures.

To achieve the development goals set out in the SDGs, it is high time that the continent takes concrete steps. The most sensible measures which have been well documented and not backed by actions include managing the rural as well as the urban environment sustainably, building capacity of countries to raise agricultural productivity (e.g. through adoption of appropriate technologies and complementing existing indigenous farming technologies), and supporting the marginalized and the vulnerable through social protection. One bottleneck is finance which forces nations to look for help elsewhere, mostly through regional and global multilateral frameworks. Some immediate policy measures that can be acted upon within the continent in an era of shrinking external assistance and resurgence of the need for domestic resource mobilization include tackling corruption and capital flight, which can provide the funds for such environment and food crisis management that the continent sorely needs.

African development policy initiatives

There are a number of recently adopted global and continental development frameworks that focus on the SDGs, such as the Addis Ababa Action Agenda, the United Nations 21st Conference of the Parties (COP21), Agenda 2063 of the African Union (AU), and the 2030 Agenda for Sustainable Development (Agenda 2030). These frameworks provide a supportive foundation for adopting and following through on national environment and climate change initiatives; however, they should also support attempts by African countries to integrate their diverse development policies and strategies.

Specifically, a number of countries have attempted to develop economic strategies that are aimed at addressing environmental and climate change concerns at least at a planning stage. Some have done a lot in terms of developing renewable energy sources (e.g. North African countries such as Morocco) and accessing some climate finance from global sources. Hence, these countries will be expected to be ahead of the pack in terms of environmental sustainability in the coming 15 years. Other countries are doing remarkably well (e.g. Ethiopia) but are faced with environmental degradation and drought recurrences that have been the dominant features of most of the dry agro-ecological zones of the country, which indicates the enormity of the challenge despite the alignment of national development visions with the global environmental and climate change goals.

Since Ethiopia is our chosen country case study, we will provide a few more details. Recognizing the challenge posed by environmental degradation and climate change, the Ethiopian government aims to make Ethiopia a carbon neutral and a lower middle-income country within the next ten years. This is articulated in vision 2025 where the annual growth rate targets for GDP, manufacturing and exports are set at 11 per cent, 25 per cent and 30 per cent respectively MEF 2015. Realizing the enormous challenge of transforming the Ethiopian economy to be a light manufacturing hub in Africa in a sustainable and inclusive manner, the government has signed a five-year technical cooperation agreement with the United Nations Industrial Development Organization (UNIDO). However, there are some difficulties and capacity challenges that hamper the process of putting environmental protection policy prescriptions into practice. There is a need to have strong institutions with personnel (i.e. at lower, mid- and high level of the organizational hierarchy) committed to green principles.

The Climate-Resilient Green Economy (CRGE) Strategy developed by Ethiopia utilizes a sectoral approach in identifying and prioritizing more than 60 initiatives, policies, strategies and action plans. Among others, these include Ethiopia's Growth and Transformation Plan, National Adaptation Program of Action, Nationally Appropriate Mitigation Actions, Ethiopia's Program of Adaptation to Climate Change, Energy Policy, Water Policy, and Agricultural and Rural Development Policy Strategies. Therefore, the second national communication of Ethiopia to UNFCCC (i.e. the input to the deliberations at CoP21 in Paris in December 2015) recognizes climate change as a cross-cutting issue affecting all sectors (MEF 2015). The overall development trajectory of Ethiopia is anchored on achieving ambitious growth targets with low-level greenhouse gas emissions.

There are several African governments taking the lead on implementing an inclusive green economy strategy, as demonstrated in their national-level initiatives (see table 9.1 below), These national development strategies combine attention to energy access, creating quality jobs with rising incomes, investing in critical environmental assets, soil, water, biodiversity, forest, and designing resilience for cities and infrastructure.

In practice, one expects committed countries to reorient sectoral development strategies along sustainability principles (e.g. green industrialization) (ECA 2016). For instance, Ethiopia is building one of the largest hydroelectric dams in the continent, and by October 2015 already had a functioning light rail network, which runs on electricity and serves the public transportation needs in Addis Ababa, the capital city.

Potential viable and beneficial pathway to attain sustainable outcomes

In terms of pathways, it is more beneficial to be specific than covering potential routes of achieving environmentally friendly development at a continental

Table 9.1 Selected African countries with development plans that incorporate environment and climate change

Country	*Strategic framework for inclusive green economy*
Ethiopia	Climate-Resilient Green Economy (CRGE) Strategy. The vision is to achieve middle-income status by 2025 in a climate-resilient green economy.
Ghana	Since Ghana's economy relies heavily on climate sensitive sectors mainly on agriculture, energy and forestry, the country designed a participatory approach driven National Climate Change Adaptation Strategy (NCCAS). NCCAS is aimed at ensuring a consistent, comprehensive and a targeted approach to increasing climate resilience and decrease vulnerability of the population; deepening awareness and sensitization for the general populace particularly policy-makers about the critical role of adaptation in national development efforts.
Kenya	Green Economy Strategy and Implementation Plan (GESIP) (2015). The objective of this plan is to guide the transition process to a green, low-carbon and climate-resilient economy.
Morocco	Green Morocco Plan, launched in 2008, has a particular focus on the agricultural sector and associated agrifood processing industry. Morocco is one of the leading nations in adopting climate-resilient growth strategies in Africa.
Mozambique	Towards a Green Economy. Roadmap for a Green Economy in Mozambique: accelerating sustainable economic, social, and environmental development. The vision of the road map is that Mozambique is an inclusive middle-income country by 2030, based on protection, restoration and rational use of natural capital and its ecosystem services, to guarantee development that is sustainable, inclusive and efficient, within the planetary limits.
Rwanda	Green Growth and Climate Resilience: National Strategy for Climate Change and Low-Carbon Development – 2011–2050 (2011). The vision is for Rwanda to be a developed climate-resilient, low-carbon economy by 2050. The strategic objective is to achieve energy security and a low-carbon energy supply that supports the development of green industry and services. The strategic objective is to achieve social protection, improved health and disaster risk reduction that reduces vulnerability to climate change.
South Africa	Green Economy Accord (2011): This partnership is signed by organized labour, community constituents, business and government and lays out 12 commitments to green the economy, including: roll out of solar water heaters and renewable energy; energy efficiency; biofuels; and waste recycling, reuse and recovery. Other commitments relate to: clean coal initiatives; electrification of poor communities; and reduction of open fire cooking and heating. The partners also commit to promote localization, youth employment, cooperatives and skills development.

Source: compiled by the author from readings of various strategies and development plans of the countries selected.

level. Therefore, we focus on a national case study that can potentially provide some lessons for other African countries. Ethiopia is one of the few African countries in sub-Saharan Africa leading the way in the area of climate change and the environment, both in continental and global forums focusing on Africa. Ethiopia ratified the UNFCCC on 31 May 1994 and the Kyoto protocol on 21 February 2005 as a non- annex I party, thereby signifying a commitment to join the international community in combating the problem of climate change (MEF 2015; World Bank 2015).

Ensuring food security and increasing agricultural productivity are the outstanding challenges of the Ethiopian economy. In 2010, the government established the Agricultural Transformation Agency with the aim to identify and address systemic bottlenecks to Ethiopia's agricultural development. Some of the core responsibilities of the agency are to promote environmentally sustainable and inclusive agricultural growth including natural resource management, sustainable land management, gender equality and nutrition, climate change and disaster risk management. Across the programmes, the Agricultural Transformation Agency engages public, private and non-governmental stakeholders to support strategic planning, manage and strengthen implementation capacity and test innovative models. With the development of eco-friendly industrial parks, not only in the capital city but also in secondary towns, the country is aiming to boost the interaction between industry and agriculture and transform the whole economy.

Based on primary data collection through interviewing various stakeholders, we present below a review of Ethiopia's experience. The interviews were carried out with the Ministry of Industry, particularly the Industrial Zone Development and Environmental Protection Directorate. The country follows a sectoral approach to addressing environmental and climate change challenges; hence, our review will cover some of the key sectors such as transport and industry.

a. Political commitment to green growth

Ethiopia has a visionary and transformative leadership committed to developmental state principles. Since there is a need to sensitize the population with the detailed elements of CRGE strategy, those who are already training in the federal ministries are tasked to train others in the various parts of the countries. Therefore, CRGE has been popularized at the *wereda*[4] level. Due to the potential challenges associated with implementation, the government has undertaken a capacity needs assessment on CRGE and discussion is under way on the best possible way of addressing the capacity gap particularly of different administrative regions across the country. The Ministry of Environment and Forestry has the primary role to operationalize CRGE.

In terms of actual operational commitment to environmentally friendly industrialization, the Ministry of Industry requires all factories to complete an environmental impact assessment for the planned industrial activity.

However, there is an acute shortage of skilled manpower, which should be a significant area of investment for Ethiopia as well as other African countries to make progress in the various sectors of the economy in relation to environmental protection. The ministry is not only interested to review the environmental impact assessment study and to approve the project to proceed to the licensing phase; it also follows up on activities of the numerous factories dotted around the country based on the environmental impact assessment report. For industries that were established before CRGE, the ministry assesses their polluting and emission levels and works towards solutions if there are problems that need to be tackled. Therefore, the scrutiny on compliance to environmental protection standards is not just restricted to new industrial establishments; it also extends to old and existing ones. The Ministry of Industry believes that the green economy provides an opportunity. The main challenges of the Industrial Zone Development and Environmental Protection Directorate in the Ministry of Industry is ensuring reduction of CO_2 emissions and the rational use of energy and increase energy efficiency.

The main strategy in relation to the green economy in Ethiopia includes a variety of environmental criteria such as energy/water-use efficiency, waste management (reduction, recycling and reuse) and energy switching. The Grand Renaissance Dam is one of the key long-term renewable, hydropower-based energy generation projects. With respect to social criteria, the government prioritizes the development of communities through training at *wereda* level to equip them with competencies in environmental issues. When it comes to governance, the existing institutional set-up allows for the promotion of mechanisms of dialogue between communities and agro-based industries. Public and private companies/factories are also reminded of the environmental regulations that they need to comply with. There are a number of relevant laws, protocols and conventions that direct the work of the Ethiopian government in the area of environment and climate change. Compliance to them and progress under the SDGs is heavily dependent upon the capacity of the staff of relevant ministries and the efficiency of institutional frameworks. These can eliminate or minimize colluding behaviour between law enforcers and private and public firms that might seek to maintain previous production systems and disregard environmental and climate change concerns.

b. The transport industry

We finalize the Ethiopian case study by making reference to the recent environmentally friendly development in the transport sector. Under the business-as-usual scenario, emissions from transport are calculated to increase from 5 metric tonnes (t) CO_2 equivalent emission of greenhouse gases (e) in 2010 to 41 t CO_2e in 2030. Leapfrogging to new technologies in transport offers an abatement potential of 13.2 t CO_2e in 2030. Major initiatives proposed are: (1) improving Addis Ababa public transport by building a light rail transit system; (2) improving vehicle efficiency through fuel efficiency standards; (3) promoting clean fuel blends (biodiesel and ethanol); (4) adopting hybrid and plug-in electric vehicles; and (5) shifting freight transport from the roads to the proposed electric rail network, which is the largest abatement lever in the transport sector, e.g. the Addis Ababa Light Rail System, which has an abatement potential of 8.9 t CO_2e.

The Addis Ababa Light Rail System is the first of its kind in Africa (excluding Northern and South Africa). With 85 per cent of funding secured from the Chinese Export and Import Bank it was completed within three years – a very reasonable time frame. The plan is to have a light rail/tram network of about 185 km that connects the whole city. The first section, which is 31 km long and serves 41 stations, was completed in January 2015 and began trial/partial operations on 1 February 2015. The initial phase has now been fully operational since October 2015 and the second phase of the project is under way. It will have only 15 minutes waiting time at a station and is planned to transport 60,000 people per hour throughout the whole city. In future, there are plans to extend the railway in all four directions. In addition, the Ethiopian government is constructing the Regional Electric rail system which will be 5,000 km long.

The light rail project's direct environmental benefit includes: offsetting 1.8 t CO_2 e by 2030; from the regional train network, the first phase three routes would avoid 5.3 t CO_2 e by 2030. In general, the total avoided emissions by 2030 are estimated to be 54 t CO_2 (MEF 2015).

Conclusion

We would like to draw attention to three areas of future work. First, SDGs are improved and universal aspirations that need *domesticating* to local realities. For instance, with respect to environment and climate change, there was only one goal under the MDGs but this has now expanded to numerous goals under SDGs, covering a wider variety of sectors and locations such as agriculture, industry, water, energy and urban areas. That is why in Africa there is an effort to review development planning visions and strategies to align them with SDGs and set out country priorities.

In addition to developing the technical, financial and institutional capacities of various economic sectors, with the aim to conduct development with environmental sustainability, one needs to keep abreast of efforts that attempt to domesticate SDGs. Equally, it is essential to monitor how country development visions and SDGs goals and targets are aligned in the realm of environment and climate change. For instance, in an attempt to provoke and lead member states in the direction of domesticating SDGs, the African Union is making an attempt to develop 'African SDGs'. Whether this is the right and successful route to improve Africa's achievement of the targets of SDGs is subject to temporal scrutiny as we witness how development takes course in the continent over the next 15 years.

Second, the success in December 2015 at the Paris CoP21 deserves careful analysis and regular monitoring of progress of the fruits it bears for the environmental sustainability of African economies. CoP21 also touched and promoted other development agenda (e.g. urbanization) and in the Paris negotiation circles the climate agenda is well argued and more developed than other agenda items.

Finally, it is very important to highlight the importance of environmental protection/damage in relation to the activities of the *informal sector* which can play a positive role (e.g. waste collection and recycling) via informal-formal sector linkages; as well as a negative role (e.g. compromising safety by facilitating congestion and creating waste).

Notes

1 Thanks to Florent Baarsch, Michiel Schaeffer, Maria Knaus, Mario Krapp, Jessie Granadillos, and Niklas Roming from Climate Analytics, Bonn, Germany for insights shared about the link between climate change and the macroeconomy. Also for sharing the preliminary findings of the 2015 'Economic Growth and Climate Change in Africa Project', a research project supported by the United Nations Environment Programme (UNEP), the United Nations Economic Commission for Africa (UNECA) and the African Development Bank (AfDB).

2 The PSNP is mainly operational in rural Ethiopia targeting vulnerable and food poor families but the government is also planning to cover the chronically poor in some urban centres in future.

3 The onset of the rainy season is expected around October time as is often the case for Southern part of Africa. At times the rains do not reach the level required in the cropping seasons but at others bring unwanted levels of downpour when not required, which exacerbates the food crisis situation, as well as causing infrastructural and other damages from flooding.

4 This is the third-level administrative unit in Ethiopia which is further divided into wards.

References

Abidoye, B. O. and Odusola, A. F. (2015) Climate change and economic growth in Africa: An econometric analysis, *Journal of African Economies*, 25 (1): 1–25.

AfDB (2011) *Climate Change Action Plan, Quality Assurance and Results Department (ORQR) Compliance and Safeguards Division*. Tunis: African Development Bank.

Barrios, S., Bertinelli, L. and Strobl, E. (2010) Trends in rainfall and economic growth in Africa: a neglected cause of the African economic growth tragedy, *Review of Economics and Statistics*, 2 (92): 350–66.

Berg, E. (1976) *The Economic Impact of Drought and Inflation in the Sahel*, Discussion Paper No. 51. Ann Arbor, MI: Center for Research on Economic Development, University of Michigan.

Brown, C., Meeks, R., Ghile, Y. and Hunu, K. (2013) Is water security necessary? An empirical analysis of the effects of climate hazards on national-level economic growth, *Philosophical Transactions of the Royal Society*, 371 (2002): 1–19.

Brown, C., Meeks, R., Hunu, K. and Yu, W. (2010) Hydroclimate risk to economic growth in sub-Saharan Africa, *Climatic Change*, 106 (4): 621–47, doi:10.1007/s10584-010-9956-9.

Dell, M., Jones, B. F. and Olken, B. A. (2012) Temperature shocks and economic growth: evidence from the last half century, *American Economic Journal: Macroeconomics*, 4 (3): 66–95, doi:10.1257/mac.4.3.66.

Deschênes, O. and Greenstone, M. (2011) Climate Change, Mortality, and Adaptation: Evidence from Annual Fluctuations in Weather in the US, *American Economic Journal: Applied Economics*, 3 (October), 152–85.

Ebohona, O., Field, B. and Ford, R. (1997) Institutional deficiencies and capacity building constraints: the dilemma for environmentally sustainable development in Africa, *International Journal of Sustainable Development and World Ecology*, 4 (3): 153–65.

ECA (2016) *Greening Africa's Industrialisation, Economic Report on Africa.* Addis Ababa, Ethiopia: United Nations Economic Commission for Africa (UNECA).

Gallup, J. and Sachs, J. (2000) Agriculture, climate, and technology: why are the tropics falling behind? *American Journal of Agricultural Economics*, 82 (3): 731–7.

Gallup, J., Sachs, J. and Mellinger, A. (1999) Geography and economic development, *International Regional Science Review*, 22 (2): 179–232.

Intergovernmental Panel on Climate Change (IPCC) (2007) *Climate Change Impacts, Adaptation and Vulnerability*. Report of Working Group II to the Fourth Assessment Report of the IPCC. Cambridge/New York: Cambridge University Press.

Kedir, A. (1995) Environment, population and agricultural development in Ethiopia, published in D. Aredo and M. Demeke (eds) *Ethiopian Agriculture: Problems of Transformation, Proceedings of the Fourth Annual Conference on the Ethiopian Economy*. Addis Ababa: Ethiopian Economic Association.

Ministry of Environment and Forest (MEF) (2015) *Ethiopia's Second National Communication to the United Nations Framework Convention on Climate Change (UNFCCC)*. Addis Ababa, Ethiopia.

Ogala, P. (2007) *Environmental Impact Assessment General Procedures, presented at Short Course II on Surface Exploration for Geothermal Resources*, organized by UNU-GTP and KenGen, 2–17 November 2007, at Lake Naivasha, Kenya.

Painuly, J. (2001) Barriers to renewable energy penetration; a framework for analysis, *Renewable Energy*, 24: 73–89.

Schellnhuber, H. J., Hare, B., Serdeczny, O., Schaeffer, M., Adams, S., Baarsch, F. and Rocha, M. (2013) *Turn Down the Heat: Climate Extremes, Regional Impacts, and the Case for Resilience*. Washington, DC: World Bank.

Schlenker, W. and Roberts, M. J. (2009) Nonlinear temperature effects indicate severe damages to U.S. crop yields under climate change, *Proceedings of the National Academy of Sciences of the United States of America*, 106 (37): 15594–8.

Turco, M., Palazzi, E., von Hardenberg, J. and Provenzale, A. (2015) Observed climate change hotspots, *Geophysical Research Letters*, 42, doi:10.1002/2015GL063891.

UNDP (2016) *Assessing the Cost of Drought in Ethiopia and the Case for Long-term Development Approach*. Policy Note prepared by UNDP Ethiopia Office, Addis Ababa, Ethiopia.

UN Foundation (2016) World Food Programme's Executive Director to Brief on El Niño and Devastating Drought and Food Crisis in Malawi – the Largest Humanitarian Emergency in the Country's History. Press Briefing. Lilongwe, Malawi

Way, D. and S. Long (2005) Climate-smart agriculture and forestry: maintaining plant productivity in a changing world while minimizing production system effects on climate, Special Issue on Climate-Smart Agriculture and Forestry, *Plant, Cell and Environment*, 38 (9): 1683–85.

WEC (1993) *Renewable Energy Resources: Opportunities and Constraints 1990–2020*. London: World Energy Council.

World Bank (2012) *Inclusive Green Growth: The Pathway to Sustainable Development*, Washington, DC: World Bank.

———. (2015) *Ethiopia's Great Run: The Growth Acceleration and How to Pace it*. Addis Ababa: World Bank Country Office.

10 Crystallizing the Africa Rising narrative with sustainable development

Kobena T. Hanson, Korbla P. Puplampu and Timothy M. Shaw

Introduction

In 2015, African Heads of State and Government adopted Agenda 2063 and the 2030 Agenda for Sustainable Development. The two initiatives constitute 'a two-pronged transition: a global-level transition from the MDGs to Agenda 2030 and a continent-level transition from NEPAD to Agenda 2063' (AU/ECA/AfDB and UNDP 2016: xix). However, as Africa tries to seize the second half of the twenty-first century, it will undoubtedly face a globe confronted with multiple crises; and the challenges for realizing the transformation envisioned by the UN Sustainable Development Goals are formidable. The challenges range from both the global to continental contexts. In the former, one cannot dismiss the events unfolding in Europe: the fallout of the Brexit vote in the United Kingdom not only in Europe, but the implications for Europe–Africa relations; the emergence of new right politics and its populist undertones; the settlement of refugees in Europe; the changing economic fortunes of several European countries, from Portugal, Italy, Ireland, Greece and Spain to Turkey; as well as Russia's assertions of its place on the globe, symbolized by its role in the Syrian conflict, and sovereignty claims culminating in the retake of Crimea from Ukraine.

Beyond Europe, there has been the election of Donald Trump in the United States of America and its policy implications for global market transactions, regional economic entities and, by extension, the place of the USA in the world. The USA and its allies, together with the broader world community, are still confronted with the twin issues of war and terrorism which are framed by the discourse of security and human rights. A persistent issue in the global imaginary is the growing disillusionment with the status quo or mainstream politics and its inability to address wage stagnation, the associated job insecurity, and the general failure to build a positive political and social environment, amid the growing gap between the haves and the have-nots (OXFAM 2017).

Closer home on the African continent, authoritarian regimes and their leaders continue to find ingenious ways to extend their mandate in power, by amending the constitution and a general lack of authenticity in leadership

Table 10.1 The longevity of selected leaders in Africa and UNDP's (2015) rank of their countries

Country	*Ruler*	*Years in office (2016)*	*UNDP 2015*
Algeria	Abdelaziz Bouteflika	17	83
Angola	José dos Santos	37	149
Cameroon	Paul Biya	34	153
Chad	Idriss Déby	26	185
Democratic Rep. of Congo	Joseph Kabila	15	176
Equatorial Guinea	Obiang Mbasogo	37	138
Republic of Congo	Denis Sassou-Nguesso	22	136
Rwanda	Paul Kagame	16	163
Sudan	Omar al-Bashir	27	167
Uganda	Yoweri Museveni	30	163
Zimbabwe	Robert Mugabe	36	155

and governance. From Southern Africa, the bright lights of South Africa in terms of governance and transparency in the early post-apartheid era have been replaced by the lethargic leadership of Jacob Zuma and an environment of institutionalize malaise. In terms of governance, while countries such as Botswana, Cape Verde, Ghana, Namibia, Sierra Leone and Tanzania are working to deepen democracy and governance, several others have leaders who defy constitutional arrangements, engineer or manufacture changes to the constitution or continue as leader of the party in order to prolong their reign (table 10.1).

One would expect the longevity of leadership to be attributed to excellent governance, uplifting of the citizenry, and broad and steady human development (see table 10.1). To the contrary, many African countries, even those with de facto presidents for life continue to occupy the lower echelons of human development (UNDP 2015). The situation is no different for those with oil wealth, especially in the case of Chad, Equatorial Guinea and Sudan (Puplampu 2014). Thus, there is no a priori assumption that the recent discovery of oil in African countries (e.g. Ghana and Uganda) would necessarily transform and uplift human development in these countries.

The above political landscape does not inspire any confidence in the ability of political leaders to shepherd the 'Africa Rising' narrative, since they have not shown any deference to their nation's constitution; an embodiment of the rule of law in any country. To be sure, many leaders find it rather convenient to tinker or engineer demands to amend their constitutions in order to circumvent term limits and increase their reign. Hence, the notion of Africa Rising has to challenge the politics that underpin the manoeuvres in changing the constitution to suit the desires of the president. The constant urge to amend constitutions in the arena of term limits accounts for the novelty of the steps towards deepening democracy in Ghana with the inauguration of the fifth president under the Fourth Republic. However, the democratic strides in Ghana and other countries need not be an abnormal situation; rather it should be the norm across the continent.

Getting the political leadership equation right would make it possible to refocus on institutional capacity. Because institutional capacity would fast-track the continental breakthroughs in mobile banking such as M-Pesa and the other strides that embrace and leverage emerging technologies and the value of data by way of the sharing economy and Internet of Things (IoT) for transformative change (Hanson and Puplampu this volume).

Political leadership and institutions would also ensure that natural resource governance, green growth, transboundary water management and attempts to address security hurdles are successful. Such developments, which also impinge on regional cooperation, would become ever more imperative as the continent strives towards 2030 and the continent's own milestone of 2063. Invariably, to meaningfully move forward with sustainable development calls for an institutional architecture that promotes, among others, inter-sectoral coordination, leverages multi-disciplinary synergies and enhances policy coherence (AU/ECA/AfDB and UNDP 2016). This view is also espoused by Besada *et al.* (2016: 5) who argue that, given the 'comprehensive agenda embedded in the SDGs, there is now even more need and more opportunity for African agency at the continental, regional, national, and subnational levels through the SDGs in the post-2015 development agenda'. It is against this background and many others that enlightened and responsible leadership at the national and continental levels assumes an added significance in Africa's efforts to attain the SDGs.

The above constitutes indispensable, necessary and sufficient conditions to shore up the Africa Rising account, a narrative that requires context, a focus on agency, capacity imperatives and other spaces.

Africa Rising narrative: agency, capacity imperatives and spaces

Africa, as a region, is often characterized by different actors for different reasons. Many news outlets, including *The Economist*, *Time Magazine* and *The Wall Street Journal* introduced and reiterated several dimensions of the Africa Rising metaphor. Not to be left out, the academic community has also been interrogating the underlining assumptions and prospects of the Africa Rising narrative. Taylor (2016, 2014) has addressed the over-optimism of African development at the start of the second decade of the twenty-first century articulated by private sector consultants and institutions such as the United Nations Economic Commission for Africa (UNECA) on 'developmental states' and 'developmental regionalism'. Specifically Taylor (2014) examines the relationship of each BRIC (note not BRICS) with Africa suggesting a variety of degrees of dependency formulated in his notion of 'levels of agency' (Taylor 2014: 33) and presents the BRIC as not homogeneous. But his critique relies on rather 'old-fashioned' ideas about national, continental, global economies as manufacturing of declining importance by contrast to the service sector, especially in Africa where cell phones are ubiquitous and mobile finance burgeoning as in M-Pesa in eastern Africa.

Blossoming high-tech centres are appearing, for instance the iHub in Nairobi where codes are written and start-ups hatched. These activities have compelled the international financial institutions (IFIs) to recalculate the GDPs of Ghana, Kenya and Nigeria in the last couple of years to take into account sectors such as Nollywood, the digital economy and second-hand vehicle imports. So, the Republic of South Africa (RSA) is no longer the biggest economy on the continent despite being one of the BRICS. Taylor (2014: 147) concurs that: 'It is not *impossible* that accrued revenues may help implant constructive change, perhaps in the division of welfare reforms pursued by some Middle East oil producers. It is just unlikely'. Taylor essentially argues that the BRICS are problematic as they are heterogeneous: neither a bloc, nor 'emerging', nor do they (BRICS) speak for the historic 'global South'. Taylor further asserts that they bring 'uneven development' to Africa (2014: 153), and dismisses the analysis or place of the Africa Progress Panel (APP) as not reflective of the 'real' African political economy (Taylor 2014: 156–7). In dismissing an 'emerging' Africa, Taylor fails to recognize the rise of an African middle class, parallel to, albeit smaller than, those in Latin America or Asia; its consumption drives mobile telecommunications, shopping malls and hotel development. Taylor (2014: 159) concludes his thesis by insisting that 'the diversification of dependency is *not* a coherent development project for the continent, even if the notion that the BRICS somehow facilitate an escape route from the historic relationship with the North is held'.

Others, such as Onuoha (2016), suggests that the Africa Rising narrative is situated in a context of natural resources. That assumes that natural resources and minerals as well as other raw materials will bring significant wealth to African countries. The problem according to Onuoha (2016: 281) is the lack of attention to the role of global powers, multinational corporations and the overarching capitalist relations at stake coupled with the related outcomes of a 'mix of extremes of wealth and poverty, power and disempowerment, profit and exploitation, global extraction and local resistance'. Hence, in many African countries, including many of those with oil wealth, patterns of inequality continue to prevail (Beegle *et al.* 2016: 122–4).

Goldstone and Obarrio (2016), employing the metaphor of 'African Futures', examine the tapestry of forces, some contradictory, sweeping across the continent. In theorizing the question of where is Africa heading, Goldstone and Obarrio (2016) examine the significant changes in the urban landscape, the unprecedented centrality of religious forces, mobility and diasporic anxieties. Yet, they present the dynamic and sometimes irreconcilable forces as an opportunity for pluralistic forms of thinking in a context that they call fluid and containing endless possibilities for rethinking the African development project.

Both the Africa Rising and the African Futures narratives cannot ignore the historical power relations that underpin the region's development trajectory. While the historical power relations are still relevant towards an understanding of the political economy of contemporary Africa development, it is also important to acknowledge that the decade before the SDGs was marked by African agency. This is the ability of a range of African state and non-state actors to impact decisions and directions at a variety of levels by expanding their room for manoeuvre (APP 2012), or to maximize reach of balancing and norm setting (Shaw 2015a), or to grow in strength (Besada *et al.* 2016; Hanson *et al.* 2012). Initiatives such as the New Partnership for Africa's Development (NEPAD), African Peer Review Mechanism (APRM), the African Capacity Building Foundation's (ACBF), *Africa Capacity Report* (previously *Africa Capacity Indicators*), ACBF and AfDB's *African Governance Outlook*, the Africa Mining Vision and subsequent establishment of the African Minerals Development Centre (AMDC), to name a few, are all testament to the growing agency. The formulation and articulation of the Africa Mining Vision, for example, would have been inconceivable before the current decade. Today the continent is better positioned to formulate its own response to the post-2015 development agenda (Shaw 2015b). African actors can now claim a degree of agency rather than endure continuing dependency (Brown and Harman 2013); the prospect of policy-making rather than policy-taking (Gyimah-Brempong *et al.* 2012).

Another area where Africa's agency is evident is in the area of confronting transnational organized criminal activities, including people and drug smuggling, which pose a significant and growing threat to national, regional and continental aspirations (Shaw 2015a, 2015b; Gastrow 2013). Transnational organized criminal markets criss-cross the continent conveying drugs, arms, trafficking women, blood minerals or endangered, protected animal parts (UNODC 2016). The illegally generated revenue, and resultant mix of alienation, fundamentalisms and small arms, end up distorting local economies, corrupting institutions and fuelling conflict. Examples include the Lord's Resistance Army in northern Uganda; Boko Haram in northern Nigeria; Ansar Dine/Movement for Unity and Jihad in West Africa, Al Qaeda in the Islamic Maghreb, the Signed-in-Blood Battalion and the Islamic Movement for Azawad in Mali; and Central African Republic along with armed pirates off the coast of West Africa and the Horn of Africa and the conflict in Darfur (Shaw 2015b). Elsewhere, 'border' conflicts around energy, water, and conflict minerals proliferate. In connection with the emergence and spread of transnational organized crime, the West African Commission on Drugs (WACD) (www.wacommissionondrugs.org) is a particularly remarkable regional display of agency to the burgeoning problem and global drug, gun, gang supply chains being routed through West Africa (Shaw 2015a, 2015b). What are the implications of such agency? And what security strategies – human, national, and regional – need to be adopted going forward?

Africa's agency is also evident in the continent's role

> in international trade negotiations, processes governing the distribution of aid and discussions over climate change, as well as military and humanitarian intervention [consequently] generating new areas of interdependence between the continent and outside powers in the form of 'new' transnational security issues – migration, environmental degradation and health.
>
> (Brown 2011: 1)

Bischoff *et al.* (2016) also highlight Africa's agency in areas such as regionalism, security management, as well as in the continent's dealing with the outside world. The continent's agency in the second decade of the twenty-first century is, thus, the collective economic and foreign policy mantra of Africa's 'developmental states', the continent's initial definition of contestation (Shaw 2015a).

At the start of 2017, preoccupations of President Trump and Prime Minister May as leaders of the USA and Great Britain respectively – notably US isolationist, protectionist stance (e.g. withdrawal from the Trans-Pacific Partnership, declaring a renegotiation of the North American Free Trade Agreement (NAFTA)), or repealing the Wall Street Reform and Consumer Protection Act of 2010, better known as the Dodd-Frank Act; the European Union's (EU) divisions, plus the attractions of multilateralism Chinese style – also have the potential to spur on Africa's agency. The Silk Road Fund and Asian Infrastructure Investment Bank, both central to President Xi Jinping's signature 'Belt and Road' vision, have generated much talk. At the 2017 World Economic Forum in Davos, President Xi Jinping called for nations to reject the protectionism threatening multilateral trade agreements and embrace the win-win potential of interconnected growth. President Jinping's statements at Davos are consistent with the higher ambitions of China's multilateralism (Ekman 2016).

The emerging multilateral initiatives will serve to hasten, not retard global change, whether Mr Trump or Ms May so wish. And while following through on USA isolationism may potentially spell trouble for the African Growth and Opportunity Act, it possibly could energize African nations to enhance cross-border and regional trade among themselves, as well as engage in more South–South initiatives, since how Africa (re)positions itself in this fluid and shifting landscape, will impact how it forges ahead on the SDGs, Agenda 2063 and its overall quest for transformation.

African countries need, therefore, to advance and entrench policies that acknowledge the realities of their national contexts, that can bring about rapid results in terms of urgent needs, and that allow for incremental improvements to their governance processes (Marcel 2013). Thus in Africa's post-2015 develop agenda, Kararach *et al.* (2016: 366) argue that if the right policy and programmatic frameworks are put in place and bottlenecks are eliminated, then the goal of eliminating poverty could be achievable within the coming decade or so.

Policies generally frame the sphere of potential constructive action, as this volume's contributing authors note; there are now new spaces for agency. The continent is gradually defining its own science and technology policies (Hanson and Puplampu this volume) including how it embraces emerging technologies and related developments of the IoT and sharing economy, and proactively planning for climate change with green growth planning (Kedir, this volume). In the area of natural resource governance, African stakeholders have been central to a set of innovations in transnational governance including Corporate Social Responsibility (CSR), from the Kimberley Process to Publish What You Pay/Extractive Industries Transparency Initiative (Hanson *et al.* 2014; Puplampu and Hanson this volume; Shaw 2015a).

For agriculture, a sector central to the attainment of SDGs 1 (no poverty), 2 (zero hunger) and 8 (decent work and economic growth), the NEPAD-inspired CAADP and Maputo Declaration represented a bold collective expression of agency by African countries not experienced before in the history of Africa's post-independence agricultural development (Puplampu and Essegbey this volume). Desirable policy and institutional outcomes in agriculture are also vital to attaining SDG 16 (justice, peace and strong institutions). Again, there is a need to devise novel ways to utilize existing skills and resources to unlock African potential, while building capacity for effective natural resource governance (Puplampu and Hanson this volume); and creating an environment conducive to the promotion of exports, a key requirement as set out under SDG 17 and associated target 12 in the 2030 Agenda for sustainable development (Tang this volume).

Finally, reconfiguring the landscape for foreign aid has become necessary, especially in view of the extent to which addressing the infrastructure deficit would contribute to the development possibilities of the continent (Odoom this volume). A central issue remains: the significance of appropriate incentive, reward and management systems that effectively leverage African potential and attract the requisite capacities (ACBF 2011: 194). Doing so also implies securing better partnerships for capacity development and enhancing development partner coordination for aid effectiveness and development results (Odoom this volume).

Imperatives going forward

Crystallizing the Africa Rising narrative and the continent's agency, requires capacity (individual and institutional) and transformative leadership (ACBF 2011; Besada *et al.* 2016; Brown 2011). Capacity or the lack thereof to implement programmes often constitutes a hindrance to the delivery on well-intentioned policies in less-developed countries (Kwon and Kim 2014: 358). Policies do not evolve in a vacuum. Hence, there is a need to enhance governance and bring about transformational leadership (Arthur this volume; Makinda 2012; Tettey 2012). Then there is the need to improve and expand the quality of leadership towards attaining development goals. Leaders at all levels of society must be savvy, dynamic and strategic thinkers. Only by ensuring that the principles of accountability, transparency, rule of law, participation and inclusion of non-state actors in the design and implementation of development activities are present, will African countries have greater prospects of making progress on the realization of development initiatives like the SDGs.

Capacity is also a critical issue for the role of regional organizations. The processes envisaged going forward have to be consistent with the idea of transformative change, which involves

> changes in economic structures to promote employment-intensive growth patterns that ensure macroeconomic stability and policy space. In order to make this economic change environmentally sustainable, profound changes are required in production and consumption patterns and energy use through legislation, regulation and policy policies. But most importantly, it requires changes in social structures and relations, including addressing the growing economic and political power of elites and patterns of stratification related to class, gender, ethnicity, religion or location that can lock people (including future generations) into disadvantage and constrain their choices and agency.
>
> (UNRISD 2016: 3)

Since transformative change is a long-term process, it means that the African Union, and the continent's regional blocs, sharpen their ability to address or mediate efforts in conflict resolution, enhance the requisite institutional capacity and expertise (Ismail 2015). This is because meeting the SDGs hinges on, among others, resolving existing conflicts, preventing new ones and guaranteeing security of people and businesses. How countries police protests, resolve conflict and eschew official corruption are all central to the attainment of SDGs and Agenda 2063 (Ayoyo and Oriola this volume). That is why it is important to acknowledge the assertive, preventative ECOWAS diplomacy that got rid of Yahya Jammeh from the Gambia in January 2017. That possibility raises the question of what next? Specifically, can the ECOWAS approach be used elsewhere on the continent, especially in the case of countries where the leaders try to engineer changes to their tenure (table 10.1)?

While Africa undoubtedly made huge strides in its quest to meet the MDG targets, it fell short in many areas. So, going forward, African countries need to enhance not only their capacity choices, but also their policy options. The key actors in the drive to ensure the continent succeeds at meeting the targets of Agenda 2063, and the 2030 Agenda need 'to raise their game to stay in the game'. First, proper governance structures (inclusion, transparency, access to information, freedom of association and participation), 'effective institutions' (state capacity, rule of law, property rights, reduced bribery and corruption), and the capacity to undertake and implement the necessary programmes and services (Arthur this volume; Hulme *et al.* 2014) need to be put in place.

Second, in fragile and post-conflict settings, the capacity of a country to provide basic social infrastructure for its people is critical (Ayoyo and Oriola this volume), and not so much in 'developmental states'. The continent could also take a page from the European Union (EU) where, recent developments seem to suggest that sustainability is getting institutionalized. Programmes such as the University of Vienna's (in collaboration with the Austrian Foundation for Development Research: ÖFSE) and the United Nations Industrial Development Organization (UNIDO) 'Global Political Economy of Sustainable Development' commencing in October 2017; and opportunities such as the Resilience 2017 Conference on the theme 'The transformation we want: Towards a global policy environment for resilient futures', taking place in Stockholm, Sweden on 21–23 August 2017, are aimed at interrogating policy reforms and innovations, which will produce environmentally sustainable and socially just solutions. Africa should not only engage these spaces and contribute to the dialogue; but it should also engender such spaces locally and institutionalize sustainability in its own planning. These are the concerted required and necessary steps to create and attain the transformative change so much desired by the present generation and thus would ensure the dignity of the future generation of Africans.

References

African Capacity Building Foundation (ACBF) (2011) *African Capacity Indicators 2011 – Capacity Development in Fragile States.* Harare: ACBF.

Africa Progress Panel. (APP) (2012) *Africa Progress Report 2012.* Available at africaprogresspanel.org/publications/policy-papers/africa-progress-report-2012/ (accessed 7 January 2017).

African Union, Economic Commission for Africa; African Development Bank and United Nations Development Programme (AU/ECA/AfDB and UNDP) (2016) *MDGs to Agenda 2063/SDGs Transition Report 2016: Towards an Integrated and Coherent Approach to Sustainable Development in Africa.* Addis Ababa, Ethiopia: AU/ECA/AfDB and UNDP.

Beegle, K., L. Christiaensen, A. Dabalen and I. Gaddis (2016) *Poverty in a Rising Africa.* Washington, DC: World Bank.

Besada, H., Xu, J., Mathers, A. and Carey, J. (2016) Advancing African agency with the new 2030 transformative development agenda, *African Geographical Review*, dx.doi.org/10.1080/19376812.2016.1138232.

Bianchi, A. (2015) *From MDGs to SDGs – Where Does Africa Stand?* ISPI Commentary, 5 October 2015. ISPI.

Bischoff, P-H., Aning, K. and Acharya, A. (2016) Africa in Global International Relations: emerging approaches to theory and practice, an introduction. In P-H. Bischoff, K. Aning and A. Acharya (eds) *Africa in Global International Relations.* Abingdon/New York: Routledge, pp. 1–22.

Brown, W. (2011). *African Agency In International Politics: Scope, Analysis and Theory.* Paper presented at the ESRC African agency in international politics seminar, *New Directions in the study of Africa's IR: Perspectives from Southern Africa* Wallenberg Research Centre, University of Stellenbosch, 2–3 November. Available at www.open.ac.uk/socialsciences/bisa-africa/files/africanagency-seminar5-brown.pdf (accessed 8 January 2017).

Brown, W and Harman, S. (eds) (2013) *African Agency in International Politics.* Abingdon: Routledge.

Ekman, A. (2016) China's multilaterism: higher ambitions. *Alert Issue*, No. 2, European Union Institute for Security Studies, January. Available at www.iss.europa.eu/uploads/media/Alert_2_China.pdf (accessed 25 January 2017).

Gastrow, P. (2013) *Transnational Organized Crime: The stepchild of crime combatting priorities*. ISS Policy Brief 45, October, Institute of Security Studies. Available at issafrica.s3.amazonaws.com/site/uploads/PolBrief46.pdf (accessed 22 January 2017).

Goldstone, B. and Obarrio, J. (eds) (2016) *African Futures: Essays on Crisis, Emergence, Possibility*. Chicago: University of Chicago Press.

Gyimah-Brempong, K., Shaw, T. M. and Simonis, V. (2012) *Is Bilateral Aid Responding to Good Governance in Africa?* Occasional Paper No. 18. Harare: ACBF.

Hanson, K. T., D'Alessandro, C. and Owusu, F. (2014) (eds) *Managing Africa's Natural Resources: Capacities for Development.* Basingstoke: Palgrave Macmillan.

Hanson, K. T., Kararach, G. and Shaw, T. M. (2012) (eds) *Rethinking Development Challenges for Public Policy: Insights from Contemporary Africa.* Basingstoke: Palgrave MacMillan.

Hulme, D., Savoia, A. and Sen, K. (2014) *Governance as a Global Development Goal: Setting, Measuring and Monitoring the Post 2015-Development Agenda*. ESID Working Paper No. 32.

Ismail, O. (2015) The Boko Haram insurgency and the changing patterns of regional security arrangements in Africa. In K. T. Hanson (ed.) *Contemporary Regional Development in Africa.* Farnham: Ashgate, pp. 201–24.

Kararach, G., Besada, H. and Shaw, T. M. (2016) African development, political economy and the road to Agenda 2063. In G. Kararach, H. Besada and T. Shaw (eds) *Development in Africa: Reframing the Lens after the MDGs*. Bristol: Policy, pp. 365–92.

Kwon, H. and Kim, E. (2014) Poverty reduction and good governance: examining the rationale of the millennium development goals, *Development and Change*, 45 (2): 353–75.

Marcel, V. (2013) *Guidelines for Good Governance in Emerging Oil and Gas Producers*, September. London: Chatham House (The Royal Institute of International Affairs).

Makinda, S. M. (2012) Africa's leadership malaise and the crisis of governance. In K. T. Hanson, G. Kararach and T. M. Shaw (eds) *Rethinking Development Challenges for Public Policy: Insights from Contemporary Africa*. New York: Palgrave MacMillan, pp. 54–82.

Onuoha, G. (2016) A 'rising Africa' in a resource-rich context: change, continuity and implications for development, *Current Sociology*, 64 (2) 277–92.

OXFAM (2017) *An Economy of the 99%.* OXFAM Briefing Paper, January. Oxford: Oxfam International.

Puplampu, K. P. (2014) The capacity question, leadership and strategic choices: environmental sustainability and natural resources management in Africa. In K. T. Hanson, C. D'Alessandro and F. Owusu (eds) *Managing Africa's Natural Resources: Capacities for Development.* New York: Palgrave Macmillan, pp. 162–84.

Shaw, T. M. (2015a) African agency? Africa, South Africa and the BRICS, *International Politics*, February, 52 (2): 255–68, doi:10.1057/ip.2014.48.

———. (2015b) Afterword: 'African agency' to maximise the continent's policy choices after a decade of the BRICS: beyond dependency? In K. T. Hanson (ed.) *Contemporary Regional Development in Africa*. Farnham: Ashgate.

Taylor, I. (2014) *Africa Rising? BRICS – Diversifying Dependency*. Woodbridge: James Currey.

———. (2016) *Global Governance and Transnationalising Capitalist Hegemony: The Myth of 'Emerging Powers'*. Abingdon: Routledge.

Tettey, W. J. (2012) Africa's leadership deficit: exploring pathways to good governance and transformative politics. In K. T. Hanson, G. Kararach and T. M. Shaw (eds) *Rethinking Development Challenges for Public Policy: Insights from Contemporary Africa*. Palgrave MacMillan, pp. 18–53.

United Nations Development Programme (UNDP) (2015) *Human Development Report, 2015*. New York: United Nations Development Programme.

United Nations Office on Drugs and Crime (UNODC) (2016) *Transnational Organized Crime*. Available at www.unodc.org/unodc/en/data-and-analysis/toc.html (accessed 22 January 2017).

United Nations Research Institute for Social Development (UNRISD) (2016) *Policy Innovations for Transformative Change – UNRISD Flagship Report 2016*. Geneva: UNRISD.

West African Commission on Drugs (WACD) Available at www.wacommissionon-drugs.org (accessed 28 April 2017).

Index

For Product Safety Concerns and Information please contact our EU representative GPSR@taylorandfrancis.com
Taylor & Francis Verlag GmbH, Kaufingerstraße 24, 80331 München, Germany

www.ingramcontent.com/pod-product-compliance
Lightning Source LLC
LaVergne TN
LVHW011132300926
849160LV00008B/623
9781032096568